Lean Six Sigma That Works

Lean Six Sigma That Works

A Powerful Action Plan for Dramatically Improving
Quality, Increasing Speed, and Reducing Waste

Bill Carreira and Bill Trudell

AMACOM

American Management Association

New York • Atlanta • Brussels • Boston • Chicago • Mexico City • San Francisco
Shanghai • Tokyo • Toronto • Washington, D.C.

Special discounts on bulk quantities of AMACOM books are available to corporations, professional associations, and other organizations. For details, contact Special Sales Department, AMACOM, a division of American Management Association, 1601 Broadway, New York, NY 10019. Tel.: 212-903-8316.   Fax: 212-903-8083. Web site: www.amacombooks.org

This publication is designed to provide accurate and authoritative information in regard to the subject matter covered. It is sold with the understanding that the publisher is not engaged in rendering legal, accounting, or other professional service. If legal advice or other expert assistance is required, the services of a competent professional person should be sought.

Library of Congress Cataloging-in-Publication Data

Carreira, Bill.
   Lean Six Sigma that works : a powerful action plan for dramatically improving quality, increasing speed, and reducing waste / Bill Carreira and Bill Trudell.
      p. cm.
   ISBN-13: 978-0-8144-7347-4
   ISBN-10: 0-8144-7347-4
   1. Business logistics. 2. Six Sigma (Quality control standard) I. Trudell, Bill. II. Title.

   HD38.5.C27 2006
   658.4'013—dc22

                                                                          2006015562

A life mate who believes in you unconditionally and has the desire, the intellect, and the chemistry to cause you to be more than you could ever imagine being, is a rare thing.

One could spend an entire lifetime searching for just one, such perfect match . . . and it would not be a wasted life.

To my love Andria . . . she is the catalyst that opens my sky.
                                                            Bill Carreira

I dedicate this book to my dad, a boat builder from Marine City, Michigan, who gave me a great childhood and inspired me to be a leader.
                                                            Bill Trudell

CONTENTS

PREFACE

The impact and effectiveness of lean six sigma operating methodologies has been demonstrated by the numerous companies around the world who have embraced this philosophy and put the tools to use. The results include record profits, dramatic improvements in lead times and internal process variation, and market share growth (to name but a few) and have been documented and are unquestionable.

However, the fundamental ingredient in this counter-intuitive soup is people. It is all about people who are brave enough to challenge their perceptions and habits, tough enough to not give up when they hit some turbulence, and passionate and disciplined enough to carry through with the very hard work required to implement their collective vision. My piece of this book is dedicated to these impressive and inspirational individuals.

Bill Carreira
May 2006

The principles of lean six sigma work. Unfortunately, their principles and methodologies are often applied by management like defibrillators in an emergency room to resuscitate a patient in cardiac arrest as a result of life-long bad habits. Sometimes the patient survives, sometimes not. If you are a business leader, keep your company out of the emergency room by beginning to apply these concepts now. If you are in the emergency room, *Lean Six Sigma* may be the paddles that get your heart beating again.

Just get going; get started this week. The results obtained by applying lean six sigma will be rewarding both financially and professionally. What is more rewarding is that satisfaction of watching your employees becoming exited about where they work and feeling like they are a part of it all, because they are. *Lean Six Sigma* gives leaders the tools they need to succeed. However, you have to provide the most important ingredient of all, leadership.

Bill Trudell, Jr.
May 2006

INTRODUCTION

THE WHY

This is a book about lean six sigma methodologies. Additionally, this is a book written in the hope that you will use some of the tools we describe and put lean six sigma concepts to work to improve your business. There are many excellent books on lean and six sigma as separate methodologies, with each addressing different needs and preferences of their readers—high level overview, basic reference guide, service industry scenario, real life storytelling, etc. Our objective with this volume is to present the hybrid of the basic tools of lean and six sigma to give you a clear view, and sufficient comfort level, to implement what we are talking about. Some assembly may be required to make the fit to your specific industry and business model, but we'll provide the nuts and bolts and enough conceptual knowledge, to make you dangerous—to your competition.

That being said, here are the questions. What is lean? What is six sigma? How do lean and six sigma complement each other and how do I know where and when to use the appropriate tools? And of course, why should I change the way I am currently doing business and incorporate these operating methodologies?" Good questions.

When a hybrid term is used such as "lean six sigma" in relation to improving a business, it kind of equates to using the term "hammer wrench ruler" in relation to building a house. You'll need all the tools to get the job done, but the trick is knowing what tool to select for the portion of the job you happen to be working on, and how to use the specific tool to your full advantage. We'll do our best.

The Fundamental Principles of Six Sigma

The engineer who invented Six Sigma died of a heart attack, at work, in the Motorola cafeteria in 1993. His name was Bill Smith. In an article I read some time ago, written by Mr. Smith's daughter, Marjorie Hook, she said, "Today I think people sometimes try to make Six Sigma seem complicated and overly technical. My father's approach was, 'If you want to improve something, involve the people who are doing the job.' He always wanted to make it simple so people would use it." We can speculate that Bill Smith might define Six Sigma as "a disciplined, statistical approach aimed at increasing profitability by reducing defects." Pretty straightforward stuff.

A more popular definition today might be that Six Sigma is an integrated, disciplined approach for improving business performance, driven by data, and based upon improving processes by understanding and controlling variation, thus improving predictability of business processes. It is a rigorous, data-driven, decision-making process. The foundation logic and approach is a systematic five-phase, problem-solving process called "DMAIC" which stands for Define, Measure, Analyze, Improve, and Control.

We like to think of Six Sigma as a large tool box alongside of a business process. This tool box contains a variety of tools available to reduce variation in the process and improve quality. Tools can range from simple brainstorming, pareto analysis, and kaizen events, to relatively complex mathematical approaches such as statistical analysis, hyper geometric distributions, Design of Experiments, and Analysis of Variance (ANOVA).

If you were cruising a Barnes and Noble book store on a Sunday afternoon and happened to open a book whose title contained the words "Six Sigma," you might encounter page after page of graphs of bell curves, calculations of standard deviations, t scores, or ANOVA tables. To the average individual, the statistical foundation for this discipline might cause you to head back to the coffee bar for an espresso and a couple of aspirins. Not to worry, our intent is to present this topic, Lean Six Sigma, with a common sense, pragmatic approach, to enable you to appreciate and take full advantage of these very valuable problem-solving techniques.

The Fundamental Principles of Lean

In discussion of the guiding principles of lean, we might start with the concept of value. In the land of lean, all value is defined from the point of view of the customer. From the customers' vantage point, does a given activity add value to their product or service, or not. When we discuss value from the customer's view, it usually takes us to the specifics of product deliverables. In simplest terms the question is, "Does this activity cause my customers product or service to become more complete, and is the customer paying for this activity to occur?" If the answer to either of these questions is no, then this particular activity should be carefully evaluated, why are you doing it?

These definitions of value lead to two of the foundation analytical terms of lean, *value-added*, and *non value-added*. The term value-added refers to those tasks that change the product or service deliverable, from the customers view, to a more complete state. The product has physically changed shape and its value to the customer has increased. Conversely, the term non value-added refers to activity or tasks that consume time (people expense), materials, and/or space (facilities expense), but doesn't physically advance the product or increase its value.

This is straightforward, common-sense logic, yet many companies have yet to develop the *"lean six sigma eye"* to identify activity and categorize it into these terms. We would emphasize that when you walk through any business entity, be it manufacturing, retail, service, medical, and on and on, all observed activity falls into two definition categories. The two high level categories for any activity are:

1. Generates revenue or
2. Adds cost

Simple as that. Value-added "adds" to the profit line, non value-added "subtracts" from the profit line. Cash in—cash out, there are no activities or tasks that do not fall into these two slots.

A second foundation principle of lean is that of a system-wide analytical view: the value stream. A value stream is the total cycle of activity to provide a product or service, from initial customer contact to receipt of payment, for a product or service that has been delivered to your customer. Many businesses direct their improvement focus on maximizing localized pieces of the process while failing to analyze the impact across the entire process. The mindset is if we improve the pieces, the whole will be better. A value stream analysis provides a total process view of activity, inputs, outputs, and disconnects, to allow for leveraging maximum financial improvement, system-wide and bottom line.

Next come the principles of "Flow" and "Pull," two critical concepts. Flow implies a "straight shot" sequence of activity through a process. The theoretical objective is: everything is performed once, correctly, the first time. Pull is a consumption-driven system, things are done when they are needed by the next customer upstream in the process, not before. A pull system is a customer demand-driven process as opposed to a forecast-driven process. We do not produce a product or service, place it in stock or queue, and deliver to our customer at a later date when ordered. This concept of pull applies to both external and internal customers, with an internal customer being the next operation up the line—we could say across the entire value stream.

We realize that these definitions are perfect world stuff; they are objectives—maybe not 100% achievable, but they are the objectives nonetheless. We could ask "How often should you kiss your kids goodnight?" The objective is "Every night." Will you achieve this goal? Maybe not, some of us travel a good bit, but it's the goal.

Perhaps the essential principle of the lean mindset is the continuous pursuit of elimination of waste. The mindset difference between a lean six sigma environment and a non lean environment is the definition of what waste is. We will cover the definition of categories of waste in a later chapter, but the chase is to eliminate waste and free up resources to spend more time on value-added activity. The lean six sigma game is about more "saleable" product or services produced with the expenditure of less resources (nobody is working harder). The strategic objectives are increased customer satisfaction, growth through the taking of market share, greater profitability for your company, and increased long-term opportunity and stability for your employee population.

Successfully implementing these concepts and principles requires the participation of all employees in a given firm. Everyone must work together toward a common vision. We would state that deployment of these principles is "Top down," while implementation is "Bottom up."

What This Book Will Do for You

This book is composed of two sections. The first section is the "what" and the second section is the "how." The "what" chapters discuss and illustrate the ideas and logic flow of what we are trying to accomplish by adopting a lean six sigma operating philosophy. The "how" chapters illustrate some of the tools of lean six sigma and how to put them to good use. The classic tools of lean address process definition, high materials velocity, and balance while the tools of six sigma address data driven variation reduction. With a continuous improvement mindset, these tools can be used in different sequence and blended in various ways, depending on the particular process being addressed. There is no "right" or "wrong"—the important message is get going and start doing something. This volume illustrates some of the lean six sigma fundamental tools in a specific, how-to manner, with the hope that you will follow our lead and make something happen in your business processes.

In response to the question, "Why should I consider altering my approach to the way I am currently doing business?" we would mention the primary objective of business in general: "Turn a profit by being the premier satisfier of customer demand in whatever market you care to compete." We all have competition. Most markets are finite and anyone who desires a particular product or service can purchase whatever it is they require—the question is, "from whom." It is not possible to stand still in an aggressive global economy and maintain market share. You are either getting better or you are falling behind. It's a game of comparison, you versus your competition. We're reminded of a classic joke, here it is.

Three hikers are camping in the mountains. Early in the morning they are awakened by a tremendous racket. As they look out of their tent, they are horrified to see a very large, and obviously upset, grizzly bear tearing their campsite apart. They quickly grab their knapsacks, cut a slice in the back of their tent, and scramble to put some distance between themselves and this frenzied animal. After running about one hundred yards, they turn back to survey the situation and are panic stricken to see that the bear has turned his attention to them and started to pursue. The oldest of the three campers drops to his knees, pulls a pair of running shoes from his knapsack, and quickly begins to lace them up. His companions shake their heads in disbelief, and one says, "Are you crazy Jim? There's no way you can run faster than that bear." To which Jim looks up and replies, "Hell, I don't have to run faster than that bear, I've only got to run faster than you." And there it is, an illustration of competitive impact at it's finest.

Price, quality, on-time delivery, whatever the important metrics are from your customer's point of view, if you weaken by comparison, you'll begin to decline. Enough said.

There are two techniques in play when you observe a business model—"Manufacturing technique" and "Production technique." Let's start with "production technique": how to produce a product or provide a service. Production technique is a level playing field. Anyone can purchase the same types of equipment and facilities, hire and train qualified people, and purchase the materials to make a product or provide a service. There are standard steps required to make a particular product or provide a specific service, and everyone pretty much performs these steps the same way. Machining a gear is machining a gear, open-heart surgery is open-heart surgery, making a pizza is making a pizza. There may be small variations to manufacture a product or provide a service across different businesses, but the skill sets, equipment and tools required, and process steps are relatively uniform across like products or services.

When we look at "manufacturing technique" we see different operating models begin to surface. Since we don't consider lean six sigma to be strictly relegated to the confines of the manufacturing arena, we prefer to call this the Process Model Technique—how we manage, synchronize, and balance people, materials, machines, and equipment across a value stream. Whether your business is classic manufacturing, a retail store or distribution firm, a hospital, or a pizza parlor, you provide a customer with something by performing a series of processes. In our opinion, it is not so much the way individual people are doing their jobs, as the way overall resources are being managed that lead to dramatic differences in competitive effectiveness.

American industry is under tremendous pressure to be an effective competitor in a global arena. Over the past few decades we have lost much of our manufacturing base to off shore competition. We feel that it is possible to compete, on an international playing field, from any geographical location that you care to operate. We are discussing some operating philosophies and tools that make it possible to be a fierce and successful competitor, should you care to adopt and practice the operating methodologies we are about to discuss. Let's go.

Lean Six
Sigma
That
Works

PART 1

The What

Chapter 1

Overview of Lean Six Sigma

Lean Six Sigma is about relentless, sustained improvement—analysis after analysis, metric after metric, and project after project. Lean causes products to move through processes faster, and Six Sigma improves quality.

On the strategic side, Lean Six Sigma is an organizational philosophy of applying relentless efforts to drive waste out of the organization at every level and improve product quality to the level of only 3.4 defects per million opportunities. In a way, it's almost like a religion for which the goal is perfection, which is nearly impossible. Yet, it is the constant striving and never-ending effort to reach it that is important.

On the tactical side, Lean Six Sigma is a very effective approach of combining the principles of Lean Manufacturing and Six Sigma. It is a continuous analysis of the organization to determine where improvement is needed followed by Kaizen events and projects. The projects are managed by means of the Six Sigma define, measure, analyze, improve, and control (DMAIC) process using the many great tools included in the Six Sigma body of knowledge. We will review the DMAIC process in detail later on in the book.

LEAN MANUFACTURING

The basic goals of Lean are high quality, low cost, short cycle times, flexibility, relentless efforts to drive waste out of the organization, and all value being defined by the customer. Waste is anything a customer is not willing to pay for. Value is anything the customer is willing to pay for.

The basic tools of Lean are process maps, baselines, value stream mapping, spaghetti diagrams, time studies, and Kaizen events. A most important tool, the Kaizen event is a focused set of actions on applying or driving one or more of the goals into an area in the manufacturing process.

Manufacturing nirvana is a factory where the only activities occurring and product attributes being produced are those that customers are willing to pay for. No waste, no rework, no nonvalue added, no unwanted features.

SIX SIGMA

Six Sigma is about improving quality by applying a methodical approach to measuring products and processes against metrics, and arriving at improvement activities through the formal DMAIC process. The analytical and improvement tools used in Six Sigma can range from simple to highly complex.

Think of Six Sigma as a big tool box alongside a process for improving quality. This tool box contains a myriad of tools available for an individual or organization to improve quality. Tools and terms can range from simple brainstorming, Pareto analysis, and Kaizen events to the relatively complex such as statistical analysis, hypergeometric distributions, design of experiments, and analysis of variance.

One of the benefits of using the Six Sigma approach is that it is a *data-driven* improvement process. Processes or areas are measured, data are gathered, and progress is tracked against metrics derived from available data. During all of this, the data are sorted and displayed in charts and analysis that make it meaningful and valuable. It will tell a team where to focus their improvement efforts. This approach is beneficial because it minimizes situations in which precious resources are applied toward *feel good* projects that create the aura of things getting better, but in reality nothing is changing. With the Six Sigma approach, meaningful metrics are created and tracked so we are only *feeling good* when we should be.

Unfortunately, the perceived complexity of Six Sigma methodologies can drive many people or organizations away from applying them. This is too bad and unnecessary. Most *Lean* books are a fairly easy read and can be easily understood by the majority of employees in any manufacturing organization. After all, it is the *commonsense* attributes and simplicity of Lean principles that make Lean so powerful. Opening up or glancing into a Lean book will probably reveal pictures of work cells or baselines, 5S areas, and so forth, whereas the pages in a Six Sigma book contain graphs of bell curves, calculations of standard deviations, *t* scores, and analysis of variance tables. It can be overwhelming even to those with knowledge of college-level statistics.

For these reasons, many people shy away from reading Six Sigma books or studying the methodologies. This is unfortunate, because many useful parts of the Six Sigma methodologies need not be any more complex to understand or apply than Lean manufacturing principles. Six Sigma methodologies can be applied in a simple or complex manner, or somewhere in between. Significant improvements or gains can be made using the basic tools, and without applying complex statistical analysis.

APPLYING LEAN SIX SIGMA

Lean Six Sigma is about applying a strategy to improve your business. It can be applied to improve certain areas of your business or operations on a tactical level, or to achieve strategic objectives. One way to determine where to focus Lean Six Sigma tools is to determine what your *critical success factors* are. In other words, what things (usually three to five of them) are critical to improve your business. You can then apply the DMAIC process and Lean Six Sigma tools to achieve the improvement. These types of efforts are what I call *Quick Sigma* because they follow a more informal application of the DMAIC process. They do not involve the highly complex and detailed tools of Six Sigma. They are directed to a lower level or to tactical-type projects to eliminate defects in a particular process or area in the plant. An example would be to reduce finish defects in a coating operation.

Strategic objectives, on the other hand, are those objectives that are created by top management directed at improving the business or achieving the organization's vision. These are a big deal and provide a great opportunity for the Lean Six Sigma approach using several of the tools and analysis in the toolbox. An example of a strategic project would be a project to reduce warranty costs to the business. These types of projects are important to the business. The success of these projects can be enhanced when a Six Sigma Black Belt is assigned to manage or lead them. The Black Belt has the knowledge and ability to deploy any of the complex statistical and analytical tools from the tool box. He or she can also provide training to the team as required. However, as you will read ahead, having a Black Belt is not absolutely necessary, but having someone with certain skills is. Not having a Black Belt should not keep you from applying the Lean Six Sigma tools.

Whether tactical or strategic, all Lean Six Sigma projects should be driven by metrics. Each area the company desires to improve must be measured to develop meaningful metrics. Metrics are most effectively applied via *dashboards*. A dashboard is a cluster of charts, graphs, and other data revealing performance to key metrics. Dashboards are simple, yet powerful tools to communicate progress to everyone in the organization.

The ideal situation is when there are dashboards of integrated metrics at the operator level, supervisory/management level, and executive level. This situation and focused improvement efforts at all these levels ensure that the efforts of the entire organization are focused on achieving the strategic objectives of the company. This is powerful. One cannot over-state the value of having representation and participation from the finance and accounting department in Six Sigma teams. First, their knowledge of cost and financial data will be very valuable in executing projects. This knowledge will help ensure the validity of numbers and metrics used to measure progress. Another benefit is that it will help avoid a situation in which a project team is communicating or reporting their exciting results from their hard work while the finance guy is at the end of the table shaking his head (in the wrong direction!). This situation can take all the fun out of it. Make sure you get a *thumbs up* from accounting.

KAIZEN OR DMAIC?

The question of when to use a Kaizen event, or when to execute a Six Sigma project with the DMAIC process, is often asked. We believe that Kaizen events are best used to drive process improvements in smaller areas that are not all-encompassing. They are also well suited for applying the basic principles of Lean such as shortening cycle times, improving flow, or eliminating waste. For example, if your team would like to improve efficiencies on an assembly line, a Kaizen event would probably be the best tool. Developing a current state map, a future state map, and a set of actions to realize the latter is a great application for the Kaizen event.

On the other hand, Six Sigma projects using the DMAIC process are well suited for improving quality by reducing defects, improving yield, or attacking situations in which decisions will be made by analyzing relatively significant amounts of data. Any situation that demands or uses statistics leans toward Six Sigma. Problems that are broad-based across the organization are well suited for DMAIC. For example, a Six Sigma/DMAIC project would be the best approach if your goal is to reduce total warranty costs for the organization. This project would require considerable data and analysis to base improvement efforts on. Six Sigma offers great tools for any situation like this in which data will be used. The analytical tools range across all levels of complexity.

One of the key premises of this book is that applying Lean Six Sigma need not be highly complex. However, it is fair to say that you and your team need to become knowledgeable about Lean Six Sigma. It is a journey, and the more you know and familiarize your team with the tools the more successful you will be. It can also be enjoyable because there a lot of great publications out there. As you begin to apply Lean Six Sigma I recommend that you order a handful of the many pocket guides, books, and pamphlets on Lean Six Sigma that are on the market. There is no shortage of them. Pass them around to your staff. I find reading them very enjoyable. Get one of the pocket-size guides and put it in your brief case. They make for great reading in the airport or while your car is getting its oil changed.

DMAIC PROCESS

Here is a brief overview of the Six Sigma DMAIC process.

Define

The Define stage of the DMAIC process is where the problem or objective is clearly defined. What is it we are trying to accomplish? What are we trying to do? For strategic and higher level projects, a Project Charter is formed that lays out the intent and objective of the project. Top management signs off and designates a Champion and a Project Leader to ensure the support of the process in time and resources. This is top management's way of saying hey, this project is critical and highly important and it has our full support, and our expectation of results.

Some of the tools used in the Define phase include Project Charter, SIPOC diagram (suppliers, inputs, process, output, and customers), process mapping, and benchmarking. We will review these in more detail later.

Measure

The goal of the Measure phase is to focus the improvement effort by gathering information on the current situation. The process is measured, data are gathered, and metrics are created. For strategic projects the whole Six Sigma toolbox of tools is at your doorstep. You are only limited by your ability, or your Black Belt's ability to apply them. It can be complex, but it can also be fun. These tools are powerful and effective. They are all tied to metrics, and if used properly a movement in the metrics is matched by a movement in your financials.

On the tactical side, a simple discussion of what are we going to measure and how to do it will take place. What data are meaningful? What data are available? What is the simplest way to gather data? What measurement system should we use? This is a good place to develop dashboards. Quite simply, the dashboards tell you how well you are doing and where to direct your improvement efforts. Dashboards should be placed in areas easily accessible to everyone. Teams should be assembled to work together to improve the metrics in the dashboards. A dashboard is a great focal point for a team to gather in front of to review and discuss progress, as well as to determine future improvement activities.

Some of the tools used in the Measure phase include control charts, data-collection forms, flow diagrams, frequency plots, failure modes and effects analysis (FMEA), Pareto charts, prioritization matrix, and run charts.

Analyze

The goal of the Analyze phase is to identify root cause(s) by analyzing the data. The output is a theory that has been tested and confirmed. The information developed in the Analyze phase will be used to develop solutions and improvements in the Improve phase. Several tools or combinations of tools are used to assess the data to determine root causes of the defects or problem.

Some of the tools used in the Analyze phase include the affinity diagram, brainstorming, cause-and-effect diagrams, control charts, data collection, flow diagrams, frequency plots, Pareto charts, tree diagrams, process behavior charts or statistical process control, process maps, design of experiments, enumeration of statistics (hypothesis tests), inferential statistics, FMEA, and simulation.

Improve

The goal of the Improve phase is to test and implement solutions to address or eliminate the root causes. The output is an improvement plan that eliminates or reduces the frequency of the root cause(s) or improves the process.

Some of the tools used in the Improve phase include brainstorming, consensus, control charts, data-collection forms, flow diagrams, frequency plots, FMEA, planning tools, Pareto charts, prioritization matrix, process capability, sampling, stakeholder analysis, force-field diagrams, 7M tools, project planning/management tools, prototype, and pilot studies.

Control

The goal of the Control phase is to assess proposed solutions and develop controls to put in place that will ensure the desired results and prevent future occurrences of the defects, problems, or unnecessary costs.

Some of the tools used in the Control phase include control charts, data-collection forms, data-collection plans, flow diagrams, frequency plots, quality-control process charts, sampling, standardization, statistical process control, FMEA, ISO, and reporting systems.

DO YOU NEED A SIX SIGMA BLACK BELT?

This is a topic of great debate. Our answer is that if you have the room in your company a Six Sigma Black Belt certified with a reputable organization can be a big asset, given he or she has solid leadership skills and the talent required to lead Six Sigma projects and teach the tools. The concept of Black Belts is that they are professionals who have obtained the knowledge of Six Sigma methodologies and mastered the tools included in them. They have experience leading Six Sigma projects and can train others in the skills. Some organizations that are fully deploying Six Sigma believe they should have approximately one Six Sigma Black Belt for every 100 employees. Their full-time job is to manage a continuous stream of key projects in support of the company's strategic objectives while providing training for others in the organization.

Here are quick descriptions of the roles of Green Belts, Black Belts, and Master Black Belts:

Green Belt: Green Belts are employees who are trained in the fundamentals of the Six Sigma methodologies and the DMAIC process. They spend about a third of their time working on Six Sigma projects.

Black Belt: Black Belts are the workhorses of Six Sigma. They are the cornerstones. They lead project after project after project. Given that they are effective, they are incredibly valuable assets to an organization. Black Belts generally lead five to six projects per year that should bring at least $1 million to the bottom line. They coach Green Belts in accomplishing their projects.

The idea of a Six Sigma Black Belt is exciting: a professional with a high level of leadership and technical problem-solving skills who applies a continuous full force of energy at executing key projects that by their nature help the company achieve its strategic objectives and improve bottom-line performance. Because of the nature of their position, Black Belts are not distracted by the day-to-day tactical requirements of the organization that often pull managers away from their responsibilities on more traditional projects. Black Belts must be able to lead projects and interact with employees of all levels. They must be able to explain the basic tools in a way that nearly anyone can understand.

Master Black Belt: This professional has reached the highest level of technical proficiency in applying and, most important, teaching the tools used in Six Sigma.

Master Black Belts teach and train others to become Black Belts. This person is technically astute at applying and teaching the simple and complex statistical tools of Six Sigma. A Master Black Belt must have excellent written and oral communication skills. This person must be able to lead projects. This person is the model Black Belt. Often Master Black Belts focus their efforts in a specific area in an organization. They work with process owners and key people in specific areas to assist in reducing defects, tracking progress, and improving quality.

It is possible to deploy Lean Six Sigma initiatives without a Black Belt on staff given that you have someone who can understand the basic tools. This person should have excellent communication and project-management skills. This person must understand basic spreadsheets and be able to create bar charts, Pareto charts, run diagrams, etc. A solid understanding of the quality process and quality concepts is also important. Sending a person with these skill sets for Green Belt training would be very worthwhile.

GETTING STARTED

My recommendation on how to get started quickly in applying Lean Six Sigma follows:

1. Set up training for managers and supervisors in the basic tools:
    a. How to conduct a brainstorming session and certain tools such as an affinity diagram, a cause-and-effect diagram, a force-field analysis, etc.
    b. Data-collection basics.
    c. How to create a Pareto chart and what it does.
    d. How to create a run diagram and what it does.
    e. How to create a dashboard.

2. Conduct a brainstorming session with key staff to determine a list of three to five key projects that everyone agrees would be valuable to the organization.

3. Because everyone agrees that these projects are valuable, I recommend that you select the one that could be completed in the shortest period of time. The excitement of completing a project will be a great first building block.

4. Set up a project team made up of some of your best people who are familiar with the areas the project will focus on.

5. Follow the DMAIC process for each project using the basic tools of brainstorming, charting, cause-and-effect diagrams, etc.

6. Start other projects in the same manner as you feel comfortable.

Chapter 2

Customer Satisfaction

Customer satisfaction is an interesting topic. What are the facets of true customer satisfaction? What do customers ultimately want? The quick response from many people would include such things as on-time delivery, the best quality, and the lowest price. Okay, these instinctively sound like they would be important to customers. Let's noodle this around a bit.

We hear a lot of talk about customer satisfaction being the driver in many companies, but when we leave the sales office and observe activity in different areas of the business, things seem to change quite quickly more often than not.

At the center of the Lean philosophy are metrics applied from the customer's vantage point. Performance is what it is. If a customer calls with a request for delivery in 3 days and you're unable to accommodate that timeline, the typical procedure is to negotiate a delivery time based on what you can do, let's say, for example, a 10-day delivery lead time. At this point the customer has to make a decision. Accept the longer delivery timeline, or call your competitors to see if they can match the requested lead time. If your customer can find the same product (comparable quality is a given) available on the desired date, you will lose the order to your competition.

A critical message has been delivered (and demonstrated) to your customer. Your company failed to satisfy his/her needs, and your competition succeeded. The next time this customer places an order for a product, you will not necessarily be the preferred vendor in his/her mind. If your lead times are the best in your particular industry, you will be able to delude yourself that you are satisfying customer demand; however, when one of your more forward-thinking competitors figures out how to reduce the lead time, you will begin to lose market share.

We are facilitating a value stream mapping event for a company that is the market leader in their industry. We are sitting in the war room and looking at the data. . .conflicting numbers from sales, manufacturing, and logistics with regard to on-time delivery. Interesting stuff....

Bill C.: Gents, I'm not getting the discrepancy. Logistics and manufacturing are claiming on-time delivery is at 56%, but sales is saying it's at 91%?

Harold (cost accounting): Our reported on-time delivery is 91%.

Bill C.: Okay?

Jimmy (logistics): Bill, sales is reporting orders shipped. That's why their performance metric is different from mine in manufacturing.

Bill C.: I still don't understand. If the order is shipped, the order is shipped. If it hits the promise date, we're good to go.

Harold: Correct.

Jimmy: No, it's not correct! Sales are putting spin on their metrics to make their on-time appear better than it is.

Harold: These orders shipped on these dates. Here's the analysis. (Harold is holding a stack of systems data that show orders and shipping dates over the last 4 or 5 months.)

Bill C.: And?

Jimmy: Listen to me! Let me finish my point. Most of our orders are for several parts. The customer needs all of the parts on the order to provide him/her with a working system. If he/she orders 10 parts on order number XYZ and we ship 9 of the 10 and backorder the 10th, sales is claiming a 90% on-time delivery for that particular order. We are claiming a 0% on-time delivery until the order is completely delivered.

Took Martel, the sales manager had been down the hall getting a coffee. He reenters the room and hears the last half of the sentence.

Took: Are you guys beating that horse again? Listen. If you order 10 parts on an order and we deliver 9 of the parts on the request date, we have completed 90% of the order on time. That's pretty easy math, I can almost do it in my head.

Jimmy: Okay Took, here you go. If you order a new car and we deliver it on time, minus 10% of the parts, the engine for example, are you a satisfied customer? Can you take your wife for a ride in your beautiful new car?

And so it goes.

The important message here is that people consider metrics to be a *report card* of how well they are performing a given activity, and everyone wants a good grade. We want to look good in our boss's eyes and we want to look good in our reports to corporate. In Lean philosophy, metrics are a measure of how effectively we satisfy our customers, simple as that. If we spin the numbers to satisfy our internal desire to appear very effective, we lose the foundation value of metrics—to measure our ability to satisfy customer demand, to use these metrics to guide our decisions on how to change our business model to improve customer satisfaction, and to use these metrics to ascertain the market environment and show us how to take market share. It's all about cash, and the only source of cash is customers.

Here's the objective: Give your customers what they want and expect, no more, no less, and measure all performance from the customers' view.

Chapter 3

Waste

As we mentioned earlier, a Lean Six Sigma business model is characterized by a mindset of continuous and relentless elimination of waste. So, let's talk about what waste really is. When you observe a process, be it manufacturing, retail, medical, what have you, you will generally observe two types of flows occurring. The first is activity; someone is doing something that leads to a product or service being created. The second type of flow is the transmission of information; data are being generated. For ease of illustration, let's look at a typical manufacturing value stream (Fig. 3-1).

A value stream is a systemwide view of all activity from receipt of an order from a customer to receipt of payment for product or services delivered. It's the complete circle: cash out to cash in. It is important to note that activity occurs not only in the physical manufacturing flow but also in the information flow. An oversimplified view of this analysis is shown in Figure 3-2.

In the typical system, activity moves the product or service forward, and information flows backward. As we evaluate the potential for improvement of a given process or system, every observation should fall into one of two high-level categories. They are:

1. Generates revenue, or
2. Adds cost

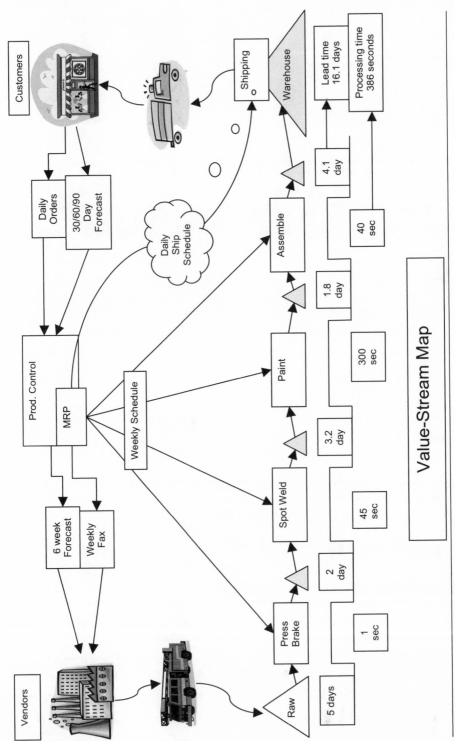

Value-Stream Map

FIGURE 3-1.

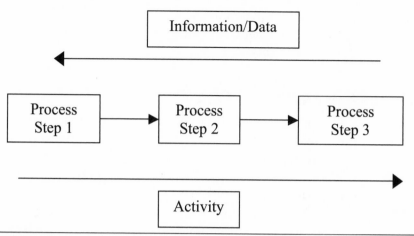

FIGURE 3-2.

This brings us to the high-level definition of waste: if an activity generates revenue, it is not waste; if an activity adds cost and generates no revenue, it is considered waste.

Let's drop down a layer and discuss the types of waste as defined by a Lean Six Sigma model. We typically categorize waste into seven boxes, namely:

1. Overproduction
2. Excess inventory
3. Transport
4. Process
5. Rejects/rework
6. Waiting
7. Unnecessary motion

These are categories that do not cause the product to become more complete and incur expense, add cost. An additional category of activity that is not waste is:

8. Work

Work is the activity that transforms the product or service to a more completed state, in the eyes of the customer. Everything observed in a process or system analysis should fall into one of these eight boxes. These categories are the foundation of the terms *value added* and *nonvalue added*. In simplest terms, work is value added, the product or service is being advanced to a more finished state, and the customer is paying for this activity to occur. The categories of waste are nonvalue added, they do not contribute to a more complete product or service, and the customer is unwilling to pay for these activities. Let's drop down another layer and discuss the types of waste in detail.

WASTE CATEGORY #1: OVERPRODUCTION

Overproduction has an internal and an external facet. The internal definition could be producing something before the next step in the process requires it. The external consideration could be producing something before a customer is prepared to purchase it. In either case, you are doing something and incurring cost before it is necessary to be done. Why does overproduction occur, we might ask? There are always reasons, and they usually sound logical. Let's look at a couple of examples of overproduction drivers.

The first driver of overproduction might be balance, or lack of it. Here's a simple process example. A three-step process with time required to do the work (Fig. 3-3).

In an unbalanced process if we use labor efficiency or machine use as our key metrics, we will want all people, and all pieces of equipment, running as fast as they can. To further exaggerate the illustration, let's say that these process steps are located in physically remote departments. Operation 1 has no visibility or linkage to operation 2 and so on. The constraint in this process is station 3 with a task time of 1.8 minutes. The most we can complete in this model is one unit every 1.8 minutes. If we launch orders into the system with a conventional materials requirement planning model, which assumes unlimited capacity, we will build up large queues of material between these steps. Operation 1 builds at a rate of 1 unit every minute, operation 2 builds at a rate of 1 unit every 1.5 minutes, and operation 3 builds at a rate of 1 unit every 1.8 minutes. To eliminate this system-driven overproduction we would have to pace operations 1 and 2 at a task rate of 1.8 minutes.

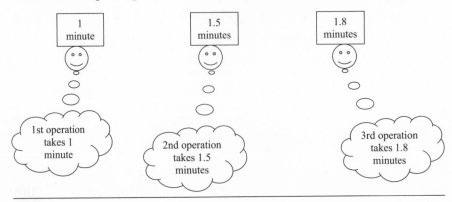

FIGURE 3-3.

This may seem to be a simple illustration, but it is all too common at most facilities—people moving parts from department to department and lots of queues of material before and after each step in the process. With this type of system there is no visible idle time; everyone appears to be working very hard. If you embrace the definitions of Lean Six Sigma, you know this *efficiency* is an illusion. These queues of materials represent overproduction; the material is being produced before the upstream operations are ready to consume.

Managing this type of system consists of launching orders and expediting them through the process. In this environment, the batches of material are not viewed as waste; they are viewed as necessary to allow people to always have something to work on. The thought processes encountered here might be, "How can I get the guys to work overtime this weekend to work through these materials build-ups?" or "How can I get my boss to invest in additional equipment so I can work down this material?"

Conversely, in a Lean Six Sigma environment the questions that come up would be, "How do we rebalance our process to eliminate the waste of overproduction?" or "When can we assign a Six Sigma team to work on reject reduction so we can better balance our flow?" A large benefit of embracing the definitions and concepts of Lean Six Sigma is that we see things differently, and this causes us to ask very different questions. The type of questions asked will lead us to take action in ways that will improve the system rather than maintain the status quo.

Okay, we're going off on a tangent; back to overproduction. Another driver of overproduction could be long setup or changeover times. In non-Lean Sigma operations with long setup times the conventional logic is to build the largest number of units possible before changing over to the next order. We want to amortize our changeovers over a large quantity of parts. The mechanism to calculate the best run quantity is called economic order quantity (EOQ). Here's the formula (Fig. 3-4).

The variables are as follows:

A = set up cost = set up cost × hourly factory cost
R = annual quantity
I = inventory carrying cost
C = standard cost of the item

$$\sqrt{\frac{2AR}{IC}}$$

FIGURE 3-4.

If you fool around with this equation and run some examples, you will find that setup cost is the primary driver from an impact point of view.

Again, in a conventional environment, typical questions might be "What is the optimum run quantity to offset my setup costs?" and "How do I manage the inventory driven by my EOQ lot size, in excess of customer orders, that I must carry in finished goods"? Once the EOQ lot sizes are calculated, when an order is received, the predetermined lot size will be run, even if it greatly exceeds the quantity ordered. Business as usual, no questions asked.

In a Lean Six Sigma environment, this overproduction would be challenged as waste. The questions might be "How do I implement a setup reduction focus team to analyze the process, drive my setup times down, and allow me to carry fewer inventories?" One mindset maintains the status quo, and the second challenges perceived waste and improves the business process.

WASTE CATEGORY #2: EXCESS INVENTORY

We often hear the question, "What do you mean by excess inventory?"

Our response is "Any material in your process that is waiting for someone to begin work on it."

"But we'll need this material tomorrow."

"Okay, so tomorrow it will not be considered excess, until then it is. What else ya got?"

As we will continue to emphasize, a ruthlessly simple definition of the categories of waste will drive a different way of *seeing*, generate different types of questions, and drive continuous improvement activity.

Another frequent question, "Isn't excess inventory the same as overproduction?"

One way to think of these two categories is, "Overproduction is the activity of producing excess inventory," whereas "excess inventory is the actual material that is not yet needed." One is the cost of people, machines, and space. The second is the cost of the actual materials and the associated carrying cost. In addition to producing excess inventory, it is also common to see companies purchase it. We've all heard of the *Great Deal* of buying in large quantities, and a common topic in purchasing circles is the old *minimum order quantity*.

"Why do you have 2 years worth of component XYZ sitting in stock?"

"Hey, nothing we could do, minimum order quantity!" This phrase is used like a *get out of jail free* card in Monopoly, no explanation required.

A question in this model might be "How do I track and control inventory accuracy of all this stock?" or "Where can we lease additional space to accommodate our inventory requirements?"

In a Lean Six Sigma environment we might be asking "How do we work with our vendors to help them "lean out" their processes and allow them to reduce their lot sizes?" or "When can we implement kanbans to define our minimum inventory requirements?"

WASTE CATEGORY #3: TRANSPORT

This category of waste is a symptom of layout and linkage. Moving an item from one location to another adds no value, yet in many environments it is never given a thought. Forklifts are simply accepted as part of the work scenario, no questions asked. Material transport devices and systems are usually very high-dollar items and incur huge cost with no value-added benefit. The questions that arise in a conventional model with high transport requirements might be, "Is it more cost-effective to buy or lease forklifts?" or "How can we pass a capital justification to automate our conveyor systems?" We tend to call this "spending money to automate waste." In a Lean Six Sigma model the typical questions might be, "How do we re-layout our process to allow physical linkage and eliminate the need to move product?" If we identify an activity as waste, we will use our collective creativity to minimize or eliminate it.

WASTE CATEGORY #4: PROCESS

It's common to have this type of waste fall under the radar. There are many interesting examples of process waste. Here's one:

"Our company policy requires the signature of five vice presidents to approve a bill of material change. We convene once a week and spend an hour or so listening to our vice president of engineering explain the changes being processed and signing the documents that are passed around. The *involved* individuals are in engineering and cost-accounting, with the balance of the executive team lacking either the technical expertise to bring anything to the discussion or the functional responsibility to derive anything of benefit from this session. This is a waste of time and energy for those individuals, yet it is our *company policy*." Process waste.

Here's another: "An assembly fixture is worn and causes the operator to spend additional time to locate and orient components during each assembly cycle." Process waste.

And another: "A chrome plating process is inconsistent and causes final grinding to run a secondary grind cycle 28% of the time." Process waste.

We categorize setup and changeover under the definition of process waste. This type of activity is nonvalue added and process-sensitive with regard to technique and type of tooling and fixturing used.

WASTE CATEGORY #5: REJECTS AND REWORK

Any disruption in a process creates a hole in time that travels across the entire system and adds a great deal of cost. The total cost incurred is very difficult to quantify (in dollars), and the impact of rejects and rework extend throughout the internal process and the external process. The high-level cause of rejects and the associated rework and scrap activity is *variation*. Let's think about a typical flow-through.

1. We purchase steel from a vendor to manufacture a precision part. This purchased material has variation in characteristics across a given batch; dimensions, hardness, and grain variation are a few that come to mind.

2. We process this material across the many steps in our internal process: forging, pre-turn, pre-grind, welding, heat treat, straighten, final turn, chrome plate, tip harden, final grind, and final inspect. Each step in our process has normal variation because of the characteristics of the material used, machines used, operator technique, and even things like changes in ambient temperature across the day. We inspect and ship our product to a customer.

3. Our customer assembles various components into his/her finished product and sells it to an end user. There is variation in the assembly process in our customer's facility.

4. The end user will experience the sum total of all the accumulated variation across this entire value stream. Some products perform well and some don't.

Variation in the process and the effects of characteristics of material will cause specification differences at each point in the system. A reject can occur at any, or all, steps in this process. So, here are the types we typically deal with.

- Materials and components rejected as they are received from vendors.
- Product rejected at any point in our internal process.
- Product rejected at final inspection.
- Product rejected at receipt by our customers.
- Product rejected by the end user, returned to our customer, with a cost incurred back to us.

These examples provide lots of opportunity to incur cost and generate rework and replacement activity. The category of rejects has a double negative attached to it. There is the cost of administrative and production resources dealing with the initial occurrence, and there is the cost of producing the replacement parts—time, resources, and capacity that could be used to produce additional new parts had the reject condition not appeared.

In a non-Lean Six Sigma environment the questions might be "How do we get our people to stop making mistakes?" or "How many final inspectors do we need to add to ensure that no nonspecification product reaches our customer?"

In a Lean Sigma process the questions might be, "How do we design our process so that the variation falls under a Six Sigma distribution curve?" or "How do we create an environment that uses Six Sigma tools and teams to minimize variation and reduce rejects?"

WASTE CATEGORY #6: WAITING

Waiting for materials, waiting for an inspector, waiting for prints or instruction, waiting for an automated piece of equipment to cycle. There are many causes of waiting, and they are symptoms of lack of process definition and balance, combined with the lack of a *point of use* mindset. When we think of the term *waiting,* most people assume this relates only to people, but that's not so. Applying the concepts of a Lean Six Sigma methodology will lead you to observe that the waste of waiting can apply to people, machines, materials, and information. You simply have to adjust your mind to see things in a different way.

In a non-Lean Sigma process, the sight of a person standing in front of an automated piece of equipment would usually not generate any questions: "Parts are being produced, we're good to go." With a Lean Six Sigma *eye,* however, the question might be, "How do we improve the linkage between additional pieces of our process so that we can balance and fill our people in relation to machine cycle times?" Two very different views, initiating two very different paths of improvement activity.

WASTE CATEGORY #7: UNNECESSARY MOTION

This category relates to people and layout. It is a measure of travel and go-gets during the course of a work sequence. The concepts of *process definition* combined with *point of use* focus will lead us to developing processes to ensure that things (tools, materials, information) are where they need to be, when they need to be there.

These are the conventional definitions of waste from the Lean Six Sigma model, and the specific tools of Lean Six Sigma provide the means to reduce and eliminate the effects of each of these profit leaks within your organization. The importance of waste elimination is lost on many conventional companies. It's common to see a focus on finding additional sales as the cure to marginal business performance: the old, "We'll just sell our way out of this mess."

We would point out that any cost eliminated through cost reduction goes directly to your bottom line. A few minor improvements by a good Lean Six Sigma focus team will usually generate hundreds of thousands of dollars of annualized cost reduction. If you are a 10% operating income business, to push $100,000 to your operating income line you would need to obtain a million dollars ($1,000,000) in additional sales.

We contend that growth is an important metric to all businesses, but it must be combined with an aggressive focus on the continuous elimination of waste to achieve dramatic financial performance improvements. Lean Six Sigma methodology supplies the tools. Simple as that.

Chapter 4

Value Added, Nonvalue Added, Required Nonvalue Added

We've touched on the terms *value added* and *nonvalue added* in the chapter on waste. We take the opportunity to expand a bit on this topic and add a third term, *required nonvalue added*.

These terms are usually a source of much tension when a group of individuals are introduced to the philosophy of Lean Six Sigma. All individuals within an organization generally take pride in their work and consider what they do to be of importance. During the course of a Lean Sigma analysis, many people find that a great deal of what they do during the course of the day falls into the category of *nonvalue added*. The usual reaction is "No way! What I do is necessary and important to running this business!" Unfortunately, this does not change the fact that the terms are the terms, and the definitions are what they are. The disconnect here is the connotation that *nonvalue added* is bad and *value added* is good. Not so.

The important message when using these definitions is as follows: Categorizing all activity from the customer's point of view focuses our approach on challenging areas that are not essential to the physical advancement of the product or service in question. We define *waste,* and the activity that falls into one of the seven categories of waste is up for challenge. We define value added, and the activity that does not fall into this narrow definition is up for challenge. It allows us to view areas of our business processes in a different light and approach performance improvement in areas that would previously never have been considered. There is no *good* or *bad*, there is only *what is*.

Let's noodle this around.

As discussed, *value added* refers to those tasks that cause the product or service to advance to a more complete stage. Pretty straightforward stuff. We machine gears, we assemble components, we solder wires, we take your blood pressure, and we make a pizza. The product or service is moving toward a complete stage. Value is being added in the eyes of the customer, and he or she is willing to pay for this activity.

Nonvalue added is also fairly black and white. This includes the activities that do not move the product forward and fall into the seven categories of waste: the moves, inspections, process waste, waiting, excess motion, and so on. We would like to design these activities out of our process when we move to a future state, improved process.

The third category we'll introduce into the discussion of value is *required nonvalue added*. You may think this sounds like a puzzle. If it adds no value to the customer, the customer has no interest in paying for this activity, and it does not advance the product, then why isn't it simply nonvalue added? An excellent question!

EXAMPLE 1

One of my favorite examples of *required nonvalue added* is payroll. Here's some foundation logic before we begin.

We would probably be pretty safe in assuming that if we stop paying our employee population for their services, sooner or later they might stop showing up for work. So our hypothesis is that to remain a viable business we need to compensate our employees. We have a choice as to the methodology used to accomplish this task. We can have 20 accountants using no. 2 pencils and hand calculators doing the work manually, or we can have a highly automated system with card scans and automatic check writers. Either way we get the task done, but at a significant difference in cost. This is truly nonvalue-added activity. Our customer does not care how we do it, it has no impact on our product or service, and this is the point.

If we allowed ourselves to rationalize this activity as value added, we would not think of challenging this process and driving for a future state that consumes minimum cost. With nonvalue-added activity, we would simply like to stop doing it. With required nonvalue-added activity, we would like to modify the process to the lowest cost possible solution.

Okay, in this example the customer was not necessarily interested in paying for the activity. Let's discuss required nonvalue that the customer is willing to pay for.

EXAMPLE 2

We're supplying a product to a government agency. The agency requires specific inspection parameters to be performed, and a detailed documentation and traceability package must accompany the product when delivered. By our rigid definition of value added (the product is changing shape), this activity clearly falls into the nonvalue-added slot. However, it is required by the customer, and he or she is paying for this service to be performed: *required nonvalue added*.

A good deal of the activity observed in a business firm is *required nonvalue activity*, much to the dismay of the administrative folks who work very hard every day. Again, the emphasis is to identify value from the eye of the customer and challenge all activity that does not fall soundly into the value-added definition. These definitions allow no sacred cows and carry no connotations of *good* or *bad*. They merely train our *Lean Sigma eye* and lead us to a better focus on improving our processes and business systems.

Chapter 5

Flow and Pull vs. Push and Batch; Balance

The words *flow, pull, push, batch,* and *balance* all have something in common. They are descriptions of the characteristics of a system. In this chapter, we'll illustrate various operating models, discuss the characteristics we observe in them, and talk to the effects that are associated with these characteristics.

There is much debate over which methodologies are better (the old "It won't work here" argument). We do not recognize the word *better* as a term that has meaning. In business there is cost and there is revenue. Change is hard. The reason to engage in change is to promote different results. Remember the operating model definition of insanity: "To keep doing the same thing and expecting a different result." This is an exploration of the *what. What* is it we are trying to accomplish? And *what* are the effects we would like to see in our business models?

BATCH AND QUEUE

Let's start with batch, or more commonly called *batch and queue*. What is it and what are the effects of a system with batch methodology? Let's start

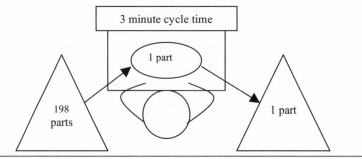

FIGURE 5-1.

with a one-station analysis. We have received a customer order for 60 units, part number 123; the money clock is now ticking (Fig. 5-1).

The setup time on this piece of equipment is 35 minutes. We've taken the order, our logistics department has calculated the economic order quantity (EOQ) of running an order across this piece of equipment, given our setup time and factory costs, and a production order has been issued for 200 parts. Of these 200 parts, 60 will be shipped to satisfy our hard order, and the balance, 140 parts, will be sent to finished goods inventory. We have satisfied our EOQ requirement, amortized our setup over the quantity of parts that we think is financially acceptable, and are confident that future orders will consume these finished goods.

What are the characteristics observed in this process; what waste do we see with this example?

- The layout is nice and tight, so let's say that excess motion is not an issue.
- We can't talk to rejects because we do not have information on this topic.
- No waiting here; our operator is working at a steady pace.
- Process waste; not enough detail to comment.
- Transport; we're only moving the parts across the work station, no transport issues.
- Overproduction? Okay, that's a yes. We are producing 140 parts that we have no hard orders for and will place them in storage. We are spending money on materials, labor, and storage space before we need to, or we could say, for no return in revenue. In addition to the expense of materials, labor, and storage, we will spend additional money on managing the accuracy of finished goods inventory, cycle counts, computer systems, etc., and may even buy a forklift to transport the

material to the stock room. Oh, wait, I guess we will have some transport waste after all.

■ Excess inventory, our last category of waste. You could argue that because this material is being worked on, it's needed. We could counter that we have 140 units worth of material, inventory, which is excess—not needed. We would also make the observation that as this order is being processed, only one unit is being worked on; the other 199 parts are either waiting to be worked on in the incoming bin or sitting in the finished bin waiting for the balance of the order to be completed and sent to shipping and finished goods, respectively.

■ Time through the manufacturing process (velocity) for this order is 600 minutes + setup time for the station (200×3 minute cycle time + setup).

It may sound like we're splitting hairs on this observation; however, a rigorous application of the definitions and categories of the Lean Sigma model will lead us to question what we see in a different way.

So, you might ask, how does this describe a batch model? Let's expand this illustration to four workstations and create four physically separate departments. In a batch and queue operation it's common to see departments, or work groupings, with similar operations located together. The logic is to group like areas together to consolidate employee skills. You'll hear descriptions like *the turning department* or *the grinding department*. This logic also prevails in most company's administrative areas, such as *the engineering department* or *the purchasing department*. At any rate, let's go, four stations, four departments (Fig. 5-2).

This model looks like a conventional non-Lean Sigma company. Let's follow the path (greatly simplified) of orders through this system.

Step 1. We bring raw materials into the facility and queue them in our receiving department.

Step 2. We release orders to the first department in our process, the drilling department. Our method of releasing orders is with a conventional materials requirement planning-driven schedule with lot sizes determined by EOQs.

Step 3. As an order is completed in the drilling department, it is moved into queue with several other orders staged for the second operation, the milling department.

Step 4. Orders are completed in the milling department and moved to the staging queue for the third operation, the grinding department.

Step 5. Orders are completed in the grinding department and transported to the staging area for the fourth operation, the turning department.

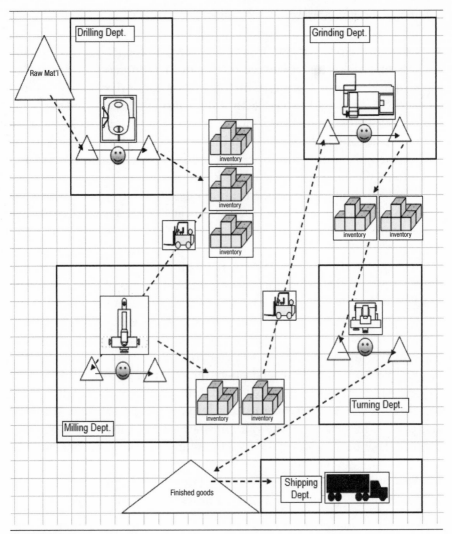

FIGURE 5-2.

Step 6. As orders are completed they are moved to finished goods.
Step 7. Orders are kitted from finished goods for shipment, and inventory remaining driven by EOQ lot sizes are stored, managed, and shipped as future orders are received.

This is pretty much a conventional business model in an organization that has not embraced the philosophy of Lean Six Sigma. What characteristics are observed in this system? Let's examine it for waste.

- Excess motion—not enough detail to determine this one.
- Rejects—again, no detail on this category.
- Waiting—no, everyone is working as fast as they can.
- Process waste—again, not enough detail to comment.
- Transport—this now becomes a large yes; we're moving all orders several steps from station to queue.
- Overproduction—still a yes, but expanded in scope. In addition to producing to a lot size being driven by EOQs as opposed to customer demand, we are producing at a disconnected rate from department to department. We are moving parts in to the various queues before the next step in the process is prepared to do something with them.
- Excess inventory—another large yes; we have queues of material staged in between each step in the process.
- Time through the manufacturing process (velocity) for an order would be the cycle time for the order size across all four steps in the process + the time to consume all staged parts in queue ahead of the newly introduced order. We can't calculate the actual time with the information given, but it would be considerable.

This illustrates a classic batch and queue model. The term *push* comes into play with a batch model in that we continue to push more work into the system whether the upstream stations are ready to work on it or not. This model also drives excess inventory because of the various steps in the process not being balanced with each other, all working at different rates of production. We are processing large batches of product across the various points in the system, and at each point we process the entire batch before moving to the staging area awaiting the next step in the process. Go, go, go!

FLOW AND PULL

Let's look at a flow model of operation. We'll start with the single-station example and expand to two stations (Fig. 5-3).

Let's examine the observed characteristics of this process.

- Excess motion—not an issue.
- Rejects—no information on this topic.
- Waiting—yes, operator 2 will have to wait 0.5 minutes every cycle because of lack of precise balance across both stations.
- Process waste—no detail.
- Transport—we're only moving the parts across the work station, no transport issues.

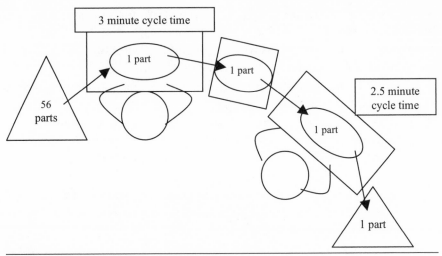

FIGURE 5-3.

- Overproduction—this model turns this category into a *No*. We are building only the 60 units that were ordered from the customer.
- Excess inventory—no, this material has been launched to cover a hard order. We can still make the observation that as this order is being processed, only two units are being worked on. The other 58 parts are either waiting to be worked on in the incoming bin or sitting in the finished bin waiting for the balance of the order to be completed. However, we've reduced the idle material by 70% and none are going to finished goods.
- Time through the manufacturing process (velocity) for this order is 182.5 minutes + setup time for the stations (5.5 minutes for the first piece and one piece every 3 minutes thereafter). Because we are not building excess units in this example, the time consumed building nonsalable product to satisfy EOQ quantities (as in the previous example) can now be spent to produce additional product with hard orders. Our on-time delivery will improve.

Let's expand this example to four stations. In this illustration we have physically linked the four stations together and flow parts from one machine to the next. Because of the size of the equipment, we have placed a small conveyance between machines to transport parts to the next operator. The operators are feeding parts directly to the next operation, and the rule has been implemented, "When the two holding containers on the conveyor are full, stop producing until one is consumed" (Fig. 5-4).

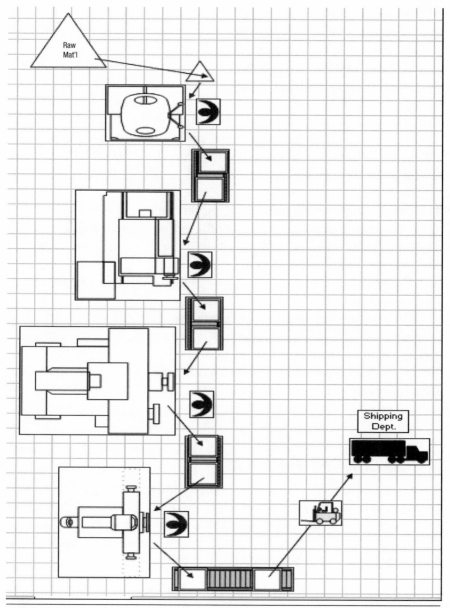

FIGURE 5-4.

Let's examine the characteristics of this system.

- Excess motion—not an issue, but we do not have low-level detail.
- Rejects—no information on this topic.
- Waiting—yes, operator 2 will have to wait 0.5 minutes every cycle because of lack of precise balance across both stations.

- Process waste—no detail.
- Transport—we're only moving the parts across the work stations, minimal transport.
- Overproduction—no, we are building to customer order and are supplying upstream internal customers based on a physical pull model.
- Excess inventory—no, this material has been launched to cover a hard order. We can still make the observation that as this order is being processed, only four units are being worked on. The other 56 parts are either waiting to be worked on in the incoming bins or sitting in the outgoing bins. However, we are flowing a single order across several workstations.
- Time through the manufacturing process (velocity) for this order. We have not established cycle times for the individual machines and would simply make the observation that an order that is launched into this work cell will process through rapidly to a finished state. Materials velocity through a process designed in this manner will be very high.

The illustrations of operating models presented so far have been extremely simplified, intentionally so. Our interest is to illustrate batch and flow with a comparison of characteristics—waste and velocity (at the concept level). The design of any system will result in outputs that reflect the nature of the specific process under analysis. With that in mind, let's summarize and discuss the ups and downs.

EFFECTS OF A BATCH SYSTEM

With a batch operations model, the simplified foundation logic is as follows: Group similar operations and machines together to localize skill sets and work as fast as you can. The metrics that are generally in play in this type of environment are machine use, labor use, and on time to schedule. Some of the effects that this system creates are as follows.

Overproduction

Because we are measuring machine and labor use, we want each piece of equipment, and each person, running as many parts as possible in a given time bucket.

"Okay, seems to make sense so far."

The traditional accounting logic in this type of model is usually the *standard cost system*. This accounting system is based on a database of *bills of material, predetermined labor content,* and *pre-allocated overhead costs.* As product is developed, the materials used in this product are defined, a *bill of material* is created that defines the specific materials and components used to create this particular part number, and the costs are assigned. This is the *standard material cost* for this part number.

In addition, the number of labor hours required to produce this particular part number is defined, transposed to dollars, and assigned, *standard labor cost.* This labor is usually called *direct* labor because these people are actually building the product. The third piece of the costing puzzle is *overhead.* In simple terms, overhead cost is everything that does not fall into the material and direct labor categories: all salaried people; indirect labor jobs such as inspection, maintenance, and material handlers; all facilities costs, such as lights, power, taxes, and so on. Overhead allocation can get complicated in real life, but we'll just make the point that overhead cost is usually assigned across all product made, in proportion to the amount of *standard hours* required to make the particular product.

"We're off on a sidebar here, but this is an important point."

All right, let's turn this method of costing around and examine how it drives behavior. When the production team in this type of facility produces a given pat number, they *earn* the amount of cost that has been locked into the standard cost database. For example, if part number XYZ contains 50 standard hours, when a unit of XYZ is completed through the last step in the process, this department *earns* 50 standard hours and *absorbs* the amount of overhead allocated to 50 hours. If the actual time worked to produce this unit was 50 hours, the department is given the efficiency rating of 100%. Job well done. This efficiency rating is earned if the product is shipped to a customer (revenue being generated) and also if part is sent to finished goods (cost is being added).

This metric system does not differentiate between sold goods and goods sent to stock; thus, the activity of overproduction is not viewed as having a negative financial impact on the business. In this operation you'll hear the people in finance saying things like, "Man, we've got to reduce our inventory levels," and you'll hear the people in production saying, "If we can just get larger batch sizes we can change over less and improve our efficiencies." A fundamental disconnect.

"Okay, back to the effects."

Excess Inventory

This is the second effect you'll observe, which is kind of a cascade effect of overproduction. With our functional departments disconnected, parts are being produced at the rates that each piece of equipment and/or person is capable of producing, no balance. This will cause large queues of work in process to accumulate in between departments. If we apply the same logic to our purchasing group, they might buy in large lot sizes to get the best piece price, lots of raw material. They will also be forced to bring in material before it is needed to support our overproduction activity.

Transport

All of this material needs to be moved from department to department and from production to stock. We'll see lots of transport, and possibly some interesting capital expenditures as we attempt to automate the material movement processes.

Cost of Quality

We haven't taken our illustration to the detail that would let us talk about reject impact. However, when we discover a quality issue in a batch environment, there are usually large quantities of product in play. We may have to rework several batches of product, depending on where the reject occurs.

Lead Time

If a new order is launched into a batch model, the time it takes to make it to finished goods—without an extensive expedite effort—is the process time to make it plus the process time of all orders queued up ahead of it in the system. Because we're building a combination of hard orders and stock product (have to satisfy the EOQ requirements), a large part of the lead time for a hard order is spent building product that we intend to merely place in stock.

Cash Flow

With all of this product in process and queue, and the associated long lead times through our system, we have *locked* a bunch of money in our *cash out* box with no associated *cash in* on its way from a customer. A simple analogy; you can do the math.

"We could expand, but let's move to the flow systems observation."

EFFECTS OF A FLOW SYSTEM

With a flow operations model the simplified foundation logic is to link processes together to produce a part from start to finish with the highest materials velocity possible through your process, and build to hard orders only (customer demand). Every *cash out* is driven by a hard *cash in.* When the required material hits your incoming dock, you don't want it to stop moving until it is placed on a truck to ship to your customer. The metrics that are generally in play in this type of environment could be sales dollars shipped per employee hours worked, on-time delivery to customer request date, and parts per million reject rate. Some of the effects that this system creates are as follows:

1. **Overproduction.** Because we're building only to hard orders and we've linked processes together, we are not overproducing in this model.

2. **Excess inventory.** Minimal excess inventory is carried in a flow operation model. With the elimination of a departmentalized layout and processes physically linked together, the model does not create excess inventory; there's nowhere to put it.

3. **Transport.** Again, minimal transport. We have physically linked processes and are building start to finish in production cells.

4. **Cost of quality.** If a reject condition is discovered in a flow operation, there are no batches to sort, only the units in the cell. Cost of quality is greatly reduced.

5. **Lead time.** With the very high velocity of a flow process, lead times are dramatically shortened.

6. **Cash flow.** Again, high velocity and short lead times result in a much faster turn on dollars locked.

BALANCE

And so we come to the starter ingredient in the flow soup—balance.
A few thoughts on balance....

- With an objective of *highest velocity,* a Lean Six Sigma system will cause you to schedule the constraint in your system, *balance up against Takt Time,* and pull from everywhere else.

- A pull system will cause you to pace all nonconstraint work areas in the system.

- A pacing analysis, driven by Takt Time, will require the comparison of machine cycle times and labor time required, with a *balance up to Takt* approach.

- Where operations cannot be balanced to an acceptable degree, line-balancing kanbans will usually be inserted into the process.

- Because variation will be disruptive to balance, a Lean Six Sigma process will use Sigma tools on reject variation reduction combined with Lean tools such as 5S for process variation reduction.
- Setup and changeover times will be disruptive to balance across the system. A setup reduction focus is critical to a successful flow process.
- The more balance you can achieve across a system, the more opportunity you will have to eliminate waste and increase velocity through the system.

Let's discuss velocity and lead time in more detail. On we go.

Chapter 6

Velocity, Throughput, and Lead Time

Okay, we've discussed *flow* versus *batch* methodologies. Let's look at the effects of these systems with an expanded discussion on time and speed. You may see these terms used in slightly different ways and that's OK, it's all in the interpretation. Here are the words:

Velocity is the speed at which an order of product or service moves through your system. The important point here is that the longer an order stays in your process, the more cost it accumulates. Another consideration is the rate of return on investment during a specific time bite. The faster you can move through your system, the faster you can complete your service or order and start the invoicing and receivables cycle into play. Fast turns on money *locked up* is the game.

Throughput is usually a term used with regard to constraints or bottlenecks in your process—your high station, if you will. We're measuring how much finished product can be made available to a customer within a finite amount of time. A common analogy here is water flowing through a pipe with different diameters (Fig. 6-1).

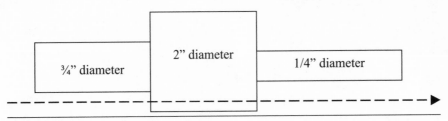

FIGURE 6-1.

No matter how much water you try and run through this pipe, the most you can run is what the quarter-inch diameter (smallest) section is capable of passing. This would be your throughput.

Lead time is the time it takes to process and order or service through your complete process, from initial customer contact with an order to delivery to your customer. It is not uncommon to see the processing time through sales, engineering, and materials exceed the velocity through the manufacturing piece. At any rate, lead time is what your customers see when they place an order. "How long does it take to get me what I want?"

In Lean Six Sigma these three terms are critical metrics. We would also add that the only reason to measure anything is if you intend to support those measurements with action plans to improve on them. Whenever you observe run charts or graphs measuring various areas of a business, the first question out of the gate should be, "Where are your action items to support and improve on these metrics, the who is doing what, and when will it be done?" If there is no detailed plan to perform activity that will make the numbers change, there's really no sense in wasting your time by compiling the measurements in the first place. So, what do we see as the importance of these terms? Let's go.

MEASURING VELOCITY

The first term, *velocity*, is important with regard to the fundamental objectives of any firm or business. Receive the maximum amount of cash into your business, from product shipped or services rendered, with the minimum amount of cash invested (we like the term *cash locked*), in the shortest time window possible. Here's a simple visual in four process steps (Fig. 6-2).

The path of materials is from raw through step 1, into queue for step 2, through step 2, into queue for step 3 and so on, into finished goods. This is a very simple process illustration in a batch mode. Several orders are in process, and they proceed in the order they are launched.

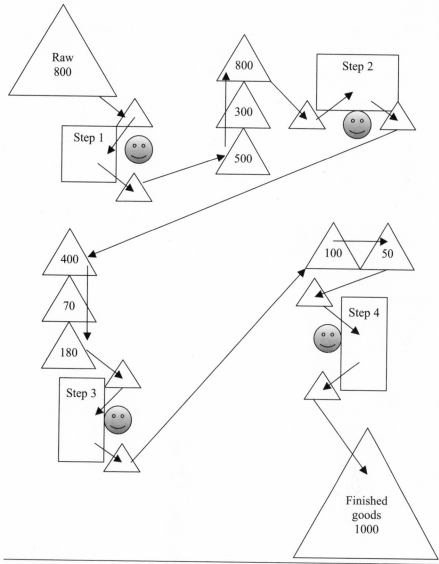

FIGURE 6-2.

For ease of numbers, let's say that each order being processed at steps 1 to 4 are 100 units each (the small triangles) and process times are as follows:

Step 1 = 1 minute
Step 2 = 2 minutes
Step 3 = 2.5 minutes
Step 4 = 1.5 minutes

We have made no attempt to balance the individual process steps; everyone works at their own individual pace and feeds the upstream queues.

- Step 1 is being fed from raw materials stock, so we'll call raw material the queue @ 800 units worth of material, plus 100 at the station being produced.
- Step 2 has three orders queued ahead @ 1,600 units plus 100 units at the station being produced.
- Step 3 has three orders in queue @ 650 units plus 100 units at the station being produced.
- Step 4 has two orders in queue @ 150 units plus 100 units at the station being produced.
- Step 4 feeds finished goods or shipping if there are hard orders in the mix.

If an order is introduced into this process and sequenced without expedite, the velocity through the process—to finished goods—is like so, starting from finished goods and working backward.

Step 4 must process all work in the system:

$$\begin{array}{r}
1 \text{ new order} = 100 \text{ units} \\
4 \text{ orders in process at the stations} = 400 \text{ units, plus} \\
3 \text{ queues of work in process (WIP)} = 1,600 \text{ units} \\
+650 \text{ units} \\
+150 \text{ units} \\
\overline{2,900 \text{ units} \times 1.5 \text{ minutes} = 4,350 \text{ minutes}}
\end{array}$$

Step 3 must process all work in the system:

$$\begin{array}{r}
1 \text{ new order} = 100 \text{ units} \\
3 \text{ orders in process at the stations} = 300 \text{ units, plus} \\
2 \text{ queues of WIP} = 1,600 \text{ units} \\
+650 \text{ units} \\
\overline{2,650 \text{ units} \times 2.5 \text{ minutes} = 6,625 \text{ minutes}}
\end{array}$$

Step 2 must process all work in the system:

$$\begin{array}{r}
1 \text{ new order} = 100 \text{ units} \\
2 \text{ orders in process at the stations} = 200 \text{ units, plus} \\
1 \text{ queue of WIP} = \underline{1,600} \text{ units} \\
1,900 \text{ units} \times 2 \text{ minutes} = 3,800 \text{ minutes}
\end{array}$$

Step 1 must process:

$$\begin{array}{r}
1 \text{ new order} = 100 \text{ units} \\
1 \text{ orders in process at the station} = \underline{100} \text{ units, plus} \\
200 \text{ units} \times 1 \text{ minute} = 200 \text{ minutes}
\end{array}$$

$$\begin{array}{r}
\text{Total} = 14,975 \text{ minutes} \\
= \underline{249.5} \text{ hours} \\
\text{At a 3-shift operation} = 10.3 \text{ days total system velocity}
\end{array}$$

There are many companies that would be quite happy with a 2-week velocity through their manufacturing process. If we again use simple math and say that a unit represents $1 of material cost, we would have $4,600 locked in materials and WIP in this system. In addition, a one day snapshot requires us to pay for 4 operators across 3 shifts or 12 operators at 8 hours each = 96 labor hours at whatever rate you care to assign; let's use $15.00 per hour + 35% fringes. Our labor cash lock for a unit of time (1 day) is $1,944.

Here are the stats for a one day snap:

        Labor = $1,944.00   ($3.37/unit shipped)
      Material = $4,600.00
      Velocity = 10.3 days
Units shipped = 576 (24 hours × our high station, step 3, at 2.5 minutes)

IMPROVING VELOCITY WITH LINK AND BALANCE

Let's compare the possibilities with a process that's linked and balanced (Fig. 6-3).

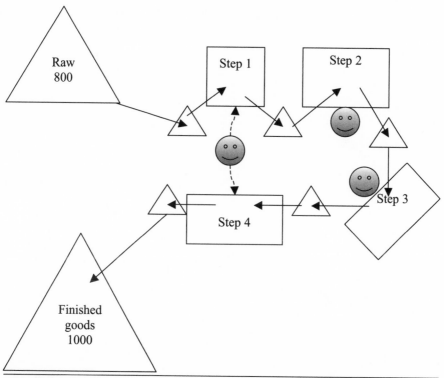

FIGURE 6-3.

With this illustration we have linked the process together and are flowing one order (100 units) across all four steps. We have combined steps 1 and 4 and assigned these tasks to one operator; you'll recall our task times.

Step 1 (1 minute) + Step 4 (1.5 minutes) = 2.5 minutes total
Step 2 = 2 minutes
Step 3 = 2.5 minutes

We'll leave raw and finished goods as they were, although in real life we would reduce finished goods if our velocity increased, at any rate. Let's introduce a new order.

Step 4 must process

$$
\begin{array}{r}
1 \text{ new order} = 100 \text{ units} \\
1 \text{ orders in process in the cell} = \underline{100} \text{ units} \\
200 \text{ units} \times 1.5 \text{ minutes} = 300 \text{ minutes}
\end{array}
$$

Step 3 must process

$$
\begin{array}{r}
1 \text{ new order} = 100 \text{ units} \\
1 \text{ order in process in the cell} = \underline{100} \text{ units} \\
200 \text{ units} \times 2.5 \text{ minutes} = 500 \text{ minutes}
\end{array}
$$

Step 2 must process

$$
\begin{array}{r}
1 \text{ new order} = 100 \text{ units} \\
1 \text{ order in process in the cell} = \underline{100} \text{ units} \\
200 \text{ units} \times 2 \text{ minutes} = 400 \text{ minutes}
\end{array}
$$

Step 1 must process

$$
\begin{array}{r}
1 \text{ new order} = 100 \text{ units} \\
1 \text{ order in process in the cell} = \underline{100} \text{ units} \\
200 \text{ units} \times 1 \text{ minute} = 200 \text{ minutes}
\end{array}
$$

$$
\begin{array}{r}
\text{Total} = 1{,}400 \text{ minutes} \\
= \underline{23.3} \text{ hours} \\
\text{At a 3-shift operation} = 1 \text{ day total system velocity}
\end{array}
$$

Same math; a unit represents $1 of material cost; we would have $2,000 locked in materials in this system at 800 raw, 1,000 finished goods, 200 WIP. In addition, a 1-day snapshot requires us to pay for three operators across three shifts or nine operators at 8 hours each = 72 labor hours at $15.00 per hour + 35% fringes. Our labor cash lock for a unit of time (1 day) is $1,458.00

Here's the new stats for a 1-day snap:

Labor = $1,458.00   ($2.53/unit shipped)
Material = $2,000.00
Velocity = 1 day

Units shipped = 576 (24 hours × our high station, step 3, at 2.5 minutes or, steps 1 + 4, also 2.5 minutes)

A lightning analysis shows that we reduced our labor by 25%, materials locked per unit shipped is cut in half, and our velocity went from 10 days to 1 day. Big numbers—that's the *what* we're trying to accomplish.

LEAD TIME

If we expand our model to evaluate lead time through the entire system, we'd be looking at time through sales and order entry, engineering, materials and scheduling, and so on. By applying value stream mapping techniques against waste observed, we would follow the same logic and develop a plan for a future state with process linkage and balance. We would also apply Six Sigma techniques to minimize variation across the system and allow for predictable balance. Same logic, same type of results.

THROUGHPUT

Our throughput is defined by our high station—step 3 in this example. If we needed to increase our throughput to satisfy customer demand, we would need to add an additional station (or machine) to reduce the 2.5-minute current state requirement at this step.

Those are the terms. They represent a very real opportunity to improve an operational model if they are used to drive systems design of a future state model. Link and balance, minimize the areas of waste, minimize variation in the process, increase speed through the system, and the cash will take care of itself.

Let's move on to cost and profit.

Chapter 7

Cost and Profit—Cash Flow

As we analyze a business process or system for value-added content, the subject of cost turns into an interesting area of discussion. As we prepare our quarterly reports to the board of directors and our stockholders, profitability turns into an even more interesting area of discussion. Let's examine the relationship between cost and profit for a bit before we proceed to *true cost*.

There are those who believe profit can be predetermined. You establish your cost, you add whatever margin you desire for profit, and then you establish your selling price. We would comment that it's usually not quite that easy.

In today's global marketplace, the cost of various types of materials, taxes, running expenses such as heat, electricity, water within a given region, and labor are all predetermined by the prevailing market rates for each commodity. If your company is very large, you may get some pricing leverage through volume and corporate partnerships. But within a certain window, it's a level playing field for all competitors within a given market. So much for the cost of commodities; we're inside the curves.

At the same time the selling price for any particular product or service is locked by the range of comparable products or services being offered by the various companies and firms that provide those offerings. Quality is usually considered to be a given, and with that considered, we could say that our selling price (window) is also set by prevailing market conditions.

If we consider our profit to be the difference between our cost and our selling price this leads us to some interesting questions. Namely, how do we increase our profit when the two variables that produce this effect are controlled by forces largely outside of our span of control?

If we expand on this thought and think of the equation:

$$\text{Profit} = \text{Selling Price} - \text{Cost}$$

We might drop down a layer and make the observation, "If our selling price is truly set by the marketplace, and our profit is the *effect* of selling price minus cost, then I guess we better figure out how to reduce our cost!" Good observation!

We think the answer lies in the riddle of establishing our *true cost*, not to be confused with what we observe as our *actual cost*. This brings us back to the seven types of waste and the definitions of value added and non-value added.

ESTABLISHING THE TRUE COST

What is the true cost to produce a product or service? If we were to observe the value-added content of a work sequence to make a given product, we would observe only those steps that physically forward the product or service to a more complete state. Ruthlessly simple definition! When we observe the typical value stream (baseline) mapping event, it is common to see that the value-added portion of the map comprises only a small amount of the activity observed (30 minutes of touch time, 8 weeks of lead time?).

Let's peel the *value onion*:

1. We assemble three parts together, paint the product green, and apply a name label.

   "This is great stuff, value-added work always belongs in our true cost."

2. We pay the light bill so the power company doesn't turn off the lights. (It's usually slower to work in the dark, without heat, and our electric coffee pot won't work.)

   "Oh, oh, nonvalue added, but we could argue that it's required, so let's develop the most cost-effective way to get this task done and include it into our true cost."

3. We work with our customers to define their desired product characteristics.

"Nonvalue added by our strict definition, but definitely required because we build a lot of custom product, let's add it to our cost."

4. We run payroll so that our employees can be paid every week.

   "We did stop this nonvalue-added activity for a short time, but our Human Resources Director (Maritza Aleman) convinced us that there was a direct correlation between our skyrocketing turnover rates and this activity. We resumed with an automated low-cost process; let's add it to our cost."

5. We decide to break up our *three parts* assembly into three separate departments and physically locate them in different parts of our facility.

   "Shorter learning curves, less education/training cost, skill-set consolidation and all that sort of thing. However, we seemed to have added the waste of transport into or process. We had to buy a couple of forklifts too."

   What else? "Hey what are you waiting for?" "I'm waiting for our materials handler to bring some parts over; don't worry, he said he'd only be 15 minutes." "This is not part of our true cost, this is waste."

6. We also decide to move our paint process into the building next door because our assembly folks don't like the way the fumes smell.

   "More waste, transport, facilities expense, and such, not part of our true cost." "Oh yeah, we had to add one more forklift and a material handler."

7. We choose to lease 100,000 square feet of warehouse space to store partially assembled components in between steps because the three assembly areas can't seem to work at the same pace and we need temporary storage. And because we have the room, let's put our name label on in the warehouse so that when we bring the parts to the last assembly area, we'll have the jump on it.

   "We needed this space to be able to store our overproduction, although it sure seemed to fill up with inventory awfully quick!" "Plus, we got a great price, only $5.00 per square foot." "Oh, almost forgot, we had to buy three more forklifts, hire three forklift operators, buy four computers with the associated software, and hire the materials coordinators to manage, count, and control this inventory, and buy a small truck to transport parts back and forth. (Did we forget the truck driver?)"

8. For some reason, we never seemed to develop an effective maintenance process, we have preventative maintenance, but our equipment still breaks down with alarming frequency (thank God for FedEx), and as our machines age, we experience a growing level of rejects and scrap.

"Not a problem, we are definitely on top of this one. We recruited five highly skilled inspectors (top of the pay scale for our company) and purchased state-of-the-art laser measuring devices. Our quality is superb! We inspect all products 100% before they are shipped to our customers!" "Waste, or should we include it in our true cost?"

That's a tough one, let's noodle it around for a while.

Reduce cost? Improve profitability? As we reduce our cost (this is activity we engage in, we *do* the work), we increase our profitability (we don't *do* anything here, better profitability is the *effect* of us reducing our cost).

And so it goes. . . .

CASH FLOW

We've been talking to true cost and its relationship to profitability, which brings us to another piece of this financial puzzle: cash flow. We've all heard the old statement "I'd rather have good cash flow than be profitable." To some people this would sound like a strange thing to say, but it's all in the timing. Obviously an unprofitable business will, at some point in time, run up on the rocks. At the same time it's possible to be extremely profitable and simply go out of business. Again, to some people this statement might not make any sense. "How can you be extremely profitable and go out of business?" Let's take a look at how cost, nonvalue-added activity, waste, and cash flow fit together.

Example 1

Company A has a traditional batch and queue, departmentalized production operating philosophy. We'll use a time-line analogy and, as usual, keep it simple. Here are steps in the value stream:

1. Company A receives an order from a customer.

   "It's March 1."

2. It's a standard order, so they process it through their normal system—sales, order entry, materials, and scheduling; materials are ordered, and configuration puts a manufacturing order/package together to release to manufacturing.

   "It's March 22, the normal 3-week lead time through the administrative processes."

3. Our materials arrive.

   "It's April 5, the *money clock* starts ticking. Our payables are running at 35 days, which means we have to pay our vendors (on average) for these materials in 35 days—sounds like May 10, give or take."

4. We launch our order into our manufacturing process. Because we batch orders we have 190 orders on the floor (2500 parts in the system) in queue at the various steps of the process. Our manufacturing lead time is the normal (in our industry) 8 weeks. The order works through the process and is completed, shipped, and invoiced.

   "It's May 31. You'll remember that we had to pay for these materials back on May 10. We also paid all of our employees during this time period, administrative people since March 1 and production people since April 5."

5. We receive payment for this order.

   It's July 19, our receivables are running at 49 days, which is the time our customers take before paying us (on average).

The activity on this order spans almost 5 months. Our *cash out* began shortly after March 1 and continues through May 31. Our *cash in* occurred on July 19. When we talk of a value stream as being a *cash-to-cash* view, this is what we mean. The entire cycle from initial receipt of a customer order to the receipt of payment for product or services delivered is the value stream. The seven types of waste cause our value steam to have a longer lead time through the pipe, which negatively affects our cash flow position. We must carry a large amount of money spent in our *float* before we receive payment—negative cash flow.

Example 2

Let's look at Company B—a balanced, flow operation.

1. Company B receives an order from a customer.

   "It's March 1."

2. It's a standard order, so the customer was able to directly access our product configurator via the Internet; the order is entered into the system, and materials are ordered.

   "It's March 1, the normal 1-day lead time through the administrative processes."

3. Our materials are here.

   "It's March 1, we have a kanban process in place with our vendors on repetitive, volume business with a consignment agreement, and we pay for materials as they are consumed from the kanban. The money clock is ticking, and we must pay for this material in 35 days (April 5)."

4. We launch our order into our manufacturing process. Because we have physically linked our processes together and balanced work across the process, we have no queues of material (excess inventory) in the system and very high velocity. Our Six Sigma environment has provided us with minimal variation across our value stream. Our manufacturing lead time is 5 days. The order works through the process and is completed, shipped, and invoiced.

   "It's March 8."

5. We receive payment for this order.
   "It's April 7, our receivables are running at 30 days, which is the time our customers take before paying us (on average). We were able to negotiate a 30-day receivables agreement because our lead time is considerably better than that of our competitors. This allows our customer to reduce the damage caused by forecasting out 8 weeks and eliminates a large investment in their finished goods."

The activity on this order spans 1 month. Our *cash out* began shortly after March 1, and our *cash in* occurred on April 7. We do not suffer the cost of an additional $4\frac{1}{2}$ months of float. We have minimized the seven types of waste in our system and enjoy a very high velocity through the process with greatly reduced *true cost*. We don't spend much on transport, rejects and rework, excess inventory, or overproduction, and our space requirements are far less than those of our competition. Because our cost is so much less than our competition we have chosen to drop our prices and take some market share. Our competition has been forced to reduce their pricing to stay in the game, and their operating margins have dropped to a break-even level. They are in a painful position; they are being forced to compete with a Lean Six Sigma company.

I could go on with illustrations, but I think you get the picture: less waste, less process variation, higher velocity, better cash flow, many competitive advantages. That's the game, it's all about cash.

And with that said, let's move on to the tools required to put this type of methodology in place.

PART 2

The How

Chapter 8

The Basic Tools of Lean Six Sigma

Lean Six Sigma involves a lot of measuring, charting, and comparing. It is necessary to recognize what areas need immediate improvement, determine what projects to tackle first, keep track of your progress, and assess the success of your initiatives. This chapter covers the basic tools of Lean Six Sigma—metrics, charts, and dashboards—and brainstorming sessions to decide what projects will provide the biggest benefit in the shortest time.

THE IMPORTANCE OF METRICS

Metrics are important because they tell you how you are doing. They tell you how you are doing in business, manufacturing, service, and in fact just about anything. Take sports, for instance. Look at the scoreboard in the ballpark: the inning, score, balls, strikes, outs, runs, hits, and errors. These are numbers that everyone understands. Even kids understand them. What's more, everyone constantly watches them throughout the game. That way they can keep up with what's going on (Fig. 8-1).

In manufacturing, metrics tell you how well your processes are performing. They tell you how fast you are getting product to your customers,

FIGURE 8-1.

how much you are spending on poor quality, and how often you ship your products on time to your customers. If you are providing a service, metrics will tell you how much your customers are pleased with your service. Metrics may tell you the average amount of rings that occur before you answer a call, the number of minutes a customer is on hold, or the number of calls handled per hour. Metrics could even tell you the average waiting time spent in the lobby of a dentist office.

Many companies have not mastered the use of metrics. Every day people go to work in hundreds of places and have little idea of how well they are doing. In fact, they may not even be sure of what it is that's expected of them or their work area. These people don't know the score of a game that involves feeding and housing their families, what they will have when they retire, how they will help their kids through college—a pretty important game, wouldn't you say? Yet, very often employees know more about how their favorite team is performing than how the company or factory they work for is doing. They know how well their teams are batting or scoring, yet they don't know the first-time pass rate of items produced in their work area.

Then there are statistics. These analyses tell you how well you are doing compared with others. If you are a part of a team, statistics let you and your teammates know what you are doing well at, and what you are not. They tell you where you need to focus your improvement efforts—what to work on individually and as a team.

DEVELOPING MEANINGFUL METRICS

Developing meaningful metrics is an important function. It has been said that the most important decision we make every day is deciding what to work on. You can work all day and not move closer to your goals. It only makes sense that another important decision is what we will measure. After all, in most organizations the metrics will drive behavior and focus people's efforts. It has also been said, "What gets measured, gets done." There is a lot of truth to that.

Metrics should complement each other and balance each other out. For example, if you just measure labor efficiency and nothing else, operators will focus on speed, sacrifice quality, and use excessive materials in the mean time. A heavy focus on labor efficiency will drive inventory levels high. Foremen earn high efficiencies by producing products whether they are needed or not. To achieve balanced results, the organization should also focus on on-time delivery, cost, and quality. These metrics complement each other and will produce better results.

Metrics should be clear and understandable to the people managing the process driving them. It doesn't do any good to post *Rolled Throughput Yield* if the people in the area don't understand what it is. You must clearly communicate the meaning of metrics to operators and staff. They must understand what the metrics mean and what behaviors or situations drive them. Everyone should understand what actions they need to take to move the metrics in the right direction. Again, everyone understands balls, strikes, outs, and runs, so shouldn't they understand the metrics important to their jobs?

Metrics have to be meaningful. If a metric is improving, then the performance of the process should be improving or getting better. In other words, if you are measuring the amount of defects in an area and they are going down, it would make sense that the payroll expense for the department doing the rework is going down. Be careful. Once again, you could be all fired up while advising your boss that a department is making great progress in improving quality. Meanwhile, your controller is shaking his/her head, because he/she knows that the department's payroll hasn't gone down. In fact it might be increasing. I personally like to review metrics with accounting. They often have good feedback.

Metrics are most valuable and effective when everyone in the organization understands them, at least area by area. Operators should understand what the metrics for their areas mean and how their actions directly affect them. They should understand what corrective actions must be taken to move them in the right direction, or what actions or decisions will keep them in an acceptable range.

In Lean Six Sigma, metrics are important because we are trying to measure the impact of our efforts on projects. Again, they tell us how we are doing or whether the improvement plan we are implementing is working. Lean Six Sigma views anything the customer is not willing to pay for as a defect. This opens up a broad spectrum of measurements.

EXAMPLES OF COMMON METRICS

- First-time pass
- Defects per opportunity
- Labor efficiency to standard
- Rework
- Critical process levels
- Average time to introduce a new product into production
- Number of new products introduced in a given time period
- Materials variance to standard
- Shop supplies performance to budget
- Process defects
- Error rates
- Process cycle time
- Process consumption
- Accident/incident per hour worked
- Customer satisfaction
- On-time delivery
- Number of customer suggestions integrated into a new product
- Market share
- Inventory turns
- Fill rate/stock outs
- Sales $ per employee

FIRST-TIME PASS

Plug *first-time pass* into an Internet search engine and you will see lists of hits for first-time pass for people taking bar exams after taking a preparation course. Colleges are taking credit for high rates of students passing the Certified Public Accountant exam the first time. Take our real estate course

First Pass Yield - Tachometer gage					
Date	Day	Yield	Date	Day	Yield
2-Aug	Tue	88%	16-Aug	Tue	87%
3-Aug	Wed	89%	17-Aug	Wed	91%
4-Aug	Thu	91%	18-Aug	Thu	92%
5-Aug	Fri	90%	19-Aug	Fri	89%
8-Aug	Mon	89%	22-Aug	Mon	88%
9-Aug	Tue	86%	23-Aug	Tue	87%
10-Aug	Wed	88%	24-Aug	Wed	89%
11-Aug	Thu	92%	25-Aug	Thu	90%
12-Aug	Fri	93%	26-Aug	Fri	89%
15-Aug	Mon	88%	29-Aug	Mon	86%

FIGURE 8-2.

and pass the first time! It is easy to understand why passing the bar, the Certified Public Accountant exam, or the real estate exam the first time is important. This is because if you have to take them a second time, you will have wasted your money and time preparing for it the first time.

In manufacturing, not getting it right the first time, and having to re-work an assembly or product to get it right, is called waste. It is expensive, unnecessary, and something that customers are not willing to pay for. So getting products correct the first time is important and the least costly way to manufacture. Because first-time pass is a measurement of yield in a process, it is an excellent quality metric (Figs. 8-2 and 8-3).

First-time pass yield is determined by developing a list of all possible defects for a process and applying a measurement system capable of accuracy. The system must contain equipment that is capable of meeting the requirements of the system. Repeatability and reproducibility of the measuring equipment must also be adequate.

HOW TO CONDUCT A BRAINSTORMING SESSION

One of the basic tools for developing a list of candidate projects is a brainstorming session. I recommend that you bring in key players from your organization, and make sure one of them is from accounting. This session should be conducted in a large room, preferably a conference room with a dry-wipe board and open walls. Either yourself, a Black Belt, or someone

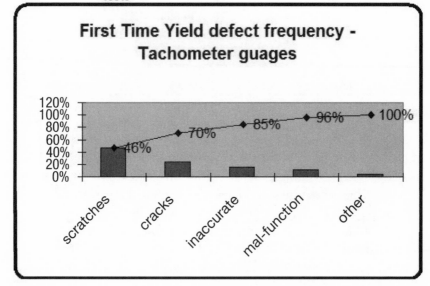

First Pass Yield defects - Tachometer gage

scratches	46%	46%
cracks	24%	70%
inaccurate	15%	85%
mal-function	11%	96%
Other	4%	100%
	100%	

First Time Yield defect frequency - Tachometer guages

120%
100%
80%
60%
40%
20%
0%

46% 70% 85% 96% 100%

scratches   cracks   inaccurate   mal-function   other

FIGURE 8-3.

on your team with good facilitation skills should lead the session. Bring some of those yellow Post-it notes and something to write with. Have everyone sit where they can face the board or an open wall. Advise the group that the object of the meeting is to determine a list of key candidate projects that will help you achieve your current strategic objectives or solve some key issues affecting the performance of your business or plant. These projects will be made up of important tasks that will greatly improve the results of the business or solve some major problem.

Communicate to the group that you will be soliciting ideas for projects and key issues affecting the business by going around the table from right to left one person at a time. Each person will suggest only one idea at a time. Each time a suggestion is received the facilitator will write it on a Post-it and put it on the wall, only putting one idea on each Post-it. There is no talking, discussion, or debating issues during this process. The only talking should be as each person makes their suggestion. The facilitator will write each suggestion on a Post-it note and stick it on the wall. If someone cannot think of a suggestion they can just say *pass*. Follow this process until everyone has passed twice.

Next, the facilitator leads the group in sorting the ideas into categories. Category headers can be made with additional Post-it notes.

SELECTING THE PROJECT

Project selection is an important process. The company is going to deploy valuable and scarce resources such as time and money. There has to be a payback for the effort. The matrix below can be an aid in selecting the project that will provide the biggest benefit in the shortest amount of time. As a team—and, again, remember to get a member of your accounting staff involved—take care in placing the projects on the matrix according to how easy or hard they will be to implement, how long it will take to finish them, and how big the payback is. Initially, it is best to pick a project with a relatively big payback that will get done in the shortest time period (Fig. 8-4).

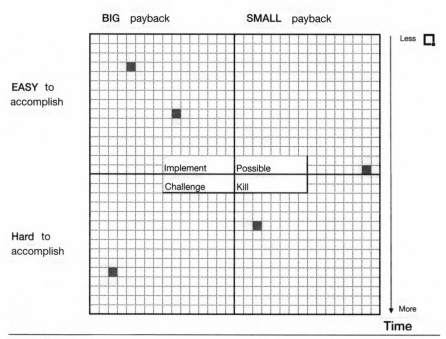

FIGURE 8-4.

PARETO CHARTS

A Pareto chart is a bar chart that shows the ranking or importance of a particular category of something. The categories might be types of defects, expenditure categories, and reasons for a situation, categories of complaints, and on and on. Pareto analysis allows us to see the relative importance against or occurrence of the different categories in a group. The Pareto principle says that 80% of problems or defects are driven by 20% of the causes. The idea is that if you know what category of defects or causes you are experiencing the most, you will know what to work on. Working on the category with the highest occurrence has the potential to give you the most benefit.

One word of caution is in order. When using a Pareto chart to analyze defects it is helpful to measure the dollars in rework each category is driving as opposed to what category is occurring most often. This is because some defects cost a lot more to rework than others. Your most frequently occurring defect may be the least costly to rework. Addressing the top defects by rework cost will usually yield the biggest payback.

To create a Pareto chart such as the one below, do the following:

1. Collect measurement data such as defects.
2. Categorize the data.
3. Determine the percentage of occurrence of each category relative to the total amount of defects.
4. Put the data in spreadsheet form as indicated, and create a bar chart with a bar and a line. The line should indicate the cumulative percentage across the categories from the most to least frequent (Fig. 8-5).

Notice that when categorized by the hours of rework generated by defect category, that cracks are driving more rework. In this case you would gain the most benefit by root causing and taking corrective action to eliminate the number of crack defects (Fig. 8-6).

RUN DIAGRAMS

A run diagram is a chart that tracks one or more variables over time. It is used to track variation and trends in the occurrence of a defect over time. It provides a meaningful visual that can signal something at a glance. It could be the number of defects per shift or the number of hours of overtime per shift. Below is an example of a run diagram indicating the number of orders processed per day in a shipping department. This may be helpful for the supervisor. It may signal the number of orders declining,

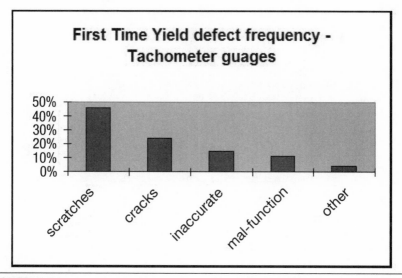

First Pass Yield defects - Tachometer gage					
				# defects	
scratches	46%	46%		612	
cracks	24%	70%		319	
inaccurate	15%	85%		200	
mal-function	11%	96%		146	
Other	4%	100%		53	
	100%			1330	

FIGURE 8-5.

which could signal a problem in the shipping area. It may signal a slow-down and the need to adjust staffing downward (Fig. 8-7).

Run diagrams are useful if the defect or situation they are tracking is a meaningful metric. They are only as helpful as the metric is meaningful.

DASHBOARDS

Dashboards are clusters of information relating to a particular area's performance. If it is done right, there will be a common theme that ties all individual department or area metrics to the company's strategic goals or objectives. The idea is if all departments are improving their metrics, the company is making progress toward its goals. Lean Six Sigma projects should be tied to the company's overall objectives. So, if a project team is making progress toward their metrics then the company is progressing toward its goals.

First Pass Yield defects - Tachometer gage					
				hours rework	
cracks	48%	48%		612	1679
scratches	36%	84%		798	1679
inaccurate	9%	93%		150	1679
mal-function	5%	98%		88	1679
Other	2%	100%		32	1679
	100%			1679	

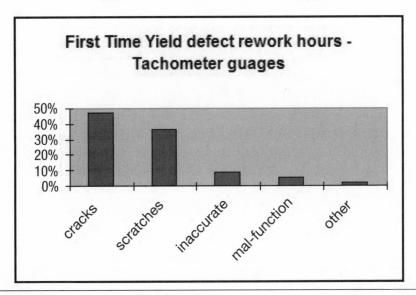

FIGURE 8-6.

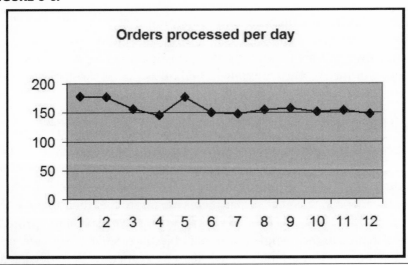

FIGURE 8-7.

A dashboard is a cluster of charts, graphs, or information relative to a certain area or areas. It displays meaningful information that operators, supervisors, and management can observe to determine the areas performance. Quite simply, the dashboard tells an operator how things are going and, when necessary, where to focus his or her improvement efforts. For a metric to be meaningful, an operator must be able to affect the metric through his or her performance. It must also be clear how the operator's performance is tied to the metric.

When placing a dashboard in an area for the first time, you can explain it to operators with the analogy of a dashboard in a car. The dashboard in a car indicates speed, temperature, oil pressure, revolutions per minute, and so on. If a driver observes low oil pressure or a warning light, he or she must pull the car to the side of the road to address the problem. If the driver does not, the results could be catastrophic to the car's engine.

A dashboard in a process or work area can be observed the same way. If the operator notices that a key metric is out of control or spec, then he or she should stop the process or *pull it to the side of the road*. At that point, a member of the Quality staff—think of a *Good Samaritan*—happens to pull up to offer roadside assistance to get the process back under control. This is a good way to explain dashboards when first introducing them.

One problem is that operators can be very defensive when a dashboard is first put in their area. It is important that you encourage them to become *offensive* and work to improve the process or area's performance. Dashboards can create a great deal of positive energy in employees. They can be such a valuable tool and can be used very effectively to focus the efforts of a group. If your organization doesn't have dashboards in the different areas, you are missing out.

Dashboards are relatively easy to create using the popular spreadsheet programs. Determine what data to gather, and enter the data into spreadsheets. Highlight the spreadsheets and create charts. Then print the charts and put them up in a cluster. If you have a plotter you are in business. Place the charts on one page of a spreadsheet. Set the print area to include all of them. Print them on a C- or D-size document. You can put company logos on them or even digital pictures of the operators.

A dashboard is created by presenting a cluster of charts, data, and information relative to an area, process, or group of people. It provides them with meaningful information on how their process is performing, what is driving defects or problems, and where they need to focus their improvement efforts. Below is a dashboard for a purchasing department (Fig. 8-8).

Other helpful templates are shown in Figures 8-9 and 8-10.

Dashboard - Purchasing Key performance metrics

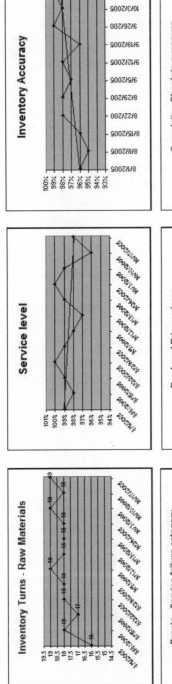

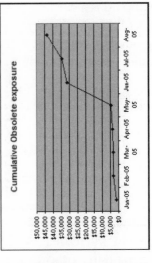

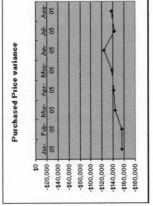

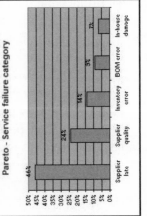

FIGURE 8-8.

Project Charter	
Project :	
Project Leader :	
Problem/s to be solved :	
Process/es impacted :	
Process/es not impacted :	
Process measurements:	
Team Member/s :	
Project goals / deliverables :	
Project Start :	
Project End :	
	Milestones
Define	
Measure	
Analyze	
Improve	
Control	

FIGURE 8-9.

Meeting Agenda				
Date	Start	End	Action items	Assigned to:

FIGURE 8-10.

Chapter 9

Value Stream Mapping (Baselining)

A fundamental tool of the Lean journey is a *baseline analysis*. The flyby objective of this powerful tool is to define the current state of a chosen business process, evaluate the system for waste and opportunity, create a future (proposed) state of the process, and formulate a plan of action to get there.

Before we get into some of the nuts and bolts of this process, we've got an interesting introduction written by a long-time client and good friend, Marty Paino. Marty is the Lean mastermind for BAE Systems, Ground Systems Division in York, Pennsylvania. Having spent his career in manufacturing, with a heavy emphasis on industrial engineering, Marty is a dangerous guy if your name is *waste*. His implementations are the best we've seen, and we've seen a few. Here's his piece. Enjoy.

NOT A COOKIE-CUTTER APPROACH

Becoming Lean is challenging; it requires the dedication of time and resources. Companies must know what their customer expects and be committed to providing that. You don't have to look any further than the BAE Systems, York, Pennsylvania, Assembly, Test, and Integration Plant to find a great benchmarking example of how to implement Lean manufacturing and the improvements that can be achieved as a result. The following dissertation is our journey, our approach to implementing Lean. It may work for your organization or it may not. The point here is simple. *There is not a one-time fix all formula for implementing Lean.* What works for one company may not work for another. It's not a cookie-cutter approach.

STARTS FROM THE TOP

Lean transformation, whether in the office or on the manufacturing floor, just doesn't happen. It starts from the organization's top management. We have all read the standard books and impressive magazine articles. We have talked to, visited, and benchmarked other successful Lean companies. When all is said and done, the one common denominator, the common theme we see in the companies that are making great progress, is commitment from the Top!

CHOOSE AN AREA

In the beginning of a company's Lean journey, it is critical for everybody to *buy in*. To achieve this, choose an area that has a small scope of work, not many parts to deal with, and make that area a *showcase*. Create a baseline, map the current state, propose a future state, and move out. As far as I'm concerned, one of the most critical features in the future state is visual management. We will touch on this later. The key here is this area has to be the *envy* of the remainder of the facility. Everybody will want to work in this area. Everybody will enjoy coming to work.

EDUCATE, EDUCATE, THEN EDUCATE AGAIN

Past lessons learned: You can't educate enough! Change is difficult. The risks may be perceived as personal. "What's going to happen to my job? I have been doing it this way for several years. . ." are initial reactions of many employees. Because everyone internalizes change at a different rate, education and reeducating over and over again is critical.

As our journey continued at BAE Systems, every employee, both hourly and salary support staff, received an 8-hour class on Lean theory and Lean participative exercises. We chose to use an outside consultant for this. Choosing the right professional here is critical. We believed that this person had to have not only excellent facilitation skills but also outstanding shop floor experience. This person must be one who shared with the pains and could empathize with the demands of the shop floor.

CREATING THE BASELINE

With the assistance of our consultant, we chose to do a nontypical value stream of our current state. To achieve this, we assembled into a room the area supervisors, engineers, and most important, the *true experts* of the process, the assemblers.

The scope of the value stream was not the typical cash-to-cash approach from the time an order is placed to when it is shipped. We chose to map the manufacturing steps, including all the nonvalue *go-gets* in the process. As the picture below shows, we used Post-it notes. We thought that this method of mapping would be less intimidating for the assemblers to use. Every process received a Post-it note, even if one of the notes said "go get crane." Every note received a value in minutes and a color-coded sticker. Green represented value added, and red represented nonvalue added. The totals for each category were tallied and reviewed by the participants (Fig. 9-1).

This two-day exercise was an eye-opener. Not because we had a large amount of nonvalue-added activities taking place. We knew that. By having the assemblers participate in the value stream analysis, they began to realize

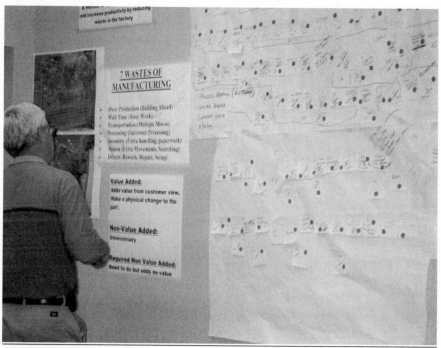

FIGURE 9-1.

how much time was being spent waiting, transporting, and going to get various component parts and/or tools—all waste!

WORKPLACE ORGANIZATION: THE 6S SYSTEM

Every book and magazine article stresses the 5S program. For the purpose of this article, I would like to stress the sixth "S"—safety. The number one priority has to be safety. It is our job as management to ensure that an employee goes home every day in the same condition he/she came to work in. No longer is it acceptable for an employee to bend over and obtain a part from the floor or reach 12 inches over his/her head. Parts are to be located in the *strike zone*.

Ergonomic solutions do not have to be expensive. Simple transport carts assist in moving parts from point A to point B. A table to set a skid on eliminates the need to bend. The following illustrations show how inexpensive solutions can be a warm welcome to the assemblers on the production line (Figs. 9-2 and 9-3).

CREATING THE VISUAL FACTORY

In our factory, the goal was to create what we call a *visual factory*. Within seconds of entering a production bay, you can tell what condition the shop is in without communicating with a single person. Does every station have work? Is there a kanban cart staged for the next station to pull from? I can

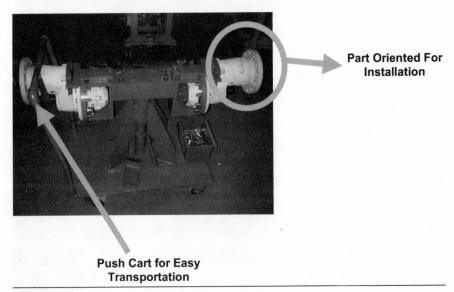

Part Oriented For Installation

Push Cart for Easy Transportation

FIGURE 9-2.

Adjustable Height

FIGURE 9-3.

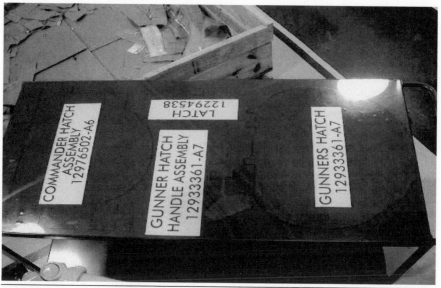

COMMANDER HATCH ASSEMBLY 12976502-A6

LATCH 12294538

GUNNER HATCH HANDLE ASSEMBLY 1293361-A7

GUNNERS HATCH 1293361-A7

FIGURE 9-4.

tell if we are on schedule or behind schedule, and view other critical metrics because there is a *white board* displaying the status of each work station.

We also control inventory levels and production schedules visually. The picture below shows how a simple cart, outlined with red silhouettes of the component part, can be used to control both overproduction and work in process inventory levels (Fig. 9-4).

FIGURE 9-5.

When the assembler sees red it is his/her trigger to build that specific product. Once all the silhouettes are covered, that's the signal to stop producing. That simple! There are two carts. The first cart with all silhouettes full is being consumed by the assembler on the production line. The second cart, located with the sub-assembler across the aisle, is being filled and staged ready to support the assembler on the assembly line. The carts go back and forth between the assembly line and the sub-assembly line.

Another major benefit of the cart system is safety. The above example eliminated overproduction and excess inventory levels. The following example adds safety to the equation (Figs. 9-5 and 9-6).

Figure 9-5 shows parts next to the floor, resulting in many assemblers reaching and being out of position. In addition to the long reach, there are many pinch points to be concerned about. Figure 9-6 eliminates that risk. Parts are within reach, easily accessible, and at an increased height.

JUST DO IT!

The single, most difficult thing to do is to get started. You just have to do it. Be wary of *paralysis by analysis*. You will find organizations spend a great deal of time planning, making sure every "t" is crossed and every "i" is dotted. A big waste of resources.

Do an event. Simulate the proposed process. Get out on the production floor. Don't be afraid to move fixtures, benches, and other items associated

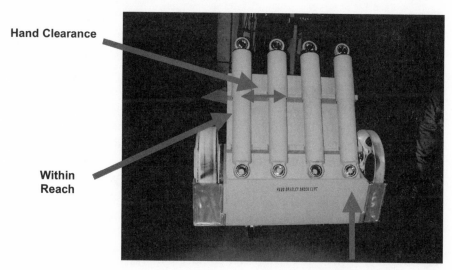

Hand Clearance

Within
Reach

Increased Height

FIGURE 9-6.

with the process over and over again. We are fortunate at BAE; our management measures our success on how many times racks and benches are relocated on the production floor. "This demonstrates continuous thinking and improvement." Just do it, and don't be afraid to do it again. Remember, there is no cookie-cutter approach.

Marty Paino
Lean Manager
BEA Systems
Ground Systems Division
York, Pennsylvania

> Good stuff!
> Okay, let's expand on the baseline process.

DOING AN INITIAL BASELINE

To allow enough time to get through the event process, a typical initial baseline requires a 5-day block of time, preceded by some data collecting, planning discussions to define the segment of the business to be analyzed, and choosing a good cross-functional team. Because we're going to be looking at the total process, the members of the team should represent all functions across the value stream.

The reason we used the term *initial baseline* is when you perform the first baseline in a company that is new to this tool, you should map a chosen process through the entire value stream. For example, you may have determined that the products provided by this company fall into four major families. A family is defined as a group of reasonably similar products that run across a like grouping of process steps. When choosing the initial family to baseline, you'll map the process from initial customer contact through receipt of payment for product or service delivered. As additional baselines are performed, the information and administrative portions of the business are universal; you'll only need to map the manufacturing processes of the remaining three families. With this said, let's construct a typical first baseline team. Areas of focus are as follows:

1. Sales and order entry (customer contact activity)
2. Engineering and configuration
3. Materials, purchasing, and logistics functions
4. Scheduling and production package release
5. Manufacturing processes
6. Shipping and distribution
7. Finance and accounting systems (front end and back end of the process)

We'll want individuals from each of these areas who are familiar with the task-level details of the work being performed. As you can see, the typical team will consist of a group in the range of 14 to 16 individuals. The manufacturing representatives should include reps from manufacturing and tooling engineering, setup people if appropriate, and direct operators who actually do the work. If you include knowledgeable people in the core team, they can call in additional resources as needed to detail the map in progress.

A generic agenda for the week will look as displayed in Figures 9-7 to 9-9.

This agenda is a guideline and will invariably move, plus or minus, depending on the team and the process being evaluated. Not to worry, just keep it in mind to stay on track as you work through the week. The overview objectives could be simplified as follows:

■ First and second days: Map the current state process.
■ Third day: Evaluate and quantify the current use for value added, nonvalue added, undesirable effects (UDEs), distances, space use, lead times and systems velocity, and people utilization sampling. Get into root-cause analysis of UDEs.

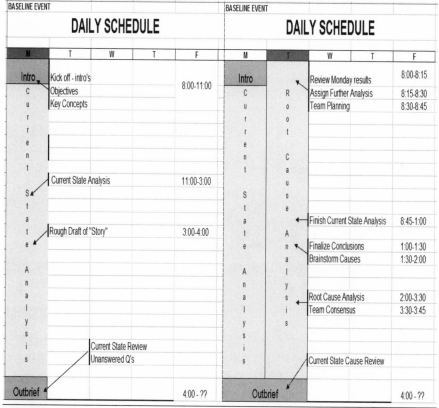

FIGURE 9-7.

- Fourth day: Begin to formulate the future state and project activity to go to the future state.
- Fifth day: Finalize the future state and develop a rough plan of action with as much cost and payback data as time allows.

Okay, let's detail the tool out and run through the week. We have the team and a large room with lots of wall space to work the week.

STARTING OUT

We always start out a team event of this nature with an overview of the terms that we'll be using, a common language if you will. Words are tricky; they always mean different things to different people (always!). Take the first hour of the week and discuss the seven types of waste with a few examples of each, and cover the definitions of value added and nonvalue added (Fig. 9-10).

DAILY SCHEDULE   **DAILY SCHEDULE**

M	T	W	T	F	
Intro		P	Review Tuesday Results		8:00-8:15
C	R	r			
u	o	e			
r	o	l			
r	t	i			
e		m	Form Solution Teams		8:15-10:00
n	C	i			
t	a	n	Problem Statements		10:00-1:00
	u	a	Solution Specifications		
S	s	r			
t	e	y			
a			Group Discussion		1:00-2:30
t	A	S			
e	n	o			
	a	l			
A	l	u			
n	y	t			
a	s	i	Preliminary Solutions &		2:30-3:45
l	i	o	Rationale		
y	s	n			
s		s			
i					
s			Review & consensus		
		Outbrief			4:00 - ??

M	T	W	T	F	
Intro			F	Review Wednesday Results	8:00-8:15
C	R	P	i		
u	o	r	n		
r	o	e	a		
r	t	l	l		
e		i		Develop Rough Plan	8:15-12:00
n	C	m		Create Scope Statements	
t	a	i	S		
	u	n	o		
S	s	a	l		
t	e	r	u		
a		y	t		
t	A	S	i		
e	n	o	o		
	a	l	n		
A	l	l	s		
n	y	u			
a	s	t	Improved State Analysis	12:30-3:45
l	l	i	Plan Overview	
y	s	o	Impact Definition	
s		n			
i		s			
s			Review & consensus		
		Outbrief			4:00 - ??

FIGURE 9-8.

With the definitions of waste and value added fresh in the team's mind, have them take a 15-minute tour of the manufacturing area being analyzed and observe and categorize what they see on this quick tour. When you reconvene in the war room, throw up a sheet of paper on the wall, have the team write their observations on Post-it notes, and arrange these Post-it observations under the seven categories of waste. The purpose of this initial walkabout is simply to gather some observations that show that the seven categories of waste do indeed exist in your process. This is a great introduction to the week in that we've started to develop a common language and note some examples of the terms we're discussing.

Okay, let's move along.

MAPPING THE CURRENT STATE PROCESS

The initial task for the baseline team is to detail a map of the current state. The deliverable of this current state map is to provide actual data to evaluate

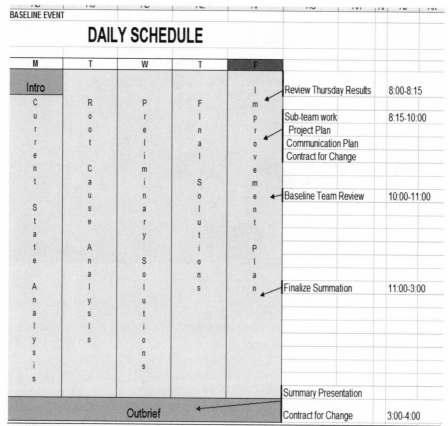

FIGURE 9-9.

for opportunity and potential in developing a future state. For us to be able to evaluate the current state process map in a meaningful manner, it must show activity at a level that allows us to assign a category of activity, such as transport, inspect, assembly, go get something, and so on, and to assign time to the task or activity.

"What are we doing? What category does the activity fall into, waste or work? And, how much time does it take?"

Given this approach, the two most common bumps in beginning this process are

1. Breaking the map down to the task level, and
2. Overcoming the *simultaneous activity syndrome.*

The beginning of a mapping session will always start with activity at a high level. "We machine the part in a turning center." There will be comments along the lines of, "Well, it's not quite that easy to map this; there are all

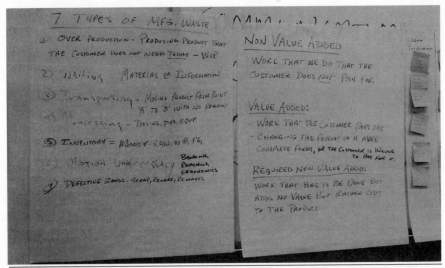

FIGURE 9-10.

kinds of things happening at the same time." The mindset we put in place with the team is the "One person in the building" scenario.

Here's the Pitch

"Imagine one individual who is capable of performing all jobs in the entire process. He or she walks into the company at 6 A.M. and performs all required tasks, one after the next, until the entire process is completed. That's what we want to see on the wall." In real life there is simultaneous activity occurring, but in our map we want a completely linear flow of tasks. This makes it easy to understand not only the activity but also the required sequence of activity. As you question down the task layers, you need to ask the questions. The example of "I machine the part in a turning center" would lead us to—

1. Where do you get the next order of parts?
2. How do you know which order is next?
3. Where do you get your work package, prints, and tooling?
4. What are the changeover steps to begin this new order?

And on and on. . .you get the picture.

So let's get the team rolling on the map. The rule is, one task per Post-it with a linear flow of activity from initial customer contact to shipment and payment receipt, left to right on the wall. The reason for the Post-it notes is that any map will start out with 20 Post-it notes, and by the end

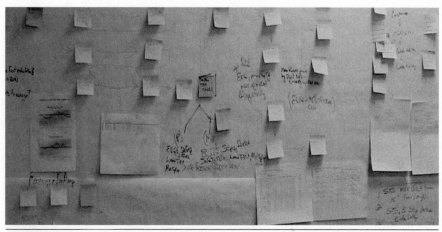

FIGURE 9-11.

of the second day will have progressed to several hundred as people bore down on the detail and add the tasks that are not defined in the first and second go-round. We need to be able to easily move and rearrange the detail. As the map begins to shape out, attach any documentation or paperwork that is used in the current process at the point where it is used (Fig. 9-11).

EVALUATING AND QUANTIFYING THE CURRENT STATE

After the preliminary team discussion on mapping is done and the group has begun the process breakdown, we need to send a few members of the team to gather some additional process data, namely, a work-sampling database to be compiled hourly over the next couple of days, a space-use visual using a CAD drawing of the shop, and a preliminary *spaghetti* diagram showing the path of materials through the process, also on a CAD drawing of the shop.

The work sampling is a walk-through at periodic times, over a couple of days, to capture the types of activity the population is engaged in (Fig. 9-12).

We want to create a visual of these data to represent a sampling of the percentage of activity at any given time. If you gather 200 or 300 data points using this sampling technique, you could say that at any given time, X percentage of the population is doing this and X percentage is doing that (Fig. 9-13).

The space use map is used to create a visual of how effectively we are using our facility, with the definition of effective relating back to the categories

Samples	7:00 AM	8:00 AM	9:00 AM	10:00 AM	11:00 AM	12:00 PM	1:00 PM	2:00 PM	3:00 PM	4:00 PM	5:00 PM	6:00 PM	7:00 PM
Transport	2	1	2	2	0	1	3	1	2	4	1	2	3
Walking	1	2	1	2	3	3	1	2	2	0	0	2	2
Communicating	3	2	2	2	4	4	1	2	2	2	3	3	3
Inspection	1	2	1	1	1	2	1	3	1	2	1	3	1
Set-up	2	1	0	1	0	0	1	0	1	0	2	2	0
Idle; machine running	5	4	5	4	3	2	5	2	4	3	4	2	1
Idle; machine not running	2	2	3	2	1	2	2	1	2	2	2	1	3
Rework	0	1	0	1	0	0	1	1	2	0	1	0	1
Working (touching product)	5	6	7	6	9	7	6	9	5	8	7	6	7
Totals	21	21	21	21	21	21	21	21	21	21	21	21	21

FIGURE 9-12.

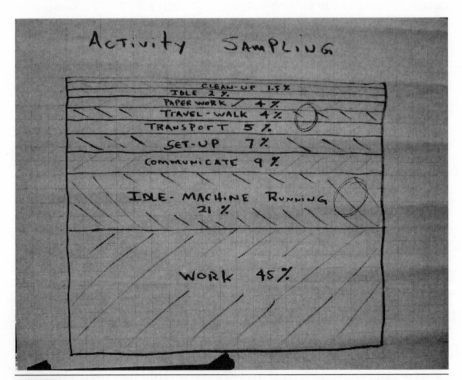

FIGURE 9-13.

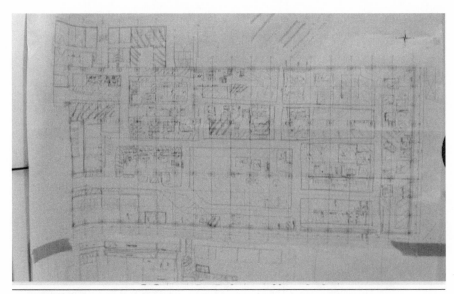

FIGURE 9-14.

of waste. For example, space used for value-added activity would be good, and space used to store work in process inventory would be not so good. Typical categories for space analysis might be materials (work in process, raw, and finished), value-added work, aisles, offices, tooling storage, etc. The visual might look like Figures 9-14 and 9-15.

The spaghetti diagram is to show distance traveled through the process and might look like Figure 9-16.

This is black and white in this book, but in real life it has various colors to show the path of different parts. With a CAD drawing to scale, the lines can be measured and the distance calculated.

Okay, the visuals are being developed of various system characteristics; let's go back to the map. As the task-level detail is nearing completion, we want to add an additional visual to the map, the location and quantities of all work in process or inventory queues in the process. These will be symbolized by a triangle and placed in the process at the point where they are physically located (Fig. 9-17).

So here's what we have so far:

1. A task-level process map showing activity and inventory queues and locations
2. A spaghetti diagram showing distance traveled through the process

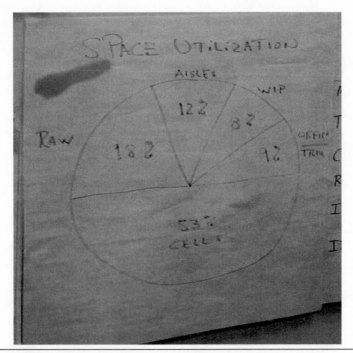

FIGURE 9-15.

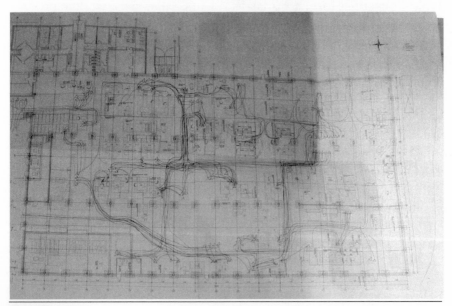

FIGURE 9-16.

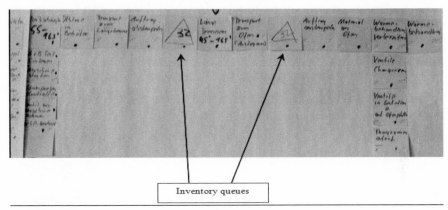

Inventory queues

FIGURE 9-17.

3. A work-sampling visual showing the percentage and type of observed activity in the system
4. A space-use visual showing facility use for various categories

The next step is to regroup the team for a collective activity: Assign time to each Post-it, and categorize all activity on the map as value added, nonvalue added, or required nonvalue added. This piece involves a group analysis and lots of discussion. Assign time to each Post-it, and use markers (red, green, and black) to color code each Post-it for the category of value that it represents. When discussing the inventory queues (triangles), the measurement is consumption time: If all new releases were stopped, how long would it take to consume the work in process? When this is done, tally up the time through the process: task, setup, and consumption time for work in process. What we're looking for here is time through the system and percentage of value-added activity. It is normal to see a process with a 15- or 20-day lead time that contains only a few hundred minutes of value-added activity. And this brings us to the opportunity!

With the data your team has compiled on the wall, it's now time to discuss observed UDEs. What do we see in the data that have been constructed? Long lead times? Excessive amounts of work in process? What are the undesirable characteristics that we observe in the current state system? Have the team list their observations of UDEs in their process. When this list is complete, we like to do a prioritization matrix, with each person on the team assigning a priority to each UDE. Take the collective numbers and create a weighted matrix. This takes us to brainstorming and root-cause analysis of the weighted effects.

Let's summarize. We have a cross-functional team who has mapped the current state process at an actionable level of detail. We have actual data on activity, space, time, value-added content, labor use, inventory levels, and more. We have quantified the databases, discussed system characteristics, and established root-cause detail against effects observed. For most of this team, it is the first time they have had the opportunity to see the process in its entirety, as opposed to seeing only their small portion of the collective value stream. We now have a team with a common vocabulary with regard to waste and value. They are prepared to work from this powerful current state map and proceed to the development of an improved future state process.

DEVELOPING A FUTURE STATE

The last portion of the baseline event is spent developing a future state.

■ In observing the current state, how do we change the process to minimize the UDEs? "Work the data!"

■ As we move from current to future state, and address the root causes we have identified, what are the specific projects that will take us there?

■ What are the timelines to accomplish these projects, and what resources are required?

■ What is the cost to implement?

■ What is the payback?

■ How do we link our processes to give us shorter lead times and inventory reductions, and eliminate the nonvalue-added Post-its in the system?

■ Are there changeover challenges, maintenance issues, or reject- or rework-related activity that must be addressed?

■ How do we recombine and balance our labor across the process to maximize our labor use?

■ How do we change our processes to reduce the cost associated with the nonvalue-added tasks, while still achieving the required business activities?

The team will spend the last 2 days of this event constructing and quantifying a future state map with an overview of the half dozen or so projects that will take them there. In working from a current state map constructed in this fashion, we have removed the opinion and emotion usually associated with discussions surrounding change. We are working from a detailed, numerically quantified value stream map and following a data-driven logic flow to an improved state.

If you'll refer back to our daily agenda, we have spent the last hour or so of each day giving a quick out-brief to our executive team. This allows for frequent input and prevents surprises from occurring at the event end out-brief. The end-of-the-week out-brief is a recap of the week's activity. The team *walks the wall* and presents the overview of the proposed future state and required projects to the executive management team. It is customary at this time to obtain approval to proceed and begin the move forward.

In most cases the week after this type of event is spent fine-tuning the proposed improvement projects, preparing an executable level of detail to the plan, and allocating the required resources. After this, it is necessary to execute the plan. Get going and *do something.*

A baseline event is a powerful tool. We suggest you give it a try, and take it to an actionable level as quickly as your organization can. Make something happen, and don't worry about doing it perfectly the first time. This is a game of *continuous improvement,* not to be confused with *one-time improvement.* We'll end this chapter with one of our favorite sayings.

> *"Everything will be okay in the end.*
> *If it's not okay, it's not the end."*
> *(Unknown)*

Chapter 10

Lean Engineering Analysis

A Lean engineering analysis is a fundamental tool to provide data on a given process. The deliverables of this technique are as follows:

1. Achieve balance across a process.
2. Maximize value-added labor content.
3. Maximize machine use.
4. Identify and quantify focus topics for Six Sigma activity.

We seek to identify and quantify the wastes of overproduction, excess motion, transport, process, waiting, and reject/rework activity. The question that usually comes up is something like, "Aren't we trying to improve the process, increase velocity, and reduce cost?" The answer might be, "Yes we are, but improving the process, increasing velocity, and reducing cost are not things that we can 'do.' They are effects of things we do and tasks we perform."

Let's talk about the words a bit. It may seem like semantics, but having a clear definition of what we are trying to do, the details we are trying to isolate, and the anticipated effects are critical to a clear implementation plan. Implementation is a stumbling block for many organizations because of the way they define objectives and perform tasks. For example, in many organizations, an industrial engineering study is performed primarily to quantify cost so that it can be applied to a particular process or product. We might observe time to complete a series of operations at a particular work station and conclude that the work inside of station number three takes 3.4 hours. We then calculate our direct labor cost, apply overhead in proportion to the standard hours assigned, and allocate that cost to the product or service—typical *standard cost* calculations. This conventional approach gives us *big box* times, but does not present the information in a format that tells us what we can do to improve the process.

With a *Lean* engineering study, we are interested in the detail of the work being performed at an *element* level, with associated time and notation of specific tools being used, specific materials being consumed, and specific identification of quality issues (noise) in the system. For the benefit of non-engineering readers, an element is the smallest unit of work that cannot be divided up across multiple people. The logic in an element level breakout is that it is the level where tasks can be categorized as value added, nonvalue added, or required nonvalue added. This is the level where tasks can be further grouped into specific categories of waste, a move or transport, a wait, a rework step, etc. A study conducted at this level also identifies tools used and materials consumed at each step in the sequence.

If you format your data with Lean Six Sigma definitions in mind, the data will tell you what to do. When we evaluate the tasks studied, this format will allow us to reconstruct the process with an equal distribution of work at each station; combine elements at each station up to the Takt Time to allow process design that meets customer demand; place required tools, materials, and components at the point of use to minimize travel; and break out non-value-added activity for corrective action activity. Powerful stuff.

SAMPLE LEAN ENGINEERING ANALYSIS

Take a look at a simple Lean study format in Figures 10-1 and 10-2.

This is an actual study with names changed because of proprietary data. The columns from left to right are:

- element number
- task description
- time to perform the task in seconds
- value-added time
- nonvalue-added time

			Category				
Element #	element-description	element time (sec's)	Value added	Non Value added	Comments/Ideas Material	QTY	Tools
		Product # XYZ			Operator: David		Tech: Scott
		Station: Rotary Rig					
1	Attach blocks with tape	900	900				
	install jamus blocks to hold wire ties	322	322		small blocks large blocks jamus-3020 mixing tip-29030	4 3 1 1	mixing tip jamus gun
2	Layout material & get air line	710		710			
	Install battery switch panel	355	355		142611 - panel 6x1 ppblk - screw-231206 washer blk-230541	1 12 12	1/8" bit, airdrill, air screwgun #1 apex
3	Install 3" stabilizer, clean & caulk	402	402		90197 - boots 150958 - ring 10×3/4"-pp-230530	2 2 12	caulk, caulk gun, 5/32" bit drill, screwgun, papertowels
4	install 4" stabilizer, & rings, clean & caulk	520	520		150154 - boot 150146 - avis ring	2 2 16	caulk, caulk gun, 5/32" bit drill, screwgun, papertowels
5	go get strap	54		54			nylon lifting strap
	hook up straps & lift transmo go get graple	399 30		399 30			graple

FIGURE 10-1A.

#	Task				Part	Qty	Tool
6	get tools & cut nylon PVC support strap	115	115	115	nylon strapping-29302	6	utility knife
	cut strap to hang wire pvc chase	115			10×3/4"-pp-230530	6	
					1/4" fender washers-230810		
7	layout material	168	387	168			air screwgun #2 apex
	install chase handle	387					
8	layout main harness	190	113	190			
	run harness for main compartment	113					
9	hook up battery switch jumpers to switch	318	318		55441 - battery cable	4	11/16 socket & ratchet 3/8" drive
	remove tape from blocks	130		130	051616-boots	4	
10	install rapport modem in holes	197	197		24715459 - rod tube	6	airscrewgun, #2 apex
	go get straps -	40		40	# 32 adel-22852067	6	
	strap down rapport modem	325	325		10×3/4"-pp-2352355	12	
11	get tools & untape harnesses	160	323	160	#20 clamps-220004	3	utility knife
	strap grundle harness	323			10×3/4"-pp-230530	6	airscrewgun, #2 apex
	untape harness	202		202	tiewraps-22221	3	sidecutters
	pull harness thru main & clip up	323		323	tiewraps-22132	6	utility knife

FIGURE 10-1B.

			Value added	Non value added			
140	get rigby and unpack	12600		12600			
	unpack riby seats						
	replace buzz saw blade				Carlos		Tech. Daryl
	cut track	6409		6409			
	deburr track	238		233			
	move line	1492		1492			
	install back rest track						
	install back rest cushion						
	install rigby seat	547		547			
	install rigby seat	3180		3180			
141	get mid tripods	3275		3275			
	upack mid tripods	233		233			
	install mid tripods	458		458			
	help co-worker install console						
	install mid tripods						
142	install tripods cover	3600		3600			
143	organize and move tools						
	get and unpack axel door						
	install axel door	1390		1390			
		1390		1390			
		469		469			
	grind door (rework)	105		105			
	install axel door						
	grind door (rework)	2723	2732		blue tape, foam	1	utility knife
144	get aft tripods (3)	1427	1472		webbing	90	utility knife
	install tripods	347	347		srink wrap, shrink wrap tape	24' × 45'	utility knife
		705	705		shrink wrap tape		utility knife
	install tripods door strap	572		572	shrink wrap tape		utility knife
		117		117			utility knife
145	unpack trivets	258	258				utility knife
		725		725			utility knife
	install trivets	300	300		door, vents, tape		utility knife
	get tools						
146	install back clips	347	347				
	get and unpack back						
	install back	293	293				
147	get wheel storage boxes	227		227	shrink wrap tape		utility knife
	light harness installed backwards (rework)	460	460				torch
	storage drawers won't fit, wrong part	89		89			
	install channel box and chalk	167	167				
	wait for storage drawers	75	75				
	install storage drawers	271	271				
	clean up	373		373			
	TOTALS		Value added	Non value added			
4681.3	60	280876	**156434**	**122605**	99%	78.02	
Totals/min's	xx	Total/sec's	**56%**	**44%**	279039	total hrs.	

FIGURE 10-2.

- materials/components used
- quantity of components
- tools required

I have not included the numerous pages in the middle of this study, but if you'll note at the bottom of the second page, this particular study captured 78.02 hours of demonstrated activity of which 56% involved value-added time and 44% involved nonvalue-added time. That's the first-pass observed process; we could call it the current state.

There are a couple of things to consider when doing this type of study. The first is the desired result of a completely linear flow of tasks observed to complete the job. When you observe a real-life process, there are always multiple simultaneous tasks being performed, which are sometimes tough to see. If you think about how any product or service is made or performed, the actual flow is one task after the next until you're done. An easier way to visualize a process is to imagine *one* person performing the entire sequence of operations. If a study is conducted with this in mind, you'll end up with a task-level, linear study of demonstrated activity.

Once the analysis begins you will be free to break out pieces that can be performed simultaneously by a second or third person, but the initial study has to be presented as a one-person flow. This takes you to the orchestration piece of a good study. If you are observing activity in an area where there is one person working, you're good to go, easy and clean. If there are two operators working, you'll either have one person do the sequence for the study or have two engineers available to do the observations ("one engineer per operator"). You cannot come back and catch the second operator on a second study; you'll get garbled data that will be difficult to construct.

Another important note is the detail of an element. For example, "I go get part number DRF and install it to the axle plate" is not an element. The get is a transport (nonvalue added), and the install is an assemble (value added). We need to ensure that the pieces are identified in a way that we can categorize each step into one of the seven wastes or into the eighth category, *work*. Let the clock run, and write start time, tasks observed, and materials and tools used as you follow the product through the process.

Okay, we've compiled the study data and entered them into our spreadsheet format as illustrated above. What's next? What do we do with these observed data?

The second step in this exercise is to observe all activity that you've compiled and assign it to the value-added and nonvalue-added columns on your spreadsheet. Our format identifies column 3 as element time, with columns 4 and 5 identified as value added and nonvalue added. As you work through the elements, copy the times observed into the appropriate columns. This gives you the breakout and process percentage of value added versus nonvalue added. This is the demonstrated activity piece. Allow me to throw a small wrench into the logic flow at this point. With this approach we are categorizing elements that involve taking the product to a more complete state as *value added*. We could more accurately describe these elements as *touch* elements. Here's what you'll see. . . guaranteed.

- An operator assembles a part to another part with six Allen-head fasteners. The tool the operator uses is a hand wrench, with a time of 65 seconds. Value added? You bet, the operator is assembling the product. But, if we were to methodize the element a bit and provide the operator with a battery pack or air driver, we can reduce the element time to 21 seconds.
- An operator is assembling fasteners that have a torque requirement. He or she drives 10 bolts using an air driver, sets the driver down, gets a standard torque wrench, and finishes the assembly by torquing all bolts manually. "Element time, 340 seconds." If we provided the operator with an air torque wrench, he or she would be able to torque to the specification on the first drive and eliminate the entire secondary sequence of manual torque to final specification. "Element time, 120 seconds."

I won't beat this one to death; the important message is, as you observe the value-added column keep an eye on opportunity to methodize and improve the touch time.

The next step is to take an exploded bill of material (BOM) for this process and work through the study to ensure that you have either consumed the entire BOM or identified components being used that reflect inaccuracies in the BOM. Either way, clean up the data. We need a completely accurate BOM going forward.

So far so good; we've got a clean linear study, time, tasks, tools, and materials. Let's start the analysis. We are at the point where we want to involve our assembly people, the folks who know this process better than anyone in the company. We've got a pretty good size conference room with lots of wall space, lots of hot coffee, and a good group of experienced people assigned to the team. The session begins.

DOING THE ANALYSIS

Bill C: Good morning. We've sidetracked you people to give us a hand with the analysis on our "Z" line. I'd like to thank all of you assembly folks for your patience over the last couple of weeks as we did the study. We know it's not easy having someone leaning over your shoulder with a stop watch and asking all kinds of questions while you're trying to get your days work done. (This gets a few "hear hears" from the group.) We have a couple of people here who weren't involved up until today, so I'd like to start off with some quick intros if you don't mind, just name, job, and maybe length of time with the company. Let's go; Stu, start us off.

Stu: Okay Bill, I'm Stu Knowles, quality engineer, been with ICT (company name) for 1 year. Started in the forge department, moved to fabrication, and came into this quality spot about 3 years ago.

Bill: Thanks, Stu. Next?

Oscar: I'm Oscar Aquilar, final assembly and wire. I've been here 8 years.

Bill: Always in assembly, Oscar?

Oscar: Yes. I've worked in different areas, but all assembly.

Bill: Thanks. (People are fidgeting, I'm looking around.)

Sam: Hey everybody, I'm Sam Rainer. Worked at ICT 18 years. I started in the cabinet department and came to final assembly about 10 years ago.

Red: Red Sykes, industrial engineering, 5 years.

Jack Tyler: I'm Jack Tyler. I'm in primary, been here 12 years. I started in electrical, went to patterns, and came to assembly about 2 years ago.

Bill: I'm Billy Davis. I'm in tool engineering. Been here 10 years, always in the manufacturing engineering group.

Jimmy: Jimmy Hayes, industrial engineering, but I also work the machine side for justifications and technical evaluation of new equipment.

Hank: I'm Hank Trombley. I'm the group lead on the "Z" line; been here 17 years.

Bill: Okay guys, thanks. Here's what we want to get done. We've got the engineering study done on your process (I'm handing out copies of the study), and we want to work out two pieces today. We want to take the elements from this study, transfer them to these stickies, and arrange them on the wall so we can see the entire process, start to finish. (I've got several boxes of 2" × 2" Post-it notes on the table, a dozen pencils, and red, green, and black felt markers.) On each Post-it we want only one task and the time that it took. The second thing we want to construct today is a current state distribution of the work across the various stations and graph it out. Questions?

Jack: I got the first one Bill. Why are you tying us up in here? We've got work to do. (Ah yes, now we know why people are fidgeting.)

Bill: You're right Jack, we've got important work to do. There's two ways we could do this. The first is to have industrial engineering do the study, reconstruct the process, implement the new flow, and stand back and listen to you guys tell us the 12 reasons that the new process won't work, and the 17 things that we overlooked or forgot about when we thought through the redesign. Or, the second, which is to involve the people who know the process down to the smallest nuance help us break it up and redesign the process so we can get it right the first time. That would be you guys. We chose number 2.

Oscar: Bill, we're assemblers, not engineers.

Bill: Exactly, and this process of improvement is supposed to provide you people with a process plan that works. You're the experts, and you're also the customers. Any other questions?

Sam: Okay, we're past that. Why do we need to copy all this information onto these Post-its?

Bill: Good question Sam. We're going to move them around, and we need them to be in element bites. Task and time. You guys ready to go?

The group is beginning to accept their fate, and we get some *yes* nods.

Bill: Alright, let's break into two groups. Stu would you, Oscar, and Jimmy build us a visual of the current distribution, and would the rest of you guys get rolling on the Post-it transfer to the wall. Oh yeah, let's do one more breakout. Red, while the group is working on detail and distribution, would you fire up your computer and sort out the go-gets and any tasks that were tagged as rework? Thanks, let's go.

The group begins to Post-it the process, work up a distribution, and split out the nonvalue-added transports and rework/quality issues. It starts to look like Figure 10-3 and progresses as shown in Figure 10-4.

In the meantime, Stu, Oscar, and Jimmy have finished the current state distribution illustrating balance across the process with the existing work station definition. It looks like Figure 10-5.

A breakout session such as this will generally take a couple of days but is well worth the investment when you weigh the educational benefit of involving your operators, with a cross-functional team, in the thought processes and tools of redesigning their work areas.

And so it goes. We have the process on the wall, the current state distribution is complete, and the go-gets and reworks are broken out of the process.

FIGURE 10-3.

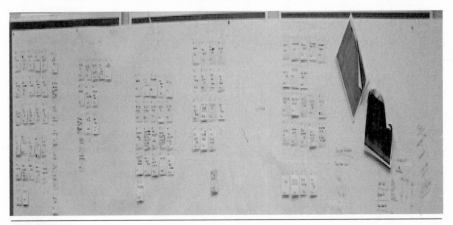

FIGURE 10-4.

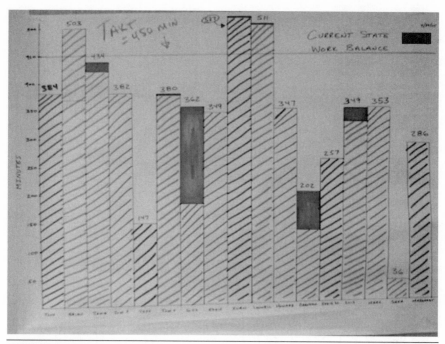

FIGURE 10-5.

Bill: Okay gather up guys. Let's look at what the data are showing us. We have a process that has a standard of 140 hours of work. The study showed us that the demonstrated time is in the neighborhood of 78 hours. The distribution shows us imbalance from one station to the next. The go-gets amount to about 5 hours (Figs. 10-6 and 10-7). And the rework/reject-related elements come to around 21 hours (Figs. 10-8 and 10-9).

Bill: What do you guys think? Questions, observations?

Stu: Why is there such a big difference between the standard hours and the demonstrated hours? Doesn't make sense.

Bill: Not uncommon, Stu. You're running a mixed model line so there's some variation, and your costing procedure is to compare with similar models. Those are a couple of thoughts. Another cause that I see frequently is the creep-over time to use actuals to update annual standards. Your accounting people look at last year's actual times and update to the new year's standards. When they do this they continue to add cost without really defining the process.

Oscar: So Bill, you're telling us we've got an 80-hour product?

Bill: Nope, I'm not telling you anything. The data are telling you we have an 80-hour product, with 21 hours of time opportunity if we solve some of the quality issues, and

Date: 2/14/2005		Station #	Rotor Rig	Operator: James		Tech: Scott	
		element time (sec's)	Value added	Non value added	Comments/Ideas Material	Quantity	Tools
Element #	element-description	Part # XYZ					
5	go get strap	54		54			nylon lifting strap
	go get grandle	30		30			grandle
	go get straps -	40		40	# 34	6	
12	go get harnesses - engine harness'	310		310	579291 - harness	4	
15	get tools & speakers	105		105	22555103 - speakers	4	
	go get hoses & material	512		512			
19	get tools & material	195		195			
22	get materials	85		85			
	get air hoses & materials	100		100	2-5/16 nut, 4-10/24 taper		
26	get parts	140		140			
28	look for part	127		127			
	get screws	77		77			
32	get drill fixture	68		68			
	get parts	62		62			
33	look for passenger seat-not here	105		105			
34	get findle box	125		125			go to next process
	get rags	106		106			
	locate seat	315		315			pencil

FIGURE 10-6.

		element time (sec's) added	Value	Non value added		
	look for parts	368		368		
	get console parts	147		147		
	get parts & hadware	337		337		
	get gasket for grodo	186		186		
	get materials	129		129		
	get materials	30		30		
	get materials	93		93		
	get new drill bit	21		21		4 drill bit
112	get weasel draw	112		112	1-weasel	
120	get parts and supplies in unit	840		840		
125	get parts	174		174		
	get supplies	74		74		
	got get hose	86		86		
128	get new jig saw blade	67		67		
	go cut end caps	262		262		bandsaw
132	get rigging ass'y	149		149		
	go get	51		51		
134	go get charger	314		314		
	take back carger	450		450		
	go get forklift	256		256		
	bring engines to line	311		311		
	get overlay	106		106		
	get tools	99		99		
	get engines	356		356		
	get hoist	85		85		
	look for tool	69		69		
	go get	261		261		
	get tools for step #41, get fuel clamps	420		420		
	get tools & test equipment	424		424		
	get parts	101		101		
137	get pilot seat	112		112		
138	get rail	140		140		
139	get cushions	144		144		
140	get cooler and unpack	250		250		
141	get mid frames	150		150		
	get and unpack hatch door	158		158		
144	get gyro's (3)	230		230		
	get tools	88		88		
147	get storage boxes	67		67		
	TOTALS	element time (sec's) added	Value	Non value added		
310.9	60	18656	0	18656	100%	5.18
Totals/min's	xx	Total/sec's	0%	100%	18656	total hrs.

FIGURE 10-7.

| Date: 2/14/2005 | | | | Rotor Rig | | Tech: Scott | |
Element #	element-description Part # XYZ	element time (sec's)	Value added	Non value added	Comments/Ideas Material	QTY	Tools
	rework speaker hole	50		50			
	re-attach piping (rework)	44		44			
	rework - recut opening (gunners door)	97		97			jigsaw grinder
	grind plate-rework-wrong stand	72		72			
	grind holes out to size (wrong tool)	283		283			die grinder
	re-drill holes (rework)	95		95			
	grind holes out to size (wrong tool)	236		236			
	re-drill holes (rework)	55		55			
	grind screws off from subassembly-rework	85		85			
	rework center latch	50		50	taper		
	rework lower spring bracket	1440		1440			
	rework - grind coring behind thermo outlet	499		499			
	grind bottom of station to fit boot - rework	495		495			die grinder
	remove excess insulation - rework	70		70			
	grind area to fit drawer hardware	80		80			die grinder, carbide burr bit
43	grind area to fit drawer hardware	135		135			air grinder, carbide bit
44	grind area to install drawer forward hardware	99		99			airgun, burr
	grind bottom of rear locker hatch	257		257	1-80 grit 3" disc.		angel grinder
	grind hatch to fit	138		138	1-80 grit 3" disc.		angel grinder
48	grind area to install Fwd. hardware	99		99			air grinder, carbide bit
	grind to fit stbrd. Fwd. probe holder	92		92			air grinder, carbide bit
51	grind, drill holes & hardware	310		310			carbide bit
	stripped bolt on hardware remove & replace	160		160	1-1/4"20x2" pp bolt, 1-1/4"x20 self lock nut		vise grips, 7/16" socket, air rachet, #2 philip screw driver
	remove packing material & rework drine cap	1315		1315			angle grinder, sanding pad
	remove packing material & rework drine cap	96		96			angle grinder, sanding pad
	remove packing material & rework drine cap	262		262			angle grinder, sanding pad
	remove packing material & rework drine cap	421		421			angle grinder, sanding pad
	touch up locker hatch trim	48		48			
	touch up drine caps	164		164			

FIGURE 10-8.

Group	Description	Total/sec's	Value added	Non value added	Notes
	rework - cut hose	86		86	
	grind brackets on vhs to fit - rework	620		620	air saw
	rework - cut console for radar	88		88	
113	rework stripped screw in battery switch panel	218		218	
	fix alarm	506		506	loose ground wires
	gyro harness ran backwards (rework)	509		509	
	grind wendle top	217		217	
131	grind wendle cap	192		192	grinder
	rework adjust engine harness lenghts	113		113	
	rework-reinstall thermal tube	69		69	
	rework-reinstall thermal tube	40		40	
	go cut torque bar to correct length - rework	471		471	
	check alarm - doesn't work	255		255	
118	clean inside of runway	2718		2718	
	detail inside of stanchion	10877		10877	
	grind door (rework)	411		411	grinder
	grind door (rework)	410		410	
	light harness installed backwards (rework)	366		366	
149	storage drawers won't fit, wrong part	283		283	
	mark finish work on fenders	661		661	
	write finish work on QA sheet	195		195	
	inspect inside of unit	3764		3764	
150	finish work	13560		13560	1 cap finish work 70min.
	finish work	12600		12600	
151	QA work off	6409		6409	
	QA work off	1492		1492	
	QA work off	3180		3180	
	QA work off	3275		3275	
	QA work off	458		458	
153	clean inside of unit	3600		3600	
	TOTALS		Value added	Non value added	
		75646	0	75644	100%
		Total/sec's	0%	100%	75644

| 1260.8 | 60 | | | | 21.01 |
| Totals/min's | xx | | | | total hrs. |

FIGURE 10-9.

another 5 hours of opportunity to minimize go-gets with a tighter layout. We didn't make up the time or rate anybody's performance; we just recorded what was done. It is what it is.

Jimmy: Okay, Bill, what's next?

Bill: Well Jimmy, thanks for asking. The next steps are recombine the work, one station at a time up to Takt Time, assign these quality issues to one of your Six Sigma focus teams, and begin to develop a physical layout with materials and tools at the point of use. Our next session is scheduled for Thursday, 8:00 A.M. Let's break and we'll see you then. Go have a cold one and get some sleep.

Session Two

The next session is convening. The guys have had time to think about what we've done, and they've all discussed the sessions with their coworkers. Let's go.

Bill: Morning, everybody. Anything to cover before we get going on the rebalance?

Sam: Yes, you've used the phrase Takt Time and I see it on the distribution graph. What is that term?

Bill: Sam, you guys have all been through the Lean 101 training and the Lego game simulation, yes?

Sam: No. Everybody here has but me. I was out on vacation for 2 weeks during my area's sessions, and so I missed it. They didn't get me rescheduled yet.

Bill: Jeez, sorry. Okay, we'll cover it now. Takt Time is a concept we use when we design a cell or process. The word means *beat* or *tempo,* but it's a measure of customer demand. When we design a work cell we want to design it so that we can satisfy customer orders, make sure we have capacity to support our anticipated demand. At the same time we don't want to waste resources, so the game is balance your machine cycle times up to Takt and then add people, again up to Takt until the cell is full. Here's how it works. (I move to a white board and write the formula in Fig. 10-10.)

In formal terms this means "the frequency with which your customers consume a unit of product." Let's use our study. We need to produce one unit per day in your area, and we're running a one-shift operation. Let's start with available work hours.

$$\text{Takt Time} = \frac{\text{Available work hours}}{\text{Saleable quantity of products}}$$

FIGURE 10-10.

A shift is 8 hours, and you take two 15-minute breaks. You get a 10-minute clean-up at shift end and a 10-minute line meeting in the morning. Let's do the math: An 8-hour shift is a total of 480 minutes, then subtract 30 minutes for breaks, also subtract 10 minutes clean-up and the 10-minute meeting, and you are left with 430 available work minutes.

Because your unit demand is one per day (per shift) your Takt Time is 430 minutes. You need to complete one unit every 430 minutes to meet customer demand. Good so far.

(Everyone is nodding; it appears a refresher is in order anyway.) Okay, the next piece to design the system is work time. Again we'll use your study and say required work hours to complete a unit is 80 hours. Let's go to minutes so we can do the calculation; 80 hours is 4,800 minutes. We divide work time by Takt Time to tell us the break-up; 4,800 minutes (work time) divided by 430 minutes (Takt Time) equals around 11.2. This is the number of stations we want to design to meet customer demand with this particular process. Because we can't have 11.2 guys, we'll round up to 12. We want to take this study and put as close to 430 minutes into each station as we can; when we get to the 12th station we should run out of tasks and have a completed unit. Another way of looking at this is 430 minutes is a *beat* of Takt and that's our balance objective. Good to go?

Sam: Pretty straightforward. I'm good. Thanks. (Everyone else is nodding their heads; the lights are all on.)

Bill: Okay, let's move on. Let's set a target of 50% reduction for the quality issues and go-gets and work up the element stack up for 12 stations. When we get that done let's graph the future state distribution.

The group begins to work through the elements grouping and sequencing, and discussing the best balance as they go. At the end of the session they have constructed something along these lines (Fig. 10-11).

- They begin construction of a future state distribution, as depicted in Figure 10-12.
- The work element breakout for each station is detailed showing element flow and times through a one-shift period (Fig. 10-13).
- The rework elements have been broken out and assigned to a Six Sigma team, as shown in Figure 10-14.

Let's summarize. When we hear of the results in different companies that have embraced the concepts of Lean Six Sigma, it is common to see double-digit improvements in labor use, work-in-process reduction, and lead-time reduction. The tools in this chapter are straightforward, provide us with the necessary detail to balance out a target process, and will result in

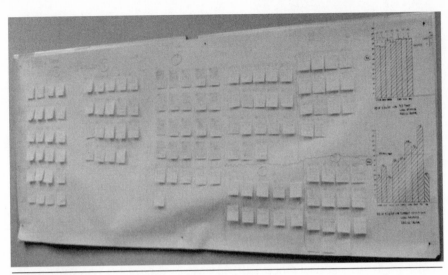

FIGURE 10-11.

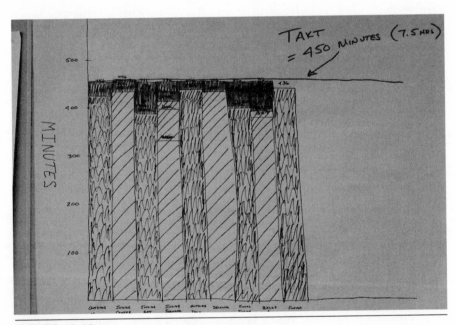

FIGURE 10-12.

Station #1A

Start Time	Stop Time	Activity Minutes	Activity
7:00	7:04	4	Drill console arm
7:04	7:15	11	Set gyro in panel
7:15	8:08	53	Drill all holes in panel
8:08	8:13	5	Install vent thru panel
8:13	8:18	5	Install platen sheets
8:18	8:23	5	Install milled thru center beam
8:23	8:27	4	Install tyron pick-up
8:27	8:30	3	Caulk thru holes
8:30	8:35	5	Install grounding plate
8:35	8:51	16	Install thru
8:51	9:02	11	Install center bracket
9:02	9:08	6	Install rear hardware
9:08	9:30	22	Install beaker tabs
9:30	9:40	10	BREAK
9:40	10:02	22	Complete install forward arms
10:02	10:04	2	Install impact sensor
10:04	10:12	8	Install rear baskets

Station #1B

10:12	10:14	2	Install post bars & adapters
10:14	10:16	2	Install power meters
10:16	10:20	4	Install rear pump
10:20	10:21	1	Install air pump
10:21	10:25	4	tie up console wires
10:25	10:38	13	Install recirc pumps
10:38	10:45	7	Install drain hoses
10:45	11:00	15	Install primary harness
11:00	11:07	7	Install vent hoses
11:07	11:17	10	Drill holes for mounting platform
11:17	11:30	13	Bolt in platform
11:30	11:36	6	Install fuel lines

Station #1C

11:36	12:00	24	Install console base, battery shelf & charger
12:00	12:30	30	LUNCH
12:30	12:48	18	Complete console base, battery shelf & charger
12:48	12:54	6	Install main floor
12:54	12:57	3	Install cabs
12:57	1:04	7	Install air lines
1:04	1:09	5	Install appliance module

Station #1D

1:09	1:20	11	Install drive stem bracket
1:20	1:55	35	Build & install filter board, install primer bulbs
1:55	2:00	5	Install rear gimble
2:00	2:10	10	BREAK
2:10	2:26	16	Install gimble hardware
2:26	2:34	8	Install reduction sensor
2:34	2:46	12	Install harness sensor
2:46	2:53	7	Install mounting flanges
2:53	3:16	23	QA

FIGURE 10-13.

Quality issue		Corrective action	Responsible person	Completion date
check alarm - doesn't work	255			
storage drawers won't fit, wrong part	283			
rework speaker hole	50			
rework - recut opening (pilot door)	97			
rework - grind shear	96			
grind area to install forward hardware	99			
grind, drill holes & fit hardware	310			
grind to fit gridle holder	92			
grind plate-rework-wrong stand	72			
grind bottom of hatch	257			
grind area to install stadle hardware	99			
grind area to fit passenger hardware	135			
grind area to fit passenger hardware	80			
touch up rear caps	164			
rework stanchion cap	1315			
rework stanchion cap	96			
rework stanchion cap	262			
rework stanchion cap	421			
glue center of forward caps	75			
grind side of fender washer to fit	219			
finish work at platen caps	8400			
rework - cut console for gizmo	88			
re-drill holes (rework)	95			
re-drill holes (rework)	55			
grind bottom of station to fit boot	495			
rework center latch	50			
grind screws off from subassembly	85			
grind door (rework)	411			
grind door (rework)	410			
fix jar off alarm	506			

FIGURE 10-14.

excellent improvements in operating performance. In looking at thousands of hours of past studies, let's talk to what is typically achieved.

It is common to see the cost of labor decrease by 20% to 40%. It is common to see work in process decrease by 60% to 80%. It is common to see lead times reduced by 30% to 50% with an associated improvement in on-time delivery. To obtain the dramatic results available, there are a couple of requirements, namely, understand your processes, involve the people who truly understand the detail of the process, and do the work. There are no silver bullets.

This team is now ready to implement. We'll expand on the discussion of taking this process to the floor in the chapter on 5S. Let's continue.

Chapter 11

Setup Reduction

We've spent a good amount of time discussing the differences between batch and flow operating philosophies. We've talked about velocity, linkage, balance, and on and on. . .all of the objectives of an operation that has decided to incorporate the principles and tools of a Lean Six Sigma business system.

Once your company has reached the point where you decide you are going to implement a flow/pull business process, you will begin the analysis of how to physically link process steps together. There are few issues that cause as much concern as setup time, or to be more specific, the differences in setup time from one machine to the next. If we are linking and balancing assembly stations, the process is relatively straightforward: Analyze the work content, recombine the work elements, and push the benches together. There is a good bit of work to be done to implement a successful transition, but there usually aren't any serious show stoppers. The process of linking machines and equipment together in a balanced flow presents a very different puzzle to be solved.

Setup reduction is a critical support element in allowing the transition from a traditional batch mode to a Lean Sigma flow mode. The longer your setup times are, the more resistance there will be to reducing lot sizes. The approach in a *traditional* company is to spend a great deal of effort on finding ways to amortize setup costs over larger and larger batch sizes, thus the conventional economic order quantity (EOQ) logic. "What is the optimum amount of parts I should run to cover my changeover expense?" In contrast, the mindset in a Lean Sigma organization is, "How do I dramatically reduce setup times to allow smaller lot sizes and eliminate the waste of overproduction and excess inventory?"

Our favored approach to setup reduction is a cross-functional event format (surprised?) and is usually scheduled over 3 days. The time frame is flexible, but we like to analyze and simulate the proposed improvements, and 3 days works for this objective. Before we jump into the approach, let's discuss setup logic a bit and look at the pieces.

Let's start with the first question:

"What is a setup (or changeover if you prefer)?"

Here's our definition: "The time between the last good piece from a production lot and the first good piece from the next production lot." Pretty straightforward.

The next question is:

"What are the typical activities that are seen during a setup?"

The answer to this one varies greatly from one company to the next; however, the general activities might include:

- Cleaning up your area and machine
- Contacting supervision or scheduling to identify the next order
- Getting tooling and parts for the next order
- Getting the information for the next order, prints, work packets, tags, or labels for parts identification
- Contacting a materials handler to bring the next order of parts
- Gathering containers for the next order
- Performing the physical setup
- Inspecting first-piece activity
- Systems transactions: clocking out on the last order, in on the setup, and in on the next job when setup is complete

These are some of the general activities. I'm sure you could add more. It's interesting to note that the activities described above all fall into the category of nonvalue added. You might want to argue that some are *required nonvalue added*, but the counter is, "Okay, but required nonvalue added is still nonvalue added."

Which brings us to the next question:

"What is the approach to reducing a setup? Our guys have already done all that can be done."

"Everything that can be done has been done." A statement such as this tells us a great deal about the environment and mindset of a company. When you hear someone say, "Everything that can be done has been done," what you are really hearing is, "We treat improvement activity as a one-time event. We do some work, consider it to be the best it will ever be, and move on." In a Lean Six Sigma environment, with a mindset of continuous improvement, you will never hear the statement, "There is nothing more that can be done to improve this area."

And so, let's answer the question. The classic approach to reduce a setup consists of:

1. Shifting internal activity to external, and
2. Eliminating nonvalue-added activity.

After our discussion on a conventional setup reduction event, we will be discussing a third category that we call "sequencing."

THE SETUP REDUCTION EVENT

Let's get our setup team together and run through an event. The team should be composed of individuals who know and do the work and/or are accountable for the outcome of the area under analysis. Some examples are operators who run and set up the equipment; setup people if they exist as a separate job classification; a rep from tooling engineering; a rep from manufacturing engineering; someone from maintenance; a programmer or two; a rep from quality engineering; and maybe a member of the supervisory team. A good size for a team of this nature is in the 6- to 10-person range. Don't forget to include representatives from all shifts if you're a multishift operation. We've got the team allocated for a 3-day session. Management is supporting the effort 100%, and we're going to follow an agenda something like this.

Day 1

- Introduction to the concepts and terms of a Lean Sigma setup reduction.
- Video the selected setup.
- Reduce the video to a Lean engineering analysis format.
- Categorize observed activity and times for internal, external, nonvalue added.

Day 2

- Continue the detail breakout if not completed on day 1.
- Brainstorm observed process for improvement solutions.
- Orchestrate a simulated future state changeover using the ideas developed.
- Complete simulation requirements in preparation for day 3.

Day 3

- Simulated setup video taken and analyzed for time and tasks.
- Improvement action plan developed with cost, timelines, and accountability.

This agenda is very fluid; on occasion we will film and analyze two setups of different parts, depending on the complexity and amount of sizzle the particular team has.

First Day

We usually begin with introductions and a casual discussion covering the general terms of waste and value added, and continue with the specific terms used in the setup process. It is important to have a common vocabulary, and we never assume that sufficient preparatory training and education have occurred. And so, on with the words.

External activity: Activity that can take place while the machine is operating, for example, bringing new dies to a machine. These are things that can be done while the previous order is being run, before the setup start.

Internal activity: Activity that must be done while the machine is shut down, like removing or attaching dies.

Nonvalue-added activity: Steps that can be totally eliminated, such as searching for tooling or walking to retrieve items.

After our introductory session, we proceed to the area of focus and video a setup. We prefer a video format in that it allows the team to carefully analyze all activity while letting the clock run to assign times, and if questions arise, or the discussion demands, we can review, stop, start, etc.

Okay, we've got the current state on tape and reconvene to our meeting room to view and analyze. On the first pass, we concentrate on documenting all the steps and times and identifying any detail that we think is important. This step is fairly noisy, and there is lots of discussion. Things look different when you are viewing them on film, and the time impact is different if you are sitting at a table viewing activity on a television screen.

There is the tendency for people to want to jump right to solutions at this point. Slam on the brakes, and focus on documenting the observed tasks. We're not ready to discuss solutions yet.

After the task and time detail, run through the elements and have the team categorize each task, external, internal, or nonvalue added. Again, this usually leads to some spirited dialog; stay focused. A typical setup format will look like Figures 11-1 to 11-4 at first pass.

SET UP #
2
10/xx/200x   Pt # 65214 to #2354   Operator   Jimmy Doyle

| Setup step # | Element | element time | Category | | | Comments/Ideas |
			Internal	External	Non value added	
1	get jaws	35		35		
2	paperwork away	5		5		
3	get new paperwork	56		56		
4	new paperwork up	49		49		
5	loaded - paperwork	43		43		
6	old jaws off	60	60			
7	t's off	73		73		
8	clean	19		19		
9	t's on	20		20		
10	jaw 1 on	14	14			
11	t's jaw 2	18		18		
12	jaw 2 on	20	20			
13	t's on	15		15		
14	jaw 3 on	19	19			
15	check jaws	56			56	
16	adjust jaws	13			13	
17	set chuck	16			16	
18	check window	14			14	
19	move out 1 more tooth	36			36	
20	adjust switch	60			60	
21	check part	31			31	
22	tighten jaws	50	50			
23	ref tool	19			19	
24	spin set zero	28			28	
25	calc zero	6			6	
26	ret tool calc zero	30			30	
27	adj. Boring bar	97	97			
28	single block	55	55			
29	machine 2 jaws off	53	53			
30	check mach. 1	1		1		
31	jaws off mach 2	19	19			
32	Program	17	17			
33	t's off	26		26		
34	mach 1 check dim's	18	18			
35	adj.		0			
36	bore adj	117	117			
37	qualify bore bar	58	58			
38	offset adj.	23	23			
39	rough bore tool					
40	rough bore out	45	45			

FIGURE 11-1.

Setup step #	Element	element time	Internal	External	Non value added	Comments/Ideas
41	mach 2 t's off	50		50		
42	check part 1	14	14			
43	depth mic's	19	19			
44	check counter bore depth	36	36			
45	adj.	17	17			
46	check bore	72	72			
47	adj.	18	18			
48	t's off mach 2	34		34		
49	get jaws	21		21		
50	mach 2 t's on	18		18		
51	mach 1 check bore	19	19			
52	finish bore	20	20			
53	check bore	86	86			
54	redo bore	28	28			
55	calc	53	53			
56	final finished bore	0	0			
57	t's on mach 2	30		30		
58	check bore	34	34			
59	next run adj	22	22			
60	groove tool call up	120	120			
61	large groove finish OD cut	34	34			
62	Deburr	53	53			
63	depth mic's	8	8			
64	Adj	8	8			
65	Check	12	12			
66	call up program	26	26			
67	run program	25	25			
68	mach 2 jaw 1	41	41			
69	jaw 2	27	27			
70	jaw 3	29	29			
71	checking jaws	36			36	
72	adj jaws	10			10	
73	Check	11			11	
74	load part	25	25			
75	tighten jaws	16	16			
76	load part	11	11			
77	zero returning	37	37			
78	tool 4 MDI	10	10			
79	zero set tool	28	28			
80	single block	48	48			

FIGURE 11-2.

You'll notice that this setup goes across three work centers, has 129 steps defined, took a total of 72 minutes, and the team called activity at 60% internal on the first pass. As you evaluate internal and external, it's important to really examine the detail with a discussion of *no constraints*. People will not consider options that are available if they are thinking of their current state operating methodology as non-negotiable. For example,

Setup step #	Element	element time	Internal	External	Non value added	Comments/Ideas
81	Adj	8	8			
82	run	16	16			
83	call tool 11	5	5			
84	adj tool11	0	0			
85	measure/calc	50	50			
86	run tool 11	29	29			
87	Calc	27	27			
88	run tool 11	25	25			
89	check/adj	34	34			
90	run tool 11	40	40			
91	check/adj	33	33			
92	Adj	8	8			
93	Run	137	137			
94	Deburr	7	7			
95	check part	15	15			
96	move to mach 3	15	15			
97	program call up	22	22			
98	qualify tool 1	27	27			
99	qualify tool 2	16	16			
100	qualify tool 3	15	15			
101	cycle start	15	15			
102	Run	0	0			
103	clean/jaws away	41		41		
104	set cmm	55		55		
105	old j16 away	70		70		
106	cmm program call up	24		24		
107	clean up tools	38		38		
108	put tools away	38		38		
109	clean jaws	24		24		
110	jaws away	14		14		
111	Organize	33		33		
112	wait for drilling	19		19		
113	clean part	22	22			
114	wipe off before cmm	19	19			
115	load cmm	25	25			
116	start program	14	14			
117	organize/clean	134		134		
118	fill coolant okuma	81		81		
119	fill dawoe	28		28		
120	wipe off mach	237		237		

FIGURE 11-3.

in many operations a setup will be done by the individual who operates the machine or cell, or by a single setup person who works an area and goes from setup to setup. You have to get your team into the mindset of "perfect world, no limitations." You'll find these types of exchanges:

You: You know guys, if you ran two setup guys through this cell, you could put quite a bit of the internal on machine #2 inside of the internal on machine #1.

Setup step #	Element	element time	Internal	External	Non value added	Comments/Ideas
121	put away tools	15		15		
122	check cmm output	55	55			
123	unload parts	2	2			
124	print out complete	177	177			
125	adj mach 1	19	19			
126	adj mach 2	19	19			
127	adj mach 1	33	33			
128	load part 2	30	30			
129	Run	35	35			
	Totals seconds	4360	2630	1364	366	4360
			Internal	External	Non value added	
		60				
	Totals minutes	72.7	60%	31%	8%	100%

FIGURE 11-4.

Team: There's no way management is going to give us more setup people; we're lucky to have the ones we have.

You: Understood. But, it's not in the scope of this team to second-guess what management will or won't give us. It's our job to present them with a plan to reduce setup time to the minimum possible. Then we'll do the cost analysis and see where it takes us.

When you start to get this type of thought process going, you'll be surprised by the creativity that will surface.

Second Day

We've detailed the current state and put the tasks into categories; the next step is to group out the drivers. We want to combine activity into groupings such as *single block, tooling adjusts, jaw changes,* etc., so we can clearly see the driving causes as a percentage of activity (Figs. 11-5 and 11-6).

We now have the current state process detailed in a manner that will allow for a good brainstorming session on the "What could be?" Kick open the chute, and turn the bronco loose! These sessions are what continuous improvement is all about: a group of process experts analyzing a current state process and letting their creativity flow as they orchestrate a future state.

- How about chuck bumps to eliminate counting grooves?
- Quick change jaws with cam-lock fasteners?
- The activity detail if two operators worked a flow-through changeover of three machines?
- Additional memory to decrease program load time?

El.	Tool Qualification	Sec.	El.	Change jaws	Sec.	El.	adjust tools	Sec.
23	ref tool	19	1	get jaws	35	27	adj. Boring bar	97
24	spin set zero	28	6	old jaws off	60	36	bore adj	117
25	calc zero	6	7	t's off	73	38	offset adj.	23
26	ret tool calc zero	30	8	clean	19	39	rough bore tool	
37	qualify bore bar	58	9	t's on	20	40	rough bore out	45
55	calc	53	10	jaw 1 on	14	45	adj.	17
77	zero returning	37	11	t's jaw 2	18	47	adj.	18
78	tool 4 MDI	10	12	jaw 2 on	20	59	next run adj	22
79	zero set tool	28	13	t's on	15	64	adj	8
85	measure/calc	50	14	jaw 3 on	19	81	adj	8
86	run tool 11	29	15	check jaws	56	83	call tool 11	5
87	calc	27	16	adjust jaws	13	84	adj tool11	0
88	run tool 11	25	17	set chuck	16	125	adj mach 1	19
89	check/adj	34	18	check window	14	126	adj mach 2	19
90	run tool 11	40	19	move out 1 more tooth	36	127	adj mach 1	33
91	check/adj	33	20	adjust switch	60			
92	adj	8	21	check part	31			
98	qualify tool 1	27	22	tighten jaws	50			
99	qualify tool 2	16	29	machine 2 jaws off	53			
100	qualify tool 3	15	31	jaws off mach 2	19			
			33	t's off	26			
			41	mach 2 t's off	50			
			48	t's off mach 2	34			
			49	get jaws	21			
			50	mach 2 t's on	18			
			57	t's on mach 2	30			
			68	mach 2 jaw 1	41			
			69	jaw 2	27			
			70	jaw 3	29			
			71	checking jaws	36			
			72	adj jaws	10			
			73	Check	11			
			74	load part	25			
			75	tighten jaws	16			
			103	clean/jaws away	41			
			109	clean jaws	24			
			110	jaws away	14			

Tool Qualification	Sec.		Change jaws	Sec.		adjust tools	Sec.
	573			1094			431
	13%			25%			10%

FIGURE 11-5.

- Repeatable tool holders to allow reduction in single blocking and tool adjusts?
- Bar coding on work packages to minimize systems data entry?

The session will invariably produce many interesting ideas. We now want to put these ideas into play and simulate what a setup would look

El.	load program	Sec.	El.	Single block	Sec.	El.	inspect qc	Sec.
32	program	17	28	single block	55	34	mach 1 check dim's	18
66	call up program	26	60	groove tool call up	120	42	check part 1	14
67	run program	25	80	single block	48	43	depth mic's	19
97	program call up	22				44	check counter bore depth	36
						46	check bore	72
						51	mach 1 check bore	19
						53	check bore	86
						58	check bore	34
						63	depth mic's	8
						65	check	12
						95	check part	15
						104	set cmm	55
						106	cmm program call up	24
						114	wipe off before cmm	19
						115	load cmm	25
						116	start program	14
						117	organize/clean	134
						118	fill coolant okuma	81
						119	fill dawoe	28
						120	wipe off mach	237
						121	put away tools	15
						122	check cmm output	55
						123	unload parts	2
						124	print out complete	177

load program	Sec.	Single block	Sec.	inspect qc	Sec.
	90		223		1199
	2%		5%		28%

FIGURE 11-6.

like if we had the improvements we have identified in place. Recruit the assistance of the necessary support groups, tooling, maintenance, and so forth, and get these simulation ideas prepared to allow a simulation video to be performed. And that's the planned end of day 2.

Third Day

On day 3 we want to video the simulation and run through a quick detail session to put the simulated flow into our Lean engineering study format. Same process, different detail. Now do the comparisons. Figures 11-7 to 11-9 are some examples of actuals with the names changed to protect confidentiality.

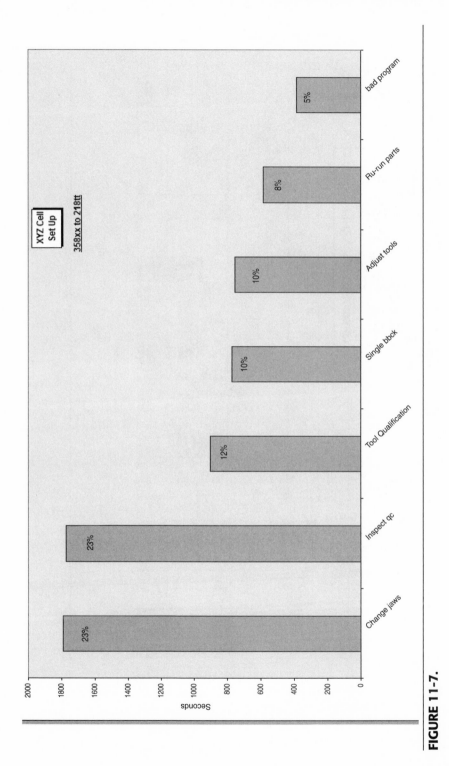

FIGURE 11-7.

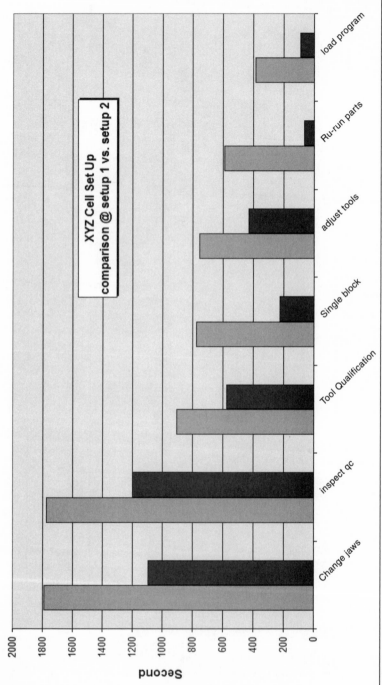

FIGURE 11-8.

XYZ Cell Changeover Event

XYZ cell Changeover team: Jim booker Team Lead, Steve Wilso, Barry Jacobs, Steve Jenkins, Mike Tyler, Billy Slater, Larry Konig, Scotty Thomes, Bill Carreira

SUMMARY of EVENTS

1. CNC changeover theory discussed - training video viewed
2. 2 changeover's video'd -
3. Process analyzed for internal/external and non value added activity
4. Quick corrections implemented to chuck change activity - visual bumps. T's. proper hand tools. etc.
5. Proposed changeover video'd and analyzed for time
6. Corrective actions identified

RESULTS

	Current C/O Time	Simulated C/O Time	Delta/Reduction	% Reduction
3756xx to 1234 mm	128.5min	55.7min	72.8min	58%
Labor Cost	$42.8. @ 128.5 man minutes	$25.4 @ 77 man minutes	$17.40	41%
$20 avg. rate				

	Current C/O Time	Simulated C/O Time	Delta/Reduction	% Reduction
5968yy to 0983ee	73.1min	55.7min	17.4min	24%
Labor Cost	$24.1 @ 73.1 man minutes	$25.4 @ 77 man minutes	$1.30	5% ↑
$20 avg. rate		(Set up man left when his portion was complete)		

CORRECTIVE ADD'S

Item	Cost (Estimated)	Time to completion	Who	Date Complete
Purchase T nuts/bolts - approx. 15 sets	$ 810.00			
Positive stop modify - jaws	$ 1,500.00			
Impact wrench	$ 100.00			
Label jaws				
Re-organize paperwork				
High speed printer - CMM and stapler	$ 200.00			
Tool qualification - standardization, 2 sleeves, 2 bars, standardized tooling, tool inserts at point of use	$ $400.00			
Investigate pressure switch application				
Shop communication, flags, lights, radio	$ $80.00			
Stardardize process - set up, work instructions				
Prove out set-up man potentials				
Misc.	$ $910.00			
TOTALS $$'s	$ $4,000.00			

NOTE: Cost reduction potential for EOQ/Inventory reduction to be quantified @ Corporate

FIGURE 11-9.

At the end of the session, we have an excellent breakout and analysis, current state and simulated future state videos, a detailed action plan to move forward, and a fired-up team who have created a vision of the future. An out-brief to management is a good way to terminate the event, with any capital requests verbally approved pending a formal cost-effectiveness analysis if necessary. Good to go. Every event is different, and every event will provide you with opportunity to improve your process.

SEQUENCING

Let's move to an interesting area of setup reduction that is not commonly seen in practice. We call it *sequencing*. We're going to take you to the scenario of a fabrication shop, but this technique will work with a variety of processes—it's characteristics driven.

The first occasion we had to use this technique was a result of a spinoff on a kanban system we were implementing for a new product family for a client who manufactured large assemblies with a large amount of fabricated sheet metal parts. As we worked through the flat pattern prints to determine the weight of parts to construct kanban containers, we were constructing a database of part characteristics (e.g., weight, size, and geometry) to allow stacking of kanban quantities with a predetermined weight limit and allow the design of custom containers and shelving systems to minimize space. There were about 90 fabricated parts in the assemblies in this family, and the product was a repetitive build. Every month this client produced X number of units. The spreadsheet looked like Figure 11-10 (I've deleted the columns depicting part numbers and description).

We had an aggressive setup reduction effort under way, and we were looking at nesting logic for turret punches and lasers, feeding flat pattern kanbans, with a pull from point-of-use kanbans in assembly looping back-through brake presses. Before this project, parts were released with conventional material requirements planning logic. No groupings were considered, simply several thousand parts released to production. As the kanban analysis proceeded, we began to compare not only the geometry of the parts but also the relationship and quantities required to make up a complete grouping of parts to produce one unit of product, a system of parts, if you will. The logic is, if you release a back for unit XYZ, you also need two sides, one top, and so on through the other 85 parts that compose a completed assembly.

We began sequencing tooling requirements for a family of parts needed to produce one completed unit of product. It is not uncommon, when

side 1	side 2	sq. in.	Thickness	weight (lbs)			weight /sq"	qty /pr	kb qty	kb height	bin weight	width	height	depth
1.900	18.250	34.675	0.060	0.6068125	#	430 s/s	0.018	1	90	5.4	55	1.900	5.4	18.250
1.160	6.200	7.192	0.060	0.12586	#	430 s/s	0.018	2	180	10.8	23	1.160	10.8	6.200
1.625	10.563	17.165	0.047	0.1201541	#	az perf. 1161014	0.007	2	180	8.46	22	1.625	8.46	10.563
5.000	11.428	57.140	0.035	0.65711	#	az	0.012	1	90	3.15	59	5.000	3.15	11.428
2.000	8.000	16.000	0.036	0.168	#	430 s/s	0.011	1	90	3.24	15	2.000	3.24	8.000
6.102	12.216	74.542	0.036	0.7826913	#	430 s/s	0.011	1	90	3.24	70	6.102	3.24	12.216
8.281	12.67	104.92	0.036	1.1016628	#	430 s/s	0.011	1	90	3.24	99	8.281	3.24	12.670
3	5.5	16.5	0.035	0.18975	#	az	0.012	1	90	3.15	17	3.000	3.15	5.500

side 1	side 2	sq. in.	Thickness	weight (lbs)			w/sq"	qty/pr	kb qty	kb height	weight	width	height	depth
3.500	5.962	20.867	0.048	0.292138	#	430 s/s	0.014	1	90	4.32	26	3.500	4.32	5.962
2.490	14.000	34.86	0.048	0.48804	#	430 s/s	0.014	1	90	4.32	44	2.490	4.32	14.000
2.543	19.200	48.826	0.048	0.6835584	#	430 s/s	0.014	1	90	4.32	62	2.543	4.32	19.200
2.000	4.558	9.116	0.048	0.127624	#	430 s/s	0.014	1	90	4.32	11	2.000	4.32	4.558
2.000	4.079	8.158	0.048	0.114212	#	430 s/s	0.014	1	90	4.32	10	2.000	4.32	4.079
0.880	2.280	2.0064	0.048	0.0280896	#	430 s/s	0.014	1	90	4.32	3	0.880	4.32	2.280
1.600	10.371	16.594	0.048	0.2323104	#	430 s/s	0.014	1	90	4.32	21	1.600	4.32	10.371
1.940	28.960	56.182	0.048	0.7865538	#	430 s/s	0.014	1	90	4.32	71	1.940	4.32	28.960
1.941	28.962	56.215	0.048	0.7870134	#	430 s/s	0.014	1	90	4.32	71	1.941	4.32	28.962
1.634	10.365	16.936	0.048	0.2371097	#	430 s/s	0.014	1	90	4.32	21	1.634	4.32	10.365
15.370	22.910	352.13	0.036	3.6973304	#	430 s/s	0.011	2	180	6.48	666	15.370	6.48	22.910
8.358	8.455	70.667	0.036	0.7420023	#	430 s/s	0.011	1	90	3.24	67	8.358	3.24	8.455
0.922	8.400	7.7448	0.036	0.0813204	#	430 s/s	0.011	1	90	3.24	7	0.922	3.24	8.400
2.231	11.625	25.935	0.036	0.2723214	#	430 s/s	0.011	1	90	3.24	25	2.231	3.24	11.625
0.750	4.212	3.159	0.036	0.0331695	#	430 s/s	0.011	1	90	3.24	3	0.750	3.24	4.212
1.378	2.375	3.2728	0.036	0.0343639	#	430 s/s	0.011	1	90	3.24	3	1.378	3.24	2.375
2.949	19.338	57.028	0.036	0.5987915	#	304_ s/s	0.011	1	90	3.24	54	2.949	3.24	19.338
3.355	8.674	29.101	0.036	0.3055633	#	430 s/s	0.011	1	90	3.24	28	3.355	3.24	8.674
11.204	22.399	250.96	0.036	2.6350632	#	430 s/s	0.011	1	90	3.24	237	11.204	3.24	22.399
8.913	9.008	80.288	0.036	0.8430272	#	430 s/s	0.011	1	90	3.24	76	8.913	3.24	9.008

side 1	side 2	sq. in.	Thickness	weight (lbs)			w/sq"	qty/pr	kb qty	kb height	weight	width	height	depth
1.150	19.95	22.943	0.06	0.4014938	#	430 s/s	0.018	1	90	5.4	36	1.150	5.4	19.950
0.650	10.23	6.6495	0.06	0.1163663	#	430 s/s	0.018	2	180	10.8	21	0.650	10.8	10.230

FIGURE 11-10.

you observe operating logic in a fabrication area, to observe brake-press operators choosing segment sizes that match the dimensional attributes as shown on the engineering prints. In addition, if parts are presented as separate pieces of work, with little or no visibility as to what parts are progressing through the process, there is no way to plan on a tooling sequence. With this operating scenario, every part represents a new setup.

The first step in this system is to identify and assign a characteristic code to each part. For example, the first two breaks on any part are *open* breaks.

The part has not progressed to the point where it has four sides broken up, so the length of the tooling bar can be any length that is longer than the part itself. Tooling segment size is one characteristic. A second important characteristic is material gauge (thickness). The cutoff for radius considerations is 16 gauge for sheet metals, so 16 gauge and down is a different tool requirement than 18 gauge and up. There can be different characteristics depending on your specific parts geometry, but for this example we'll describe some common ones. Here are some example codes.

- Code 0: A part with no fabrication, for example, a purchased rivet.
- Code 1: A part with no breaks: a flat part. After laser or turret punch to produce shape and hole patterns, it is complete.
- Code 2: An *open break,* 18 gauge and higher. These parts have only two sides broken and can be run with a segment length that is simply longer than the part itself.
- Code 3: An *open break,* 16 gauge and lower. These parts have only two sides broken and can be run with a segment length that is simply longer than the part itself.
- Code 4: A *panel bend;* a part that needs to be run across a large panel-bending brake press because of size or special geometry.
- Code 5: A *box;* a part that has multiple bends and requires segment sizes that fit inside the part after the first two breaks have been performed.
- Code 6: A *special;* a part that is a precision-fitted part or has special tonnage requirements.
- Code 7: A *hard tool;* a part that has hard tooling developed for a one-stroke or multiple-piece hit.

Figures 11-11 and 11-12 are examples of comparison matrices of codes over a family of parts, parts needed to produce one unit of finished product (again, modified to delete names and part numbers).

You will note the columns for code number, gauge of material, tooling segment size dimensions, and a running cumulative setup requirement if these parts are run in sequence. For *open* break parts we have sequenced by gauge with the entire grouping requiring no setup between parts. When we get into the *box* parts we sequence by gauge and then by tooling segment size. It is interesting to observe the grouping that appears when a family of parts is analyzed; many free setups appear even in parts with complicated geometry.

In summary, with this example, the original release model required 63 setups over the series of parts needed to build one unit of completed product.

Proc	Proc	Type	Clas	Avg	Replishment	12 Mo Usage	v	s	d	f	Date	code#	gage	mat'l	dim #1 (Inside box)	Cum tool changes - brakes		Codes
EDE	DTT	P	MV	0.75	KanBan	1432	524	0	0	###	###	1	16	430 s/s		0	0	No Fab
EDE	DTT	P	MV	2.13	KanBan	684	416	0	0	###	###	1	16	430 s/s		0	1	Flat, no breaks
EDE	DTT	P	MV	1.61	KanBan	1240	832	0	0	###	###	1	16	430 s/s		0	2	Open Brakes 18/20ga.
EDE	DTT	P	MV	0.93	KanBan	1201	839	0	0	###	###	1	18	az perf. 1161014		0	3	Open Brakes 16ga.
EDE	DTT	P	MV	2.78	KanBan	760	425	0	0	###	###	1	20	az		0	4	Panel Bend
EDE	DTT	P	MV	0.34	KanBan	753	416	0	0	###	###	1	20	430 s/s		0	5	Box
EDE	DTT	P	MV	1.71	KanBan	596	416	0	0	###	###	1	20	430 s/s		0	6	Specials
EDE	DTT	P	MV	2.3	KanBan	597	416	0	0	###	###	1	20	430 s/s		0	7	Hard tool
EDE	DTT	P	MV	0.32	KanBan	294	294	0	0	###	###	1	20	az		0		
EDE	DTT	P	MV	1.66	KanBan	762	425	0	0	###	###	2	18	430 s/s	3.500	1	1	offset?
EDE	DTT	P	MV	1.85	KanBan	1410	841	0	0	###	###	2	18	430 s/s	14.000	1	2	
EDE	DTT	P	MV	2.6	KanBan	767	425	0	0	###	###	2	18	430 s/s	19.200	1	3	
EDE	DTT	P	MV	1.34	KanBan	602	416	0	0	###	###	2	18	430 s/s	2.000	1	4	
EDE	DTT	P	MV	1.2	KanBan	602	416	0	0	###	###	2	18	430 s/s	2.000	1	5	
EDE	DTT	P	MV	0.65	MinMax	1237	54	0	0	###	###	2	18	430 s/s	0.880	1	6	
EDE	DTT	P	MV	1.31	KanBan	651	466	0	0	###	###	2	18	430 s/s		1	7	
EDE	DTT	P	MV	2.58	KanBan	652	467	0	0	###	###	2	18	430 s/s		1	8	
EDE	DTT	P	MV	2.58	KanBan	651	466	0	0	###	###	2	18	430 s/s		1	9	
EDE	DTT	P	MV	1.74	KanBan	653	466	0	0	###	###	2	18	430 s/s		1	10	
EDE	DTT	P	MV	8.58	KanBan	1663	850	0	0	###	###	2	20	430 s/s	21.180	1	11	
EDE	DTT	P	MV	1.37	KanBan	601	416	0	0	###	###	2	20	430 s/s	8.358	1	12	
EDE	DTT	P	MV	0.57	KanBan	1409	1223	0	0	###	###	2	20	430 s/s	8.400	1	13	
EDE	DTT	P	MV	1.41	KanBan	607	416	0	0	###	###	2	20	430 s/s	11.625	1	14	
EDE	DTT	P	MV	1.21	KanBan	539	416	0	0	###	###	2	20	430 s/s	0.750	1	15	gang break??
EDE	DTT	P	MV	1.07	KanBan	396	374	0	0	###	###	2	20	430 s/s	2.375	1	16	
EDE	DTT	P	MV	2.21	KanBan	689	417	0	0	###	###	2	20	304_ s/s	6.880	1	17	
EDE	DTT	P	MV	2.74	KanBan	628	424	0	0	###	###	2	20	430 s/s	7.364	1	18	
EDE	DTT	P	MV	5.02	KanBan	599	419	0	0	###	###	2	20	430 s/s	10.688	1	19	
EDE	DTT	P	MV	1.87	KanBan	684	416	0	0	###	###	2	20	430 s/s		1	20	
EDE	DTT	P	MV	1.59	KanBan	263	125	0	0	###	###	3	16	430 s/s	19.950	2	21	
EDE	DTT	P	MV	0.51	KanBan	1642	950	0	0	###	###	3	16	430 s/s	10.230	2	22	
EDE	DTT	P	MV	0.42	KanBan	2628	1740	0	0	###	###	3	16	430 s/s	0.720	2	23	
EDE	DTT	P	MV	1.36	KanBan	596	416	0	0	###	###	3	16	430 s/s	19.950	2	24	
EDE	DTT	P	MV	0.43	KanBan	94	94	0	0	###	###	3	16	430 s/s	1.500	2	25	
EDE	DTT	P	MV	0.71	KanBan	947	425	0	0	###	###	3	16	316 s/s		2	26	
EDE	DTT	P	MV	0.71	KanBan	957	425	0	0	###	###	3	16	316 s/s		2	27	

FIGURE 11-11.

After the *sequencing* database was developed, this same series required 22 setups to produce one unit of finished product, a reduction of 41 setups. We eliminated 65% of required setups.

The next step in this reduction process is to introduce these codes into your logistics/scheduling software and/or kanban process to allow for

	Type	Clas	Avg	Replishment	12 Mo Usage	Jul0	IOBS	IDEL	IDT/ Date	#	gage	mat'l	Code dim #1 (Inside box)	Cum tool changes - brakes	Codes
IT	P	MV	16.7	KanBan	761	425	0	0	###	###	4	18	430 s/s			
IT	P	MV	5.43	KanBan	636	418	0	0	###	###	4	20	430 s/s			
IT	P	MV	16.7	KanBan	762	425	0	0	###	###	5	20	430 s/s	23.286	3	28
IT	P	MV	6.95	KanBan	851	425	0	0	###	###	5	20	AZ	21.284	4	
IT	P	MV	6.57	KanBan	833	425	0	0	###	###	5	20	AZ	21.284	4	
IT	P	MV	9.05	KanBan	802	425	0	0	###	###	5	20	430 s/s	21.114	5	
IT	P	MV	4.38	KanBan	771	426	0	0	###	###	5	20	430 s/s	21.114	5	
IT	P	MV	10.6	KanBan	767	431	0	0	###	###	5	20	430 s/s	19.894	6	
IT	P	MV	5.45	KanBan	596	416	0	0	###	###	5	20	430 s/s	19.894	6	
IT	P	MV	8.17	KanBan	936	536	0	0	###	###	5	20	430 s/s	19.760	7	
IT	P	MV	5.16	KanBan	743	416	0	0	###	###	5	20	430 s/s	19.440	8	
IT	P	MV	7.53	KanBan	734	416	0	0	###	###	5	18	az perf. 1161014	19.114	9	
IT	P	MV	9.25	KanBan	761	419	0	0	###	###	5	20	430 s/s	18.474	10	
IT	P	MV	4.1	KanBan	747	417	0	0	###	###	5	20	430 s/s	18.374	10	
IT	P	MV	8.74	KanBan	561	375	0	0	###	###	5	20	430 s/s	14.030	11	
IT	P	MV	4.27	KanBan	650	332	0	0	###	###	5	20	430 s/s	13.144	12	
IT	P	MV	4.25	KanBan	450	322	0	0	###	###	5	20	430 s/s	13.142	12	
IT	P	MV	6.28	KanBan	502	417	0	0	###	###	5	20	430 s/s	13.142	12	
IT	P	MV	3.76	KanBan	1530	854	0	0	###	###	5	20	AZ	10.814	13	
IT	P	MV	2.43	KanBan	3198	1727	0	0	###	###	5	20	430 s/s	10.724	13	
IT	P	MV	2.71	KanBan	762	425	0	0	###	###	5	20	AZ	10.714	13	0 No Fab
IT	P	MV	2.71	KanBan	761	427	0	0	###	###	5	20	AZ	10.714	13	1 Flat, no breaks
IT	P	MV	4.4	KanBan	717	426	0	0	###	###	5	20	AZ	10.714	13	2 Open Brakes 18/20ga.
IT	P	MV	4.4	KanBan	797	425	0	0	###	###	5	20	AZ	10.714	13	3 Open Brakes 16ga.
IT	P	MV	4.02	KanBan	1650	852	0	0	###	###	5	20	430 s/s	10.674	14	4 Panel Bend
IT	P	MV	3.55	KanBan	1274	832	0	0	###	###	5	20	430 s/s	10.674	14	5 Box
IT	P	MV	2.8	KanBan	1536	851	0	0	###	###	5	20	430 s/s	10.568	15	6 Specials
IT	P	MV	2.31	KanBan	1240	833	0	0	###	###	5	20	430 s/s	10.568	15	7 Hard tool
IT	P	MV	3.21	MRP	623	444	0	0	###	###	5	18	430 s/s	10.493	16	
IT	P	MV	2.91	KanBan	791	422	0	0	###	###	5	20	430 s/s	9.694	17	
IT	P	MV	3.12	KanBan	1584	868	0	0	###	###	5	18	az perf. 1161014	9.565	18	
IT	P	MV	2.16	KanBan	1647	933	0	0	###	###	5	20	430 s/s	8.377	19	Note: missing dim?
IT	P	MV	2.85	KanBan	792	418	0	0	###	###	5	20	430 s/s	6.244	20	
IT	P	MV	2.58	KanBan	636	428	0	0	###	###	5	20	430 s/s	6.169	20	
IT	P	MV	2.58	KanBan	620	416	0	0	###	###	5	20	430 s/s	6.169	20	Currently @ 63
IT	P	MV	4.42	KanBan	760	416	0	0	###	###	5	18	Perf 304 s/s	6.000	21	delta @ -41
IT	P	MV	3.54	KanBan	620	416	0	0	###	###	5	20	430 s/s	5.486	22	
IT	P	MV	3.54	KanBan	620	416	0	0	###	###	5	20	430 s/s	5.486	22	63
IT	P	MV	4.5	KanBan	803	551	0	0	###	###	6	14	Ga. Galv		Note: Requires tonnage	
IT	P	MV	4.39	KanBan	1528	850	0	0	###	###	6	20	430 s/s	9.294	Note: fitted top & bottom	
IT	P	MV	7.67	KanBan	644	417	0	0	###	###	6	20	430 s/s	24 &12.806	Note: continuous bottom	

FIGURE 11-12.

release of these parts in the proper sequence and quantity. There are a lot of ways you can go with this to simplify your systems requirements. If you like a visual replenishment process, you can configure custom kanban carts that hold a code grouping of parts and turn single-part kanban logic into a kanban sequence. By using the same approach for a traditional parts release process, you can launch a *sequence code grouping* of parts, rather than individual parts. This gives scheduling the visibility they need. I won't go into the entire piece here (this is a chapter on setup reduction). However, you'll find all kinds of interesting advantages when you load these *sequenced* parts into your nesting software for punch and laser activity.

Once these codes are integrated into your scheduling logic, the next step is to get design and manufacturing engineering involved. Your manufacturing engineers can fine-tune the tooling segment requirements, most segments are chosen to the nearest one-quarter inch, and there will be dimensions close enough to move into a setup grouping.

Now take it to design engineering. This mindset and family analysis will also allow your design engineers to approach design with a target for eliminating setups in the process. Design for manufacturing and setup elimination is a very powerful approach to reducing cost and variation in the system. As engineering staff are designing new parts, or value-engineering existing parts, the more parts they can change to a code 2 or 3, the more they are capable of eliminating setups. As they look at more complicated *box* parts, they can observe family segment groupings and attempt to consolidate into existing groupings, again, additional *no setup required* parts. Good stuff; free money!

This is a fabrication area example, run specifically across brake presses, but the logic of the database construction will work in any process in which you require a series of parts to complete a unit of product, or in any process in which common characteristics can be developed. Give it a whirl, and have some fun!

Chapter 12

5S

5S occupies an important place in the Lean Six Sigma toolbox. It's an execution tool, and it's a philosophy of operation. This methodology supports the reduction of the seven categories of waste as defined in a Lean environment and has a very direct impact on the foundation objective of Six Sigma: variation reduction. There are those who think 5S is merely a tool to enhance workplace organization, and there are those who think that 5S supports every aspect of a Lean Six Sigma business philosophy. We fall soundly into the latter. Let's explore this dynamic tool.

Let's start with the basics, the 5S terms. The usual English words correspond with their Japanese counterparts in parentheses.

1. Sort (Seiri)
2. Set in order (Seiton)
3. Shine (Seiso)
4. Standardize (Seiketsu)
5. Sustain (Shitsuke)

The translations are interesting when an attempt is made to be literal. Here's our spin on the comparisons.

1. Sort: *Organization*—remove all items from the area that are not required to do the job.

   Seiri: *Put things in order*—remove what is not needed and keep what is needed.

2. Set in order: *Orderliness*—define locations for all required items. We commonly use the old saying, "A place for everything, everything in its place."

   Seiton: *Proper arrangement*—place things so that they can be easily reached whenever they are needed—the shortest path.

3. Shine: *The act of cleaning*—clean and inspect all required items. Daily cleaning is an essential form of inspection.

   Seiso: *Clean*—keep things clean and polished, no debris or dirt in the workplace.

4. Standardize: *The state of cleanliness/organization.*

   Seiketsu: *Purity*—maintain an environment that is organized and clean.

5. Sustain: *The practice of discipline*—maintain the practices that have been established in the first four steps.

   Shitsuke: *Commitment*—this translates to an attitude of pride and commitment to maintain and practice the standards that have been established in the first four steps.

We've seen this tool deployed in a Kaizen fashion: Pick an area, train a team, and work through the steps. We've also seen this process implemented as part of a Lean process reorganization. Either way works; the important point is to get it done and start reaping the benefits.

IMPLEMENTING 5S

The intent of this process is the elimination of waste and variation. The method is a highly disciplined and visual workplace. Let's work through a typical implementation.

S #1: Sort

This session starts with the formation of a team and some preliminary education. There are many excellent educational courses and videos available. Pick one up and add it to your company library. The first step in the

Cell/Area	**RED TAG**	Tag Number

Category (circle one)	
1 Raw Mat'l	6 Equipment
2 WIP	7 Furniture
3 Finish Mat'l	8 Office Mat'l
4 Tools	9 Books/Mags
5 Supplies	10 Other

Tag Date

Item Name

Quantity

Reason Tagged

Disposition Required (circle one)	3 Long Term Storage
1 Discard	4 Reduce Inventory
2 In Cell Storage	5 Sell/Transfer
	6 Other

ACTION TAKEN	**DATE**

Cell/Area	**RED TAG LOCATOR**	Tag Number

Location

Description

FIGURE 12-1.

implementation project involves having your team identify what is needed and what is not needed to perform the work being done in your initial target area, the *sort*. You may have heard the term *red tag* used in connection with the *sort*. It's the weapon of choice (Fig. 12-1).

In this initial step the team will evaluate everything located in the project area and decide whether it is essential to the tasks being performed. This includes tools and toolboxes, materials, benches, cabinets, and on and on—all the stuff that has accumulated over the years. In a non-Lean Six Sigma environment this is always a painful event. People tend to keep everything in their workplace, and the expression, "We can't get rid of that, we might need it. . .someday!" is one of the foundation comments of a sort event. Be patient, keep coaching and communicating, keep talking to the vision. As your team works through the unneeded items, attach a red tag to each one and move it to a designated quarantine area, commonly called the *red tag area*. Anything remaining in the project area at the conclusion of the *sort* must be designated as a *must have* to do the work.

Designate a red tag disposition team composed of the people who know what all the tagged items are, and have the authority to make the decision to keep or discard. Assets must be treated properly, so don't forget to include a member of your accounting department to keep you out of trouble. An important suggestion with a red tag area is make the call and don't allow things to sit around forever.

Because this method promotes a highly visual environment, we will make this a very visual chapter. A picture is indeed worth a thousand words (perhaps not so original, but appropriate nonetheless). With that said, we express our thanks and appreciation to Marty Paino (you'll recall his article in the baseline chapter) and Colonel Douglas Evans, the Commander of the Red River Army Depot. As part of the BAE/Red River Army Depot public/private partnership, Marty has recently relocated to Texas from York, Pennsylvania, to assist in championing Lean implementation initiatives on the Bradley Fighting Vehicle Program. They have graciously allowed the use of many of the following photographs, which document their extraordinary transition from a stall-built transmission process to a state-of-the-art flow build. Let's take a tour through some traditional areas—pre-sort (Fig. 12-2).

Lighting? Haphazard locations?

In addition to the obvious safety issues that we've pointed out, as we observe these photographs and the condition of the following areas, think

FIGURE 12-2.

of the seven categories of waste and the act of working in the areas outlined in Figures 12-3 to 12-8.

Okay, we're sure you've compiled an impressive list of observed waste. We won't beat it to death, but it isn't difficult to identify all seven types or conditions that will cause them. Enough said, on to the next step.

S #2: Set in Order

Although it is common practice to place the *set in order* step in the number two slot, we find that we are frequently working steps 2 and 3—*shine*—simultaneously. So let's bounce back and forth a bit. The mission for the team now is to define where the required items are to be located. Every item must have a place to be, every time. And to add to the discipline, these places must be clearly identified. We are not being nitpickers; we are attacking the waste caused by variation in our process.

The terms used here are *point of use* and *shortest path*. The logic is ruthlessly simple: If things are in the same place every time, and located the shortest distance away from where they are used, less time will be spent working the process. Less time = less cost. In a Lean Sigma environment, variation is the enemy and seconds count. Consider the mindset of a Six Sigma team

Risk of Finger/Hand Abrasions

FIGURE 12-3.

Overhead Reach & Fall
Hazard

FIGURE 12-4.

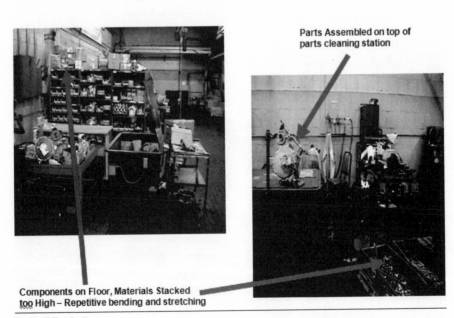

Parts Assembled on top of
parts cleaning station

Components on Floor, Materials Stacked
too High – Repetitive bending and stretching

FIGURE 12-5.

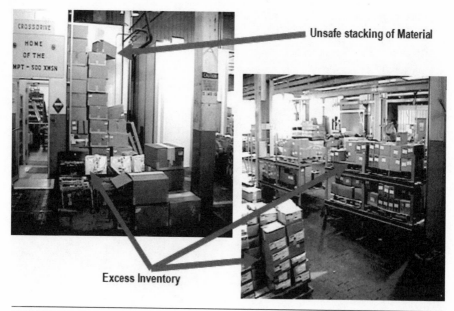

FIGURE 12-6.

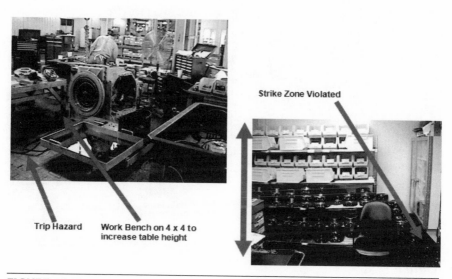

FIGURE 12-7.

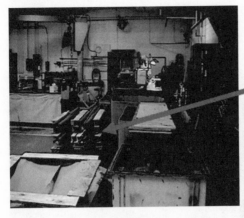

Inverted Skids used as holding
fixtures for Gun Barrels

General Housekeeping

FIGURE 12-8.

Adding Bridge Crane for
Transmission Operations

Adding door way for easy
access to Super Market

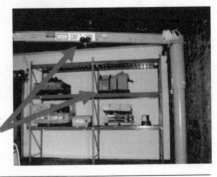

Adding Jib Crane and Shelving to Supermarket
for improved Material Handling and Kitting

FIGURE 12-9.

Prepping floor – ready for paint

Adding Anti-Slip Sand prior to painting

FIGURE 12-10.

working to reduce rejects to a few parts per million. This attitude says, "There is no level of detail that is considered insignificant." As the team is working through the "where does everything go" piece of this process, we are cleaning and conditioning all items before they are set in place. Let's go to the visuals; we're going to begin prepping the area (Figs. 12-9 to 12-12).

S #3: Shine

At this point we've worked through the *sort*. The area has been cleared of all items not required to perform the specific work being done. The team is completing the *set in order*. They have analyzed the flow of activity and developed a floor plan and location plan for all work stations, tooling, materials, cleaning stations, and equipment. Shadow boards are being constructed for hand tools; white boards are being constructed for information and area metrics; gravity racks and assembly fixture modifications are under way with particular attention to ergonomics and safety.

Concurrently, our facilities support people have reconditioned the area. It's well lighted, a fresh coat of paint has been applied, all air and power lines have been rerouted to drop from the ceiling (no cords or trip hazards on the floor), and floors have been color-coded to designate manufacturing space, materials flow, and aisles. Step 3—the *shine*—is well under way; well done, so far.

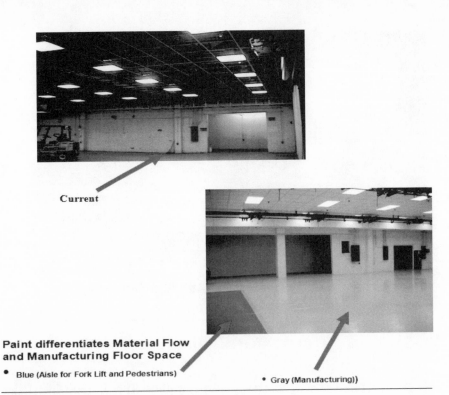

Current

Paint differentiates Material Flow
and Manufacturing Floor Space

• Blue (Aisle for Fork Lift and Pedestrians)

• Gray (Manufacturing))

FIGURE 12-11.

FIGURE 12-12.

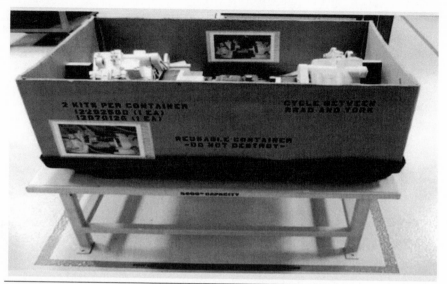

FIGURE 12-13.

Let's jump back to the *set in order*. The team will now begin to repopulate the area (Figs. 12-13 to 12-15).

A well 5S'd area eliminates the waste of looking for needed items; everything is in its predetermined location, every time. If you've ever observed an operator going to a toolbox and rummaging through seven drawers of tools to find the exact socket or wrench he or she needs, you understand the huge amount of wasted time in a non-Lean Sigma layout. In an area that is serious about 5S, there are only two places your tool can be:

1. In your hand, or
2. On the shadow board.

No noise here. The area has been reset to the team's layout and flow pattern; let's proceed to the next stage.

S #4: Standardize

Again, in practical application a good bit of this activity has been started in the previous steps; however, now that we've finished the *set in order* and *shine*, we can fine-tune the *standardize* step and complete our area at the lowest level of detail.

The *standardize* step is subject to much interpretation, with the first question being, "Just what is a standard; what are we trying to accomplish in this step?" Sorry, I guess that's two questions? Okay, a standard, in simplest terms

FIGURE 12-14.

FIGURE 12-15.

is an indicator that tells us what to do. With that in mind, the more visual a standard is, the easier it will be to follow. We like to use the example of a traffic light as a visual standard. It's hanging at the intersection, and it tells you what to do. Green means go; red means stop. You do not have to get out of your car and go to a computer monitor, open some files, and read a procedure to determine whether it's time to go or time to stop. You don't need to find a traffic scheduler, supervisor, or expediter and ask for instruction. You just follow the visual standard, easy as that.

The more effective your standards development and execution are, the easier it will be to perform the fifth S: *sustain*. The purpose of standards is twofold; they tell you what to do and where things belong. They also allow you to see immediately whether anything is not as it should be, *out of standard*. A tool is missing on a shadow board, materials are placed in the wrong location on the floor, a shadow outline for a visual replenish of a sub-assembly component is empty—time to build a replacement. You get the picture. Everything has a place, and it's clearly labeled. The purpose of a good system of standards is to eliminate variation in the workplace and minimize the waste of activity that occurs if our processes are not clearly defined. Let's continue.

S #5: Sustain

We have now completed the first 4 S's. Our area is clean, organized, items are at point of use, and locations are labeled and identified. We have a safe

FIGURE 12-16.

FIGURE 12-17.

and efficient workplace to conduct our business. Now comes the fifth S: *sustain.* The sustain effort requires the cooperation and enthusiasm of all employees in the process. We have engaged in a lot of work to put our area in fighting condition; now we must foster and maintain an attitude of pride, discipline, and professionalism.

The foundation tools for the *sustain* are clear and ongoing communication of the expected level of excellence we desire in our company and a disciplined audit procedure to keep us on track and monitor our state of being. Develop a detailed audit process, and publish the results on your 5S information board. Again, the more visual the better. Many people think that auditing a process or set of standards has a negative "we're checking up on you" connotation. We disagree. We view it as our report card on our success in maintaining a world class environment. When we get straight "A's" an audit will be cause for celebration.

With that said, we provide a summary, in our visual mode, of where we may have come from, and where we have advanced to—same work station, very different environments (Figs. 12-16 and 12-17).

Chapter 13

Total Productive Maintenance

Much of the literature on the total productive maintenance (TPM) technique places its beginnings back in the late 1960s in the Japanese auto industry. It is widely thought to have come into being at a company by the name of Nippon Denso, a supplier for the Toyota Motor Corporation. The evolution of this tool is thought to have been heavily influenced by the demands of the newly developed Toyota Production System and its emphasis on *Just in Time* delivery, short lead times, and improved quality. A gentleman named Seiichi Nakajima is credited with defining the concepts of TPM, and an English translation of one of his books on the subject in the late 1980s brought this topic onto the radar screen of western manufacturing.

TPM is another of the foundation tools required to support a Lean Six Sigma philosophy of operation. It is considered a critical component of the journey to achieve world-class equipment performance, variation reduction, lead-time reduction, and exceptional operating results.

The initial question might be, "How is TPM different than the traditional approach to maintenance?" Let's compare techniques and discuss some of the foundation logic of different operating philosophies.

TRADITIONAL MAINTENANCE ENVIRONMENT

In a traditional, non-Lean Sigma environment, as we've discussed in previous chapters, it's common to see queues of material before and after the pieces of equipment. In a "batch and queue" operating model, if a machine experiences a breakdown we just move to a different machine and work around the problem. The buildup of unnecessary inventory tends to hide machine reliability issues; the process just continues elsewhere. In this type of environment, the common mindset is "run the equipment until it fails and then call maintenance to get it going." Maintenance is largely considered to be a necessary evil, merely a cost-adder, and an area where cost can be cut in tough times. "Just lay off a couple of maintenance guys, we'll be able to work around any problems."

With this philosophy, each individual machine is treated as an independent work center. We may have a preventative maintenance process in place, but even with our periodic preventative maintenance we still seem to experience unplanned breakdowns and stoppages. We probably don't pay much attention to current equipment metrics such as overall equipment effectiveness (OEE) and probably don't have the time or the inclination to use techniques such as root-cause analysis to address downtime issues. "We just fight fires and work like hell!" is the standard mantra in this type of approach. Of course the culture in a traditional model is, "The operators just run the machines, the maintenance guys fix them."

A traditional maintenance environment is a tough place to work, and an even tougher place to run a business.

THE TOTAL PRODUCTIVE MAINTENANCE APPROACH

We bring a new game to the table—a Lean Six Sigma operating philosophy. This is a game of waste elimination, variation control, and velocity. As we begin to drive down queues of inventory and link processes together, the impact of machine reliability (or lack of it) becomes excruciatingly visible. When a piece of equipment experiences an unexpected breakdown, there's no "working around it." The entire process is affected by the performance of this single piece of equipment. We are now tightrope walkers with no safety net. Okay, there are two paths available to us now:

1. Forget about customer value-driven philosophies of operation, and get some queues of excess inventory banked up between operations, pronto! Or. . .

2. Figure out a maintenance strategy that will promote a drastic improvement in machine and equipment performance.

Those individuals who embraced the Lean Sigma model picked number 2; thus, the evolution of TPM began. Let's talk to some of the logic and drivers of this system.

One of the fundamental changes in approach evolved around "Who does what?" and "Who's responsible for the pieces of the equipment effectiveness effort?" The TPM model requires that all employees be involved and accountable for the care and feeding of the equipment and machines in their area of function. It is no longer the sole responsibility of those individuals whose job description contains the word "maintenance."

In a Lean Six Sigma environment, you will hear terms such as *quality at the source* or *prevention at the source*. These terms imply that a focus on identifying and controlling process variables, with the resulting reduction in variation, is best practiced at the point in the process where the variation occurs. This leads us to a very different view of the role of maintenance. We now expand the responsibility for daily and weekly routine maintenance to those individuals most familiar with the equipment: the operators and machinists on the shop floor. In the TPM model the operators perform the *dailys* and *weeklies*, oil checks, inspection of points where loose conditions might occur, belt and hose wear, minor adjustments, any routine maintenance, or inspection tasks that do not require a high level of technical expertise. In addition, because the frontline operators are intimately familiar with the smallest nuances of their machines and equipment, it's their responsibility to note changes in operating characteristics, noise, vibration, anything out of the ordinary, and contact maintenance to order analysis and repair.

The role of maintenance is one of performing the periodic and preventative tasks that require a higher level of technical skill, managing the preventative maintenance *process*, and continuing to effect repairs in the *catastrophe* category—the unplanned crashes, if you will.

Engineering design has the responsibility of considering new product design characteristics that can be successfully produced with existing machines, equipment, and processes. Capability studies and statistical quality measures are valuable design tools at this stage in the game.

TPM is an important component of a continuous improvement environment in that the involvement of all employees in the process enables an approach of "identify and eliminate the source of equipment and machine deterioration." The traditional mindset is "repair after the fact." In addition, when *total cost* impact is evaluated, TPM is an equally effective tool to reduce maintenance cost.

MEASURING EQUIPMENT EFFECTIVENESS

Okay, let's talk to the metrics. In a Lean Sigma company you'll probably hear the term *OEE* used in connection with the TPM process. As mentioned above, OEE stands for *overall equipment effectiveness.* You may also hear reference to the *Big Six.* There are many excellent books addressing OEE that explain this topic in far more detail than we care to get into in this volume, but let's just skim the surface and get the words up on the radar screen.

Given that TPM is a root-cause tool, OEE is a primary driver that talks to three main areas of equipment performance: availability, performance rate, and quality rate. These are commonly considered the three big boxes of machine/equipment effectiveness.

Let's take a closer look.

Availability

Availability means just that—a particular piece of equipment is *available* when needed (or not). Simple as that. The major components of availability are:

1. Breakdowns, and
2. Setup and adjustment time.

Breakdowns are pretty straightforward. A piece of equipment is unavailable when needed because of an unexpected breakdown—a motor burns up, a cylinder blows, there are a thousand things that may happen.

Setting up a machine or piece of equipment also places it on the unavailable list; it won't be *available* until the setup, or changeover, is complete. And then there are machine adjustments that are necessary for a number of reasons as we work our way through the day. These are also time killers and take a machine off the *available* roster. This sounds like three components, but typically adjustments are included in the setup category. You can reason that an adjustment is a secondary setup to bring a machine into tolerance to produce acceptable quality specifications.

Above, I mentioned the Big Six. These are the first two, *Breakdowns* and *Setup/Adjustments.*

Performance Rate

Our second big box, *Performance Rate* is composed of:

1. Reduced speed, and
2. Idling/minor stoppages.

It is common to see equipment not being run at optimum rate (reduced speed) when variation in product quality begins to occur. Idling and minor stoppages also fall into the *Performance Rate* category. And there you have the second two categories of the Big Six.

Quality Rate

The last two categories of the Big Six are the components of *Quality Rate*:

1. Defects/rework, and
2. Start-up.

These items refer to lost product. Defects and rework are self-explanatory, and I'm sure you're all familiar with the reject curve that occurs after a changeover and the fine-tuning of the start-up (production run) phase is worked through to stabilize the process.

TPM drives to eliminate or reduce these six areas of loss through the involvement of all employees in a given process, with a root-cause approach.

A good TPM process is a difficult implementation task, but given excellent communication, total employee involvement, and a disciplined Lean Six Sigma mindset, it is a process that yields significant benefits in variation elimination and cost reduction. Don't give it up when you hit the first speed bump; regroup and press on. It's a critical piece of the Lean Sigma puzzle.

Chapter 14

Practical Application of Lean Six Sigma: Indirect Expenses

The following exercise, a hypothetical conversation between Bill Carreira and Bill Trudell, is meant to provide you, the reader, with answers to some of your basic questions about Lean Six Sigma and to demonstrate some practical applications of the principles involved.

Bill Carreira: So, Bill, you really think anyone or any organization can do Lean Six Sigma?

Bill Trudell: Absolutely.

Bill C.: Well it seems like every time I peek into a Lean Six Sigma or Six Sigma book it looks like a bunch of statistical equations that are over most people's heads, and that includes mine. How is a *knucklehead* like me supposed to understand it?

Bill T.: I know what you're talking about. I have seen all of the equations. Actually, I have worked most of them. But the fact is that there is a practical side to Six Sigma that can be used very effectively by almost anyone or any organization.

Bill C.: Oh, I see, a *full factorial* experiment is practical? I can hardly wait to get started. I just remembered something. I don't know what that is.

Bill T.: Okay Bill, I get your point. But listen. Let's step back a minute. Think of one of those big tool boxes that most people's dads have. You know, the red Craftsman one with drawers and wheels in the garage? Think of that as a Six Sigma tool box.

Bill C.: Okay. I got it. All of those tools are a full factorial experiment?

Bill T.: No, Bill, listen a minute. Think about all of those tools in the box . . . hammer, pliers, channel-lock wrench, crescent wrench, flathead screw driver, Phillips head screwdriver, tape measure, drill, hack saw, saber saw, cross-cut saw, hole punch, socket set, feeler gauges, Allen wrenches, pipe wrenches.

Most all of the jobs or repairs your dad did around the house or on your car could be done with hammer, pliers, screwdrivers, socket sets, open-end wrenches, and, most likely a feeler gauge to tune up the car. These are tools that most anyone could use.

Then there are the other more specialized tools that most mechanics could use . . . brake alignment tool, clutch alignment tool, retaining ring removers, pullers, taps and dies, timing light, circuit tester. We may have heard of them, but most of us don't know how to use them. They are only needed in unique circumstances that don't happen that often. In Six Sigma, our mechanic is a Black Belt. We hire or consult a Black Belt when we are trying to solve more problems or improve processes that require the use of the more complex tools.

But if you think about it, there are a lot of jobs we could get done with the basic tools. You could tune up your car—change and set points, plugs, and condenser. You could repair a window, hang a picture, fix the screen door, fix the garage door, change the blades on your lawnmower, install a ceiling fan, assemble the kid's new swing set, or change the propeller on your boat motor. You could fix a lot of problems and accomplish quite a bit with a few simple tools.

Bill C.: Wow, thanks for the home improvement lesson Bill! I can't wait to go in and tell the CEO that our Lean Six Sigma team is standing ready to fix our lawnmower, hang pictures, and tune up the plant vehicle. He is going to be pumped!

Bill T.: Now let me continue, Bill. The tools of Six Sigma are the same. There are a few basic tools in Six Sigma that anyone can use to get a lot done. They are the hammer, pliers, wrenches, and screwdrivers of Six Sigma.

Here they are: brainstorming, fishbone diagrams, affinity diagrams, Pareto charts, run diagrams, barrier removal forms, and dashboards.

Bill C.: Actually, I have heard of these terms.

Bill T.: Tools, Bill. Not terms. These are the fundamental tools. These are in the Six Sigma toolbox. These tools can be learned and applied very quickly by nearly anyone to make valuable process improvements in any business situation, including manufacturing and service.

Bill C.: I don't know Pareto, affinity, dashboard . . . . Sounds a little intense. And then there is this DMAIC thing. That's the biggie. You Black Belts love this DMAIC thing.

You're still speaking French to me.

Bill T.: Fair enough, but give me a few minutes to change your mind. Okay?

Bill C.: Sure. Take it away.

Bill T.: Okay, let's review what Six Sigma is: a systematic, disciplined, and data-based method to get to root causes to solve problems and analyze and improve processes with the ultimate goal of achieving no more than 3.4 defects per million opportunities.

Bill C.: Data-based? Another buzzword.

Bill T.: Look, data-based just means that decisions are based on data, not on perception or opinion. This approach eliminates wasting people's valuable time and makes sure the real problem is fixed. Here's an example. One night it is raining, and while you are watching TV, water starts dripping from your ceiling. So you immediately call a roofing company and have a new roof put on the next day. The bill is $3500. Two days later the water starts to drip again, so you get on the phone and call the roofing company to give them a piece of your mind, by golly. Only thing is, while you are on hold you look outside and notice it isn't raining. On taking a closer look, you find out you have a PVC pipe in your ceiling that drains your air conditioner condensation unit, and it is beginning to leak. Now don't you think that some data, such as how often and when your ceiling leaked, what the weather was, and so on, might have been valuable? Might have saved you some money too?

Bill C.: Man, you got this home improvement thing down, Bill!

Bill T.: But see, that is all data-based decision making is. It just means that gathering and considering data when solving problems lead to better solutions. It can help you avoid spending the company's money on equipment or solutions that you don't need. Most important, it keeps you from wasting people's time in ineffective decision processes.

Bill C.: Tell me about DMAIC, Bill. Sounds a little complex. How do you "quickly" teach people to apply DMAIC?

Bill T.: Fair question, Bill. Let me explain. As I just said, Six Sigma is a systematic, disciplined, and data-based method to get to root causes to solve problems and analyze and improve processes with the ultimate goal of achieving no more than 3.4 defects per million opportunities.

DMAIC is the systematic, disciplined, data-based method used to improve quality or solve problems. It stands for define, measure, analyze, improve, and control, which are the phases of the method or process.

Define is the first phase, and in this phase the project goal or purpose is carefully defined. The scope is determined, which is an understanding of how wide or comprehensive the project will be. *(Find out why the roof is leaking and fix it.)*

Measure is the second phase, and in the measure phase information is gathered that will be needed to support finding root causes and support improvement. If it is a process, baseline data on the process's performance are gathered. If it is a problem, data that can be used to pinpoint the problem will be gathered (*e.g., recent daily histories of temperature and rain fall, days water leaked from the ceiling, how much water leaked from the ceiling, confirmation that the liquid is water, condition of roof, location of leak in ceiling, how old the roof is*).

Analyze is the third phase, and the purpose of the analyze phase is to use the data to determine the root cause or causes of the process or problem. Theories of the cause are examined and tested. (*We got together with a neighbor and brainstormed about what could be causing the leak. On several days when it rained, the ceiling leaked so we have formed the hypothesis that the roof is leaking. We test or spray water over the roof, but the ceiling does not leak, so we "reject" our hypothesis. On further review, we notice that it was very hot on the days that the ceiling leaked. Because we ran the air conditioner on those days we form another hypothesis that the air conditioner is causing water to leak from the ceiling. We run the air conditioner, and the ceiling leaks! Every time. On inspection we determine that the root cause is a leak in a pipe used to drain condensation from our air conditioning unit that travels through the ceiling.*)

The fourth phase is improve, and in this phase we test solutions until we address the root cause. Sometimes this takes several solutions. (*We apply duct tape around the leak, we put glue on the seam that is leaking, and we try a different fitting where the pipe is leaking.*)

Control is the last phase, and the purpose of the control phase is to test the solutions and develop a plan to keep the problem from recurring. (*We find the pipe leaks with duct tape applied, the pipe leaks after glue is applied, and the pipe no longer leaks when we try a new fitting. We replace the fitting permanently and implement a control plan of having a professional inspect the pipe on an annual basis in the future.*)

Bill T.: The problem is solved! And, isn't that a lot better than paying $3,500 to replace a 2-year-old roof that wasn't leaking?

Bill C.: Wow Bill, you didn't tell me you were a plumber. So now I know what a Black Belt does! Hey all kidding aside, the DMAIC process is kind of common sense.

Bill T.: Be careful, Bill. I am starting to picture you with a . . . dark-colored belt?

Bill C.: Okay Bill, fair enough, you have fixed the leak without buying a roof you did not need. But to be honest, this all still seems so much simpler than the long formulas, statistics, full factorial experiments, and all of the other high-tech terms. Is that really Six Sigma?

Bill T.: In the simplest sense yes. Let's go back again to what Six Sigma is: a systematic, disciplined, and data-based method to get to root causes to solve problems and analyze and improve processes with the ultimate goal of achieving no more than 3.4 defects per million opportunities.

Isn't that what we just did? And wouldn't it be fair to say that we never want our ceiling to leak again? If we consider every day an "opportunity" for a lead, then our desire to never have our roof leak more than 3.4 times in the next million days seems pretty close to never!

Bill C.: I'll give you that. That's pretty close to never. Okay, you are tweaking my curiosity. This still seems a far cry from what I have seen in the Six Sigma books.

Bill T.: Let's discuss that. We are back to the tool box. Here is the thing. Solving problems and improving processes with the DMAIC process is the backbone of Six Sigma. Again, there is a huge toolbox of tools from as simple as brainstorming, spreadsheets, and sticky notes on a wall all the way to statistical calculations, data distribution analysis, power tests, and full factorial design of experiments. The good news is that you can apply the DMAIC process and the simpler tools toward solving a wide variety of problems and improving processes. That is the purpose of this book: to demonstrate a more practical and simple form of applying Six Sigma that nearly anyone can understand.

Bill C.: Hey Bill, can you give me an example of how to use Lean Six Sigma for problem solving or process improvement in a factory?

Bill T.: My pleasure Bill.

Bill C.: Remember, Bill, keep it simple.

Bill T.: Okay, here we go. Simple, simple, simple. We are now working together in a company, and the president has said our overhead expenses are out of control. We must get them down and do it quickly.

Bill C.: Okay Bill, I suppose you are going to use one of those big formulas right? Maybe a standard deviation or a *t* test.

Bill T.: Bill, you just don't get it. Come on, let's go for a walk.

Bill C.: Where are we going Bill?

Bill T.: We're going to see Fred in accounting. He is going to give us the information we need to apply Lean Six Sigma. One of the tenets of the Lean Six Sigma approach is to involve accounting in all projects. This keeps your controller from shaking his or her head in disbelief during your presentation of exciting results from your project. Imagine presenting a claim of saving thousands of dollars. You are all excited, and your team is "high-fiving." You look over, and your controller is acting as if you are in fantasy land. What do you think the boss would do? If accounting is not on board with your numbers, you have basically wasted your time. If they are, it is great.

Bill C.: Okay, I've been there. I've had holes shot in my numbers before.

Bill T.: We all have, Bill. Accountants don't mean to do it, but they are skeptical by nature. It just makes sense that if you involve them from the onset they will buy in, and most important they will contribute. I've never seen an accountant who didn't love to save money. Oh yeah, one more thing, Bill. Remember our leaking roof? Well let's just say that accounting is going to help us make sure that our roof is leaking before we call the roofing company.

Bill C.: Oh, OK, I see. Boy, you are getting some mileage out of the roof thing aren't you?

Bill T.: Good morning Fred!

Fred: Good morning gentleman. And to what do I owe the honor of the opportunity to meet with you two fine individuals?

Bill T.: Fred, we are all fired up. As you know the boss has told us to cut our overhead. Do you think you could give us a hand?

Fred: I'll try guys. Can you tell me exactly what you will need, because as you know the boss has also cut our staff and we don't have an abundance of time or resources. I mean, I want to help, but I only have so much help I can give.

Bill T.: No problem, Fred. Here is what we will need. Because it is February, can you please give us the final budget performance results from last year, the financials, and get us access to the general ledger distribution accounts. Then if you can, we would like to have you attend a meeting two times per week for about 1 hour. Oh, and one more thing, we will need some data or reports periodically. What do you think, Fred? Can you do it?

Fred: Guys, I'd like to help, but is this going to be one of those endless projects? I mean, you do remember that cost-reduction committee we had last year, right? The one that met and met for hours and hours to discuss ways to cut costs? If I remember right, they started doing some things different, but our costs didn't seem to budge. Let's see, they worked on reducing office supplies, turning all the lights off throughout the plant, using fewer shop towels and drill bits, and cost-savings in other areas. They did reduce our costs for all of those, but our overall costs stayed about the same, and in a couple of months they actually went up. Honestly, it almost seemed like a waste of time. I mean, they promised the boss big-time results and created a lot of excitement. I was at the big presentation when they were excited and explaining all of their actions and expectations. I felt kind of bad when I had to report to the group that our cost had not gone down. Actually, it got kind of heated. They questioned my numbers and said they had to be wrong. There was no way they could have saved all that money and not see the results in the financials.

Bill T.: Fred you are describing the exact kind of situation that is avoided by using Lean Six Sigma.

Fred: Really. Well, I'll tell you, Bill, if you have a way to avoid those results, you will really be on to something. That was not fun at all; in fact, it was downright disappointing.

Bill C.: Fred, why do you think they got such poor results? I mean it seems like they were working on some good things, and they certainly were motivated.

Fred: You know they were working hard. I was just as disappointed as they were. It just seems that the good things they were working on didn't really amount to that much in results.

Bill T.: Guys, guys, you couldn't have said it better. The answer is in your answers! It's right there in front of you.

Bill C./Fred: We're not following you.

Bill T.: It's one of the oldest mistakes in business. The problem is the good things they were working on.

Bill C./Fred: Hold on, Bill. You're talking in riddles here.

Bill T.: Alright guys, I'll stop speaking in tongues. The problem is not that they were working on good things, but that they were not working on the right things. The fact is that in the majority of situations if you work on the right things, you will get the right results.

Bill C.: What's the difference between "good things" and "right things"?

Bill T.: Results! If you're working on the right things you will get results, almost every time.

Fred: Sounds like a bunch of semantics to me. Guys, my time is limited. I'm a team player. I'll give you 2 hours a week, and I'll give you your data if you give me a couple of days heads-up when you need it. Honestly though, if we don't get some meaningful results, this will probably be the last project I participate in. By the way, just go to Bob in Information Technology for your ledger reports. He'll give you all the help you need.

Bill T.: Okay Fred, we'll see you next Tuesday at 1 P.M. Keep the faith, Fred. We're going to have some fun and get some great results.

Bill C.: Wow, you, me, and Fred. What a dream team! This is going to be good.

Bill T.: It will, but there will be more than us three. We're going to invite two of our quality auditors along with two of our production managers to join us. Now that's a dream team!

Bill C.: I'm in!

First Meeting

Bill T.: Alright, let's call this meeting to order. As you know, our president has asked us to reduce our overhead expenses. We have assembled this team to work together to do just that. So here you are. In addition to Bill and me, we have Tony and Sam from Quality Assurance, and Jim and Don from production. Fred has graciously agreed to support us with reports, data, and time.

Don: Great, I can tell you right now we have to reduce how much soldering paste we are using. The other day I saw an operator use a half a tube on one die set. We have the same problem with solder. We just use way too much. Another thing some operators are doing is throwing solder rolls away that still have solder on them. When the rolls get low they are hard to hold onto, so they just throw them away.

Jim: Yeah, let's do it, I'll meet you in the soldering area tomorrow morning.

Tony/Fred: Great! We'll be there too.

Bill T.: I'm in!

Bill C.: So Bill, I guess you're calling the roofing company again?

Tony/Fred/Don/Jim: What does our roof have to do with anything?

Bill C.: A lot, guys. Let's give Bill a minute to explain. He's going to tell us to make sure our roof is really leaking before we call the roofer.

Tony/Fred/Don/Jim: Guys, you are making no sense at all. What are you talking about?

Bill T.: Okay, Okay. Let's see if I can help. Fred, really quick, can you tell us how much we spent on overhead expense items last year?

Fred: Sure, we spent $5.2 million.

Bill T.: Great. Okay, can you tell us how much we spent on soldering paste and solder?

Fred: Yes, we spent $30,444 on paste and $43,000 on solder. Both together, we spent $73,444.

Don: See, I told you. We spent $73,444. Now that is some cash!

Bill T.: So how much do you think we could cut our spending on paste and solder?

Don: I guarantee we could cut our spending by half. I just know it.

Jim: See, told you.

Bill T.: Okay, so if we cut paste and solder expenses in half we would save $36,722.

Don: That's what I'm talking about.

Bill T.: Fred, can you tell me what percentage of total overhead expense items $36,722 represents?

Fred: Let's see, $36,722 divided by $5,209,000 equals 0.70%.

Bill T.: See guys? I love your energy, but 0.70% is not going to help much. I mean don't get me wrong, every little bit helps, but we only have so much time and energy so we better put it where we can get the biggest bang for our buck.

Bill C.: I see it coming. Let's use the DMAIC process.

Tony/Fred/Don/Jim: The what?

Bill T.: It's a systematic, disciplined, and data-based method to get to root causes to solve problems and analyze and improve processes with the ultimate goal of achieving no more than 3.4 defects per million opportunities.

Jim: Oh boy, I think you have the wrong guy here. I operate machines and make good parts. That scientific stuff is over my head. You need one of those engineering guys.

Don: I agree. Call us when you want to work on something we can understand.

Tony: Wait a minute, guys! I have a friend who works at Electro-craft who says they've been using Lean Six Sigma and are getting great results. He says everyone from the president on down is involved. He says they are cutting costs and improving quality faster better than they ever have. He also said the operators are the ones coming up with all of the solutions. And they are using that DMAIC process you were talking about.

Bill C.: Wow! That is exciting. Bill I suggest you take us through the DMAIC process. Guys, you are going to like this!

Bill T.: Let's do it. Okay. The DMAIC process stands for DEFINE, MEASURE, ANALYZE, IMPROVE, and CONTROL. I will explain each step as we go through it.

The first thing we are going to do is to define what problem we are working on. We will develop a problem statement that will clearly indicate what problem we will be working to solve. See you Thursday.

Define Phase

Bill T.: Greetings, guys. Thanks for coming, and please let me explain the ground rules for our meetings. First, here is an agenda (Fig. 14-1). I expect to keep right to it. Everyone's time is important, and we have a lot to cover so I am going to ask that everyone be on time, complete their homework assignments, and stay with the agenda.

Meeting Agenda - Define
1:00 – 2:45 PM - Complete Project Charter
2:45 – 3:30 PM – Develop a SIPOC diagram
3:30 – 4:00 PM – Develop a high level process map
4:00 – 4:15 PM – Review requirements / actions in the MEASURE phase

FIGURE 14-1.

In the DEFINE phase, the efforts of the team will be to develop a strategy and set of actions aimed at reducing our overhead expenses. The project will focus on expenditures of items used during the production process. The team will not look at staffing or head count.

In this meeting we are going to complete a Project Charter. First we will create a problem statement.

Project Charter/Problem Statement

The efforts of the team will be to develop a strategy and set of actions aimed at reducing our indirect spending expenses. The project will focus on expenditures of items used during the production process. The team will not look at staffing or head count.

We will then determine who is on the team, key dates, and milestones.

Bill T.: We need to set a goal for spending reduction. What do you guys think would be a good goal?

Bill C.: In my experience with Lean projects, we set pretty aggressive goals. I recommend 30%.

Bill T.: What do you guys think?

Group: Hey, if we're going to work hard, let's set a challenging goal—30% sounds good.

Bill T.: Okay, here's the charter (Fig. 14-2).

Bill: Next week we will start the MEASURE phase of DMAIC. In this phase we gather information that will be needed to support finding root causes and improvement or cost reductions. In short, we are going to study all of our expenditures on expense items and learn what we are spending our money on.

I have asked Fred to get us a copy of the final budget performance results for last year, the financial details, and get us access to the general ledger distribution accounts. By the way Fred, can you please use Excel spreadsheets so we can manipulate data?

Fred: I'll have it at our meeting this Thursday. Any special color of paper?

Bill T.: Let's go with green, like the color of all of the money we are going to save. That's it guys. See you Thursday.

Measure Phase

Bill T.: Greetings everyone. Okay, today we are going to determine what we will measure (Fig. 14-3). The fact is, Fred, the majority of data for this project will come from our accounting system.

Project Charter	
Project :	Indirect spending
Project Leader :	Bill Trudell
Problems to be solved :	High expenditures on shop supplies and other expense items
Process/es impacted :	All
Team Member/s :	Bill, Bill, Fred, Tony, Sam, Jim, Don
Project goals / deliverables :	Reduce spending by 30%
Project Start :	1-Jan
Project End :	31-Mar
Milestones :	(completed by)
Define	8-Jan
Measure	5-Feb
Analyze	5-Mar
Improve	28-Feb
Control	31-Mar

FIGURE 14-2.

Meeting Agenda - Measure

9:00 - 10:30 AM - Determine what data will be gathered in Measure phase

10:30 - 11 AM - Assign responsibilities

FIGURE 14-3.

Fred: Oh, I get it. Let accounting do all of the work! Okay guys, I'll get some data. Give me a week.

Bill T.: Thanks Fred. Okay guys, here is the agenda for next week. See you then.

Bill T.: Hi everyone. Our mission today is to begin to look at what data we have to measure and analyze (Fig. 14-4). Okay, Fred, take it away. Let's hear about the data.

Meeting Agenda - Measure
1:00 - 4:00 PM
Pre-liminary review of available data
Determine any additional data needed
Task assignments as needed

FIGURE 14-4.

Fred: Sure, I have copies for everyone. First off, I would like to say that after looking at the data, it looks like we are spending too much on everything. We need to cut down on it all.

Bill T.: Fred, can I ask what kind of analysis you did on the data?

Fred: Sure, I carefully reviewed it line by line. Like I said, we are spending too much on everything.

Bill T.: Did you do a Pareto?

Fred: A what?

Bill T.: A Pareto analysis.

Fred: No I did not. I've seen them before, but I haven't really done one. Isn't a Pareto analysis just a bar chart?

Bill T.: Great question Fred! A Pareto analysis is simply a chart that allows you to see the relative occurrences of different types or categories of data.

In our case, a Pareto will tell us what groups of expenses are making up the largest part of our overall spending. This is important information because it will tell us where our biggest opportunities to cut our expenses are. Fred, can you tell us how many categories there are for overhead expenses?

Fred: Sure, there are 18 categories. Each one has a ledger number.

Bill T.: Okay Fred, great, can you do me a favor and sort them by dollars spent per category.

Fred: Sure.

Bill T.: Great, now can you put them in a bar chart?

Fred: Here you go (Fig. 14-5).

Group: Wow, look at gas.

Jim: And take a look at electric! I never realized we spent that much on electricity.

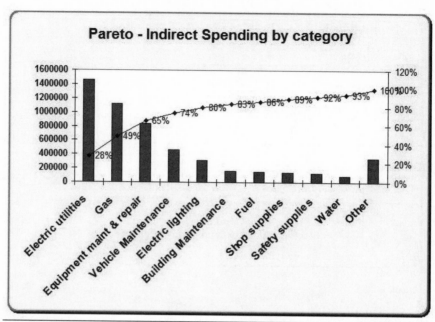

FIGURE 14-5.

Don: Lighting and vehicle maintenance are biggies.

Bill T.: Now do you see why a Pareto chart is such a good tool.

Don: Boy, it sure tells you where you are spending your money, doesn't it?

Bill T.: You know, it is so simple, yet so powerful. It seems like most people are looking for the high-tech solution. But a simple Pareto chart will show you just where you are experiencing the most cost, or problems. This is so valuable, because it tells you where to spend your efforts. You only have so much time and resources, so doesn't it make sense to spend them where you have the most to gain?

Group: Boy, it sure does.

Bill T.: So what should we work on?

Don: That's easy . . . electric, gas, equipment and vehicle maintenance, electric lighting.

Fred: Those five areas make up $4,182,000, which is 80% of our spending!

Bill T.: Good stuff, isn't it? Fred, I hate to keep putting the work on you, and I know that we are pushing the 2 hours you committed to, but could you please do a Pareto of the top spends in each category for next week? This will give us the information we need to focus our improvement efforts.

Fred: Absolutely, you know I am really getting excited. This simple analysis is so informative. You can count on me. See you next week.

Meeting Agenda - Analyze
1:00 - 4:00 PM
Continue to review data
Determine any additional data needed
Task assignments as needed

FIGURE 14-6.

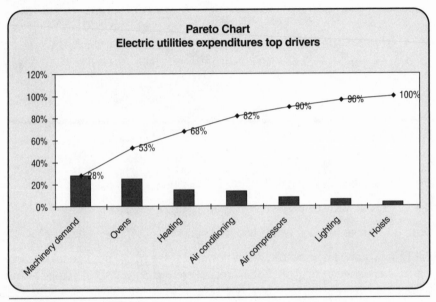

FIGURE 14-7.

Bill T.: Alright, that is enough for today. What a great meeting. I will get you the agenda for next week's meeting when we will transition to the ANALYZE phase. The purpose of the analyze phase is to use the data to determine the root cause or causes of the process or problem. We will examine and test theories of the cause(s).

Analyze Phase

Bill T.: We meet again (Fig. 14-6). Good to see everyone. Fred has called me a couple of times this week about the great data he is finding. Fred, why don't you share what you have.

Fred: Sure. Good afternoon. As requested, I gathered more data and put them in Pareto charts. As you will see, it is quite interesting and helpful (Figs. 14-7 to 14-10).

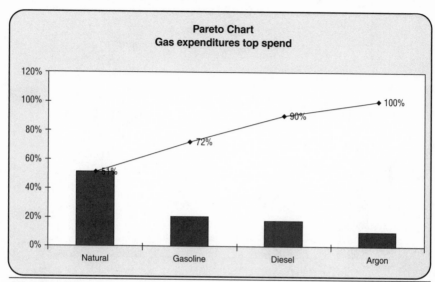

FIGURE 14-8.

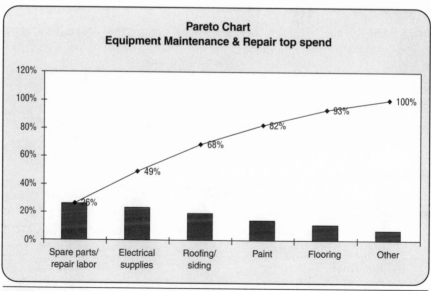

FIGURE 14-9.

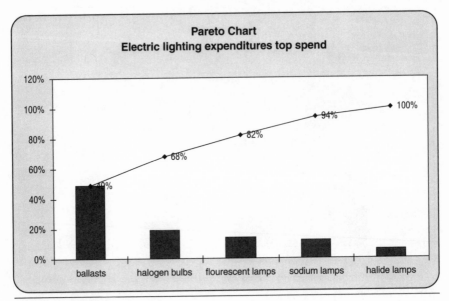

FIGURE 14-10.

Bill T.: Greetings folks. Okay, take a look at the data. Fred, what a great job! Thank you. What we are going to do now is to put together an improvement plan to generate cost reductions in each of the areas.

In the IMPROVE phase, we test solutions until we address the root cause. This may take several solutions. The purpose of the CONTROL phase is to test the solutions and develop a plan to keep the problem from recurring.

Six Weeks Later

Bill T.: Okay gentleman, let's review our improvement/control plans.

Improve Phase

Improvements in Electric Utilities/Lighting/Gas

- Conduct a complete facility lighting review with the local utility authority to ensure many of the new and improved lamp types are installed, including compact fluorescent, high-pressure sodium, metal halide, and CDM.
- Replace all possible incandescent bulbs with compact fluorescent bulbs. These bulbs last 4 times longer and use less electricity.
- Replace and upgrade insulation on all refrigerant lines in the plant.
- Install more effective insulation on all doors.
- Install upgraded insulation on factory ceilings.

- Install a low-cost solar wall to use solar energy to preheat ventilation into facility.

Improvements in Equipment Maintenance and Repair

- Set up a system to track all equipment-related warranties and eliminate situations in which the company is paying for maintenance and repairs that are covered under a current warranty.
- Implement new preventative maintenance software package to more efficiently deploy maintenance manpower resources and provide effective predictive maintenance.
- Engage purchasing to reduce the number of spare parts suppliers and negotiate high-volume supply agreement/s with one to two key suppliers/distributors.

Control Phase

Controls for Electric Utilities/Lighting/Gas

- Implement a power measurement system to provide extensive monitoring, analysis, and control to optimize the electrical systems and manage energy usage (CONTROL).
- Install power measurement software on workstations to automatically collect and process the data (CONTROL).
- Install timers/warning buzzers on all doors to signal if left open (CONTROL).
- Require security to verify that all windows are closed during rounds (CONTROL).
- Install software-driven, centrally controlled, comprehensive thermostatic control system for all areas in the facility. Review weekly/monthly output of system to troubleshoot excessive use areas (CONTROL).

Controls for Equipment Maintenance and Repair

- Add an audit point or check to annual internal control's audit to review, verify, and identify all equipment warranties in place, and further verify that the company is not paying for maintenance.
- Require facilities management to review all equipment repair invoices and ensure the service is not covered under a warranty.

SUMMARY

In this chapter we reviewed some of the fundamentals of Lean Six Sigma methodologies and attempted to explain them with meaningful scenarios. As we have stated, the purpose of this book is to "get you going" with Lean

Six Sigma. It serves as a guide to applying the more simple tools contained under the Six Sigma umbrella using the DMAIC process. Some will question whether this is Six Sigma. It's not. It's Lean Six Sigma.

In my eyes the debate over what is and is not Six Sigma is a waste of time. This is time that could be used to improve processes, improve quality, and drive defects and costs out of organizations. One thing we know, the purpose of Lean and Six Sigma is to improve the performance of your business. Sure, we are advocating a fundamental and very basic application of Six Sigma methodologies. The value is that nearly any organization can "get going" with these more simple approaches. Then later, as the organization grows, you can learn to apply the more complex tools of Six Sigma. You may want to hire a Six Sigma Black Belt and make a commitment to apply Lean Six Sigma across the whole organization.

Chapter 15

Project: Increase Throughput on an Assembly Line

Alright, let's get started. Here's the scenario. You have been recently hired as the plant manager to turn around a plant that is in big trouble. So you are now the plant manager for a plant that manufactures luxury motor homes. The kind that everyone loves. That's right, sleek, shiny, and luxurious. These are recreational vehicles (RVs) that everyone dreams of, and you are the lucky guy who is managing a plant full of assembly lines that make them. And to even make it better, you get to use one of these beauties on the weekend so you can "stay in tune with the product."

Does it get any better than this? You have it all—a great product, great employees, and a nicely equipped factory—all except an assembly line that can produce your flagship model as fast as sales is selling them. They have an order bank as far as they can see, and the only limitation on sales is your ability to build them, and build them to an acceptable level of quality. They also have a healthy 30% gross margin that, given you can build them efficiently, will bump your monthly financials quite nicely.

Here's where the excitement ends. Sales can sell six of these per month, or one every 3 days. The fact is that the factory can barely build one per month (one every 20 days), they have a large number of warranty claims and excessive rework, and there are labor and materials variances galore. The plant is losing money at a time when there are sales to support a solid level of profitability. These motor homes sell for about $450,000 each. You have been hired to increase throughput, quality, and profitability as fast as you can. To add to the drama, the president of the company mumbled during a recent visit, "I'm not convinced we should even keep this plant open."

This is a great and exciting opportunity to apply the concepts of Lean Six Sigma. We are going to take the approach of applying the principles of LEAN manufacturing (e.g., low cost, short cycles, high quality, and flow) while at the same time following the DMAIC process: define, measure, analyze, improve, and control. Let's get the team in the room.

THE TEAM

- You: Plant Manager
- Ron: Production Manager
- Joe: Quality Manager
- Rodney: Sub-Assembly Manager
- Chris: Flagship Assembly Line Supervisor
- Dick: Plant Accountant

INITIAL MEETING

You: Hi guys. I've asked you to meet so we can discuss the many challenges we currently have. We are missing sales on our flagship left and right, and as you know we have issues with quality, labor, and materials variance on the line and throughout the plant. Corporate has directed us to take action and fix this plant, and they want us to start with this line. Folks, there are people's jobs in jeopardy here. We have a golden opportunity to fix a plant. So, with that in mind I am asking for your help in participating on a team to get this line performing. To help keep us focused and ensure we get the results we need, I would like to apply the tools of Lean Six Sigma. This means applying the principles of Lean while following the DMAIC process to address inefficiencies in our process and poor-quality situations.

Ron: The what?

You: The DMAIC process. It is a formal method for solving problems and improving quality, and is based on data-driven decisions.

Ron: Isn't it all statistics that are probably way over our heads? Our employees don't understand that stuff. It's way over their heads.

You: Not at all. It is true that there are some pretty complex applications of statistics and mathematics in Six Sigma. Even the names sound complicated, but the tools and techniques really don't have to be. There are many tools in Lean Six Sigma that are practical and relatively easy to apply. The best thing to do is to just get started.

Joe: For what it's worth guys, I have had training in charts, graphs, cause-and-effect diagrams, and a lot of the things we are going to use. I have been to at least three seminars in the last 18 months that have covered it all in some form or fashion. I was concerned about being able to understand the material at the beginning of almost every course. Each time, I was surprised at how basic most of the stuff was. It would be nice to use some of it, instead of forgetting about it like a lot of others have. Look, I can do charts and graphs. I'm willing to do anything I can if it will help us turn this plant around.

You: Guys, let's take it one step at a time, and the first step is the DEFINE phase. In this phase we will define the project and determine its scope. We will create a Project Charter that will outline the purpose of the project, the scope, who the players will be, and what the expectations of the project are. Obviously, this is just common sense. Before we deploy valuable resources, let's make sure we have a plan that specifically explains what problem is going to be solved, who is going to be working on what, and what the boundaries are. Background information and data will be collected. To help us stay focused we will create a Project Charter form. It is a simple form that does a nice job of framing up all of this information.

You: I am passing out a blank form for us to use. We will work together to complete it.

Okay, what are we going to call the project?

Ron: How about the Flagship Line Improvement Project?

You: Sounds great. In goes the name. Time is of the essence, so we are going to start immediately. Let's plan on meeting next tomorrow at 1 P.M.

DEFINE PHASE

You: Okay guys, let's get right to work. In managing a Lean Six Sigma project it is important to be well organized and conduct carefully planned and efficient meetings. A Lean Six Sigma project will take a lot of time and energy, and team members will lose interest and fall short in supporting the project if it wanders or loses focus. I know you guys have jobs to do and need to be on the floor as much as possible. So to assist us I have provided an agenda (Fig. 15-1).

You: We need to define and list the problem or problems that we must solve.

Ron: Well, the number one issue is throughput. We just cannot seem to get the RVs out. We are letting our customers down. What's crazy is that I'm out there every day. I mean it's not like the guys aren't trying. They're working their butts off. It just seems like we are getting beat by a million little problems.

You: I agree. Throughput is a key requirement for our success. What else?

Meeting Agenda Define
1 – 1:45 PM - Complete Project Charter
1:45 – 2:30 PM – Develop a SIPOC diagram
2:30 – 3:15 PM – Develop a basic Process Map
3:15 - 4PM – Review requirements / actions in the MEASURE phase

FIGURE 15-1.

Joe: Well, to get the line profitable, we have to eliminate the labor and materials variances on the line. I mean we all know we have about twice as many operators on that line than the standards dictate. I also know for a fact we have damaged at least four motherboards on navigational systems in the past 2 weeks. That's about $8,000 right there. Not to mention replacing the whole salon seating in number 47 last week. The vinyl was cut in seven different places from things being set or dropped on it while working overhead. It seems like no matter how hard the guys try, the seating seems to get damaged. The same goes for cabinetry. The guys in the cabinet shop said they built the entertainment center and hallway walls three times on 46. Dick, we must have quite a usage variance on vinyl and veneer.

Dick: You bet it is. The variances for vinyl and veneer are over 30% on the flagship line. It's bad. It was so bad last month that I thought maybe we had a receiving error. But after double checking, we in fact used that. Corporate purchasing called last week and was raising Cain. They don't know how much to order, and we keep running out.

You: Alright, let's go with:

1. Improve quality
2. Improve throughput
3. Reduce labor variance
4. Reduce materials variance

Chris: How long is this going to take?

You: I'd say about 6 months, and that is with a lot of hard work on the right things. Okay, the Project Charter form is complete (Fig. 15-2).

You: Okay guys, next we are going to prepare a SIPOC diagram.

Chris: You just went over my head.

Project Charter	
Project:	50' Flagship line improvement project
Project Leader:	Bill Trudell
Problems to be solved:	Insufficient throughput. Poor quality. Labor variance. Materials usage Variance
Process/es impacted:	Final Assembly. Fabrication
Team Member/s:	Bill, Joe, Dick, Chris, Ron
Project goals / deliverables:	Increased throughput, improved Quality, elimination of Labor variance, elimination of Materials usage variance
Project Start:	17-Sep
Project End:	31-Mar
Milestones:	
Define	24-Sep
Measure	22-Oct
Analyze	19-Nov
Improve	28-Feb
Control	31-Mar

FIGURE 15-2.

Joe: Hang on Chris, a SIPOC diagram is just a name for grid that helps a project team more clearly identify the processes that will be focused on in the project. It is a high-level process map used to make sure everyone on the team clearly understands the process that will be improved. SIPOC stands for Suppliers, Inputs, Process, Output, and Customers. It makes sure we are all looking at the process the same way. It takes the process/es that will be focused on and identifies the Suppliers to the process, the Inputs to the process, the Process itself, the Outputs, and finally the Customers of the process. Once you break it down, it's fairly simple.

Chris: Alright, make it simple for me.

Joe: Do you mind if I take it?

You: Hey guys, this is a project team. Run with it Joe.

SIPOC Diagram

Suppliers	Inputs	Process		Outputs	Customers
Stock room	Component kits	Install plumbing	Audit / verify compliance to specs	Motor home	Dealership sales staff
Purchasing	Engines	Install electrical wiring	Test all functional items		Dealership service staff
Laminated parts	Bulk materials	Install hardware / sub-assemblies	Leak test		Retail customer
Sub-Assembly	Sub-Assemblies	Mate cabin to chasis	Systems test		
Cabinet Assembly	Cabinets	Install cabinets	Clean		
Upholstery	Cushions	Install cushions	Shrink wrap		
Quality	Pads	Install pads	Load on trailer		
Manufacturing Eng	Check sheets	Install sub-assemblies	Transport to dealer		
	Specifications	Install electrical components	Dealer preparation		
		Install engines	Deliver to customer		

FIGURE 15-3.

Joe: Alright. Chris, help me out. Write the following on the board and give yourself some room under each one: SUPPLIERS, INPUTS, PROCESS, OUTPUTS, CUSTOMERS.

Let's go around the room and fill in. Who are the suppliers to the flagship line?

You: Wow! Great job on the SIPOC diagram (Fig. 15-3). Hey Chris, still think this is over your head?

Chris: Actually, this is kind of interesting to me. Keep going, this is fun.

Dick: I have to admit I was a little skeptical too. Good stuff.

You: Guys, this phase is all about focus. One of the things I appreciate about Lean Six Sigma is that it is a focused approach, and like anything else, once you get used to using it you get better and better at it.

You: Alright, the next item up is a high-level process map of the process we will be focusing our improvement efforts on. Once again, this is just to help us all keep clear in our minds the process we are focusing on. This is again a higher level overview or graphic representation of the process (Fig. 15-4). We will get to a more detailed version in the MEASURE phase. Okay, let's do it.

You: Great job guys. The last thing we need to do today is to review the requirements and actions in the MEASUREMENT phase, which we will begin in our next meeting.

The purpose of the MEASURE phase is to measure the current state performance of the process to be improved. We will gather data that will be of use during our improvement project, measure the current way of doing things, and set up data-collection methods. It will help us determine defects and problems occurring, and provide a basis to create metrics for us to track progress.

Process map for Flagship Assembly Line - Current state

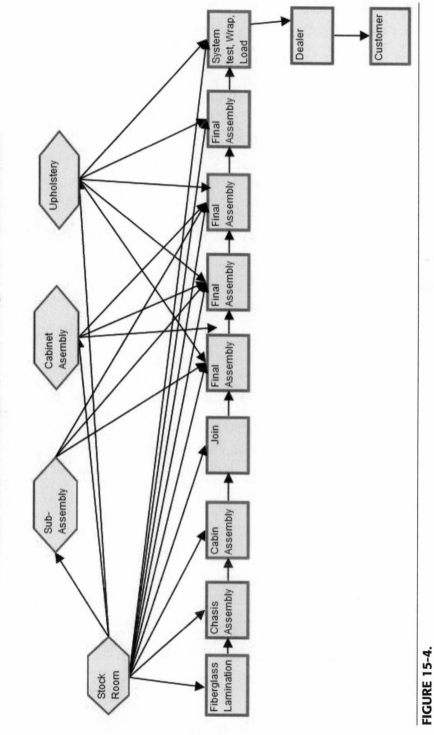

FIGURE 15-4.

MEASURE PHASE

You: Good morning. Okay guys, as you see, our agenda is fairly simple today (Fig. 15-5). The objective of today's team meeting is to determine what data we will gather to use as a guide in our improvement efforts. Let's review what our objectives are: **increased throughput, improved quality, elimination of labor variance, and elimination of materials usage variance.** Let's talk about what data or information will be valuable to us with this in mind. Any suggestions?

Based on the team's responses, here is the list of information that will help meet the objectives for this project:

- Records of completions
- Performance to schedule
- Sales dollars produced over time
- Cycle times (how long it takes for a product to go through the process)
- WIP values
- Labor efficiencies
- Overtime
- List of excess issues of materials
- Staffing
- Interviews of line workers
- Standard hours allotted for RV
- Industrial engineering analysis of the work being accomplished with a *Lean slant* (categorize in value added, nonvalue added, *go-gets*)
    - Observe and record all preparation work done to any component before installing in an RV.
    - Observe and record all work other than basic installation in assembly.
    - Observe and record all nonproductive time.
    - Observe and record all nonvalue-added activity.
- Engineering specifications
- Value stream map

Meeting Agenda
9 - 10:30 AM - Determine what data will be gathered in Measure phase
10:30 - 11 AM - Assign responsibilities

FIGURE 15-5.

You: Okay, let's assign responsibilities and methods for gathering each type of data. We will also schedule a value stream mapping exercise for next week. We will plan on a whole day. I know this may seem like a long time, but the information we will get will be invaluable. Lunch will be provided!

Value Stream Mapping Exercise

You: Let's talk about value stream mapping guys. In short it is a tool that maps and displays the flow of material, product, and information through a process. A value stream map can be constructed with magic markers, butcher paper, and sticky notes. A common approach is to gather the process owners and participants in a room and line all four walls with squares of easel paper. Participants write all steps in the process on sticky notes and put them up on the easel papers in the order of the process. The finished product will resemble a road map. Any relevant information or decision loops should be annotated over the actual steps. The team can then analyze the map and look for opportunities to improve the processes, or in this case, opportunities to reduce cycle times. During the analysis, projects can be identified to support suggested improvements or to capitalize on opportunities to reduce cycle time.

Alright, let's get started (Fig. 15-6).

You: Alright, we have not mapped out our process and identified relevant information and decision points. As you can see we identified some real opportunities in our process and particularly those related to situations that lengthen our cycle times. Let's take a look at what we found out during our value stream mapping exercise.

- Work content in final assembly is very high.
- Countless numbers of holes are being drilled into vehicles in the assembly line.
- Building utility room in first chassis station—water heater, water tank, waste tank.
- Installing vinyl on ceiling in the last assembly stations.
- Installing ceiling in last assembly stations.
- Putting bridge on deck after mating.
- Only hardware done in deck assembly—no padding, cabinets, and so forth.

Meeting Agenda
7 – 5 PM - Value stream mapping exercise

FIGURE 15-6.

- Hauling all electronics/appliances into coach to install.
- Hauling toilets, sinks, and so forth into coach to install.
- Not testing plumbing in sub-assembly (should appear in quality data).
- No testing of electronics such as stereo/radar until final test.
- A lot of preparation work going on outside of RV.
- A lot of preparation work going on inside of RV.
- Numerous "manufacturability" issues exist in which operators have to develop "work-arounds" to make components fit or go together.
- Rework levels at the end of the line are very high, actually taking days to accomplish.

ANALYZE PHASE

You: Good morning everyone. We are at the analyze phase of the DMAIC process. This is where it starts to get fun. The thing I like about the analyze phase is that some of the drivers of your key problems really start coming to light. A lot of times these drivers or situations are right in front of everyone. The problem is that everyone is so caught up in the inefficiencies and day-to-day activities of the process that they just don't see them. They really "can't see the forest for the trees in front of them." The analyze phase is where the formality and methodology of DMAIC starts to take hold. The tools of the analyze phase start to shake out the drivers. Alright, let's review what information we have at this point. Then we can begin our analysis. We have the following:

- Records of completions
- Performance to schedule
- Sales dollars produced over time
- Cycle times
- WIP values
- Labor efficiencies
- Overtime
- List of excess issues of materials
- List of quality defects for past production
- Staffing
- Interviews of line workers
- Standard hours allotted for RV
- Engineering specifications
- List of quality process checks
- Benchmarking information from sister plant

One thing I like to do in the analyze phase is *check in* on the goals, or expectations of Lean. We will also again review the problems we are trying to solve as stated in our Project Charter. Keeping one eye on Lean principles during the DMAIC process is an effective approach. This is important because Lean works. So if you improve your business's progress in achieving the goals of Lean, you will no doubt improve your business's results. Remember, the goal of Lean manufacturing is to produce the highest quality products in the shortest possible cycle times, at the lowest possible costs, while maintaining the flexibility for change. Recall from our Project Charter the problems we are trying to solve are insufficient throughput, poor quality, labor variance, materials use variance. Our project's success will be a result of our progress toward the goals of Lean, and solving the problems from our charter. At the end of this project we should have:

1. Goal: Improved quality   (Problem: Poor quality)
2. Goal: Shortened cycle times   (Problem: Insufficient throughput)
3. Goal: Lowered costs   (Problem: Labor and materials variance)
4. Goal: Improved our flexibility   (Avoid solutions that reduce flexibility)

With this in mind, let's begin to ANALYZE.

Analyze: Quality

You: Okay, folks. Our efforts have provided quality-related data and information. Let's review it.

- The quality process consists of auditors reviewing product at the end of the process and writing lists of conditions that in their opinion deviate from process and product standards. They then provide it to the operators who in turn "work off" the defects and then contact the auditors to verify that they are in fact addressed. Any defects not addressed to the auditors' satisfaction are compiled into a second or third list, and the same process is followed until all defects are eliminated. A defect is any deviation to the standards or any condition the auditor believes is a defect. There are significant inconsistencies from auditor to auditor in what is considered a defect.
- Other than providing a list of defects to be worked off, audit scores or defect experience are not communicated to operators or operators.
- A high level of defects and rework are being experienced on every unit produced.
- The highest occurring defects in house are damage, leaks, and fit and finish. The majority of damage comes from moving big parts, cabinets, furniture, and other items into the RV. The next largest driver of damage is incurred when operators scratch, dent, and cut components while working in a crowded RV.

- There are a high number of defects being passed into assembly from upstream departments, particularly from the fiberglass lamination department. The panels and small fiberglass parts contain a great deal of mold marks, air, and other defects that require a tremendous amount of rework or auto-body type repair to these parts. This rework is being accomplished while the RVs are in the assembly line. The fiberglass repair technicians are often in the way of the assembly line workers; this has the impact slowing them down and drives inefficiencies. It often takes 1 to 2 days to complete the fiberglass rework after all assembly line tasks have been accomplished.
- There are deviations from critical structural dimensions that are driving hours of rework and work-arounds to fit cabinetry and key components.
- Warranty claims tend to reflect the same types of defects in the field as identified in the plant with the exception of a high number of complaints that functional components such as air conditioners, gauges, auto-pilots, pumps, blowers, hot water heaters, etc., are not working correctly. The president of the company has said he would "give anything, if one time we could get an RV to a dealer with everything on it working correctly."
- The company does compile and measure Customer Service Indexes, and the plant's performance is going down.
- The plant is dirty and unorganized.

An analysis of available quality data yields the following results, as shown in Figures 15-7 to 15-11.

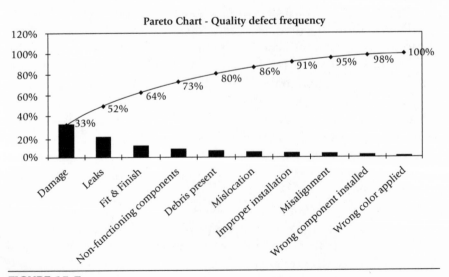

FIGURE 15-7.

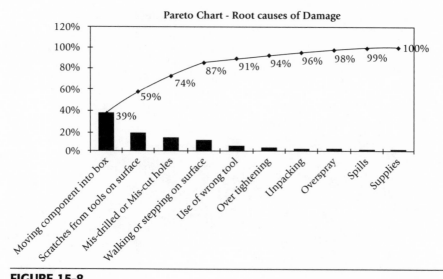

FIGURE 15-8.

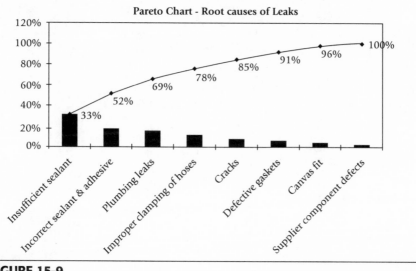

FIGURE 15-9.

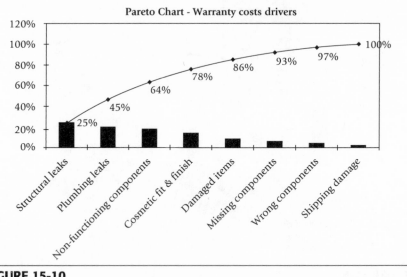

FIGURE 15-10.

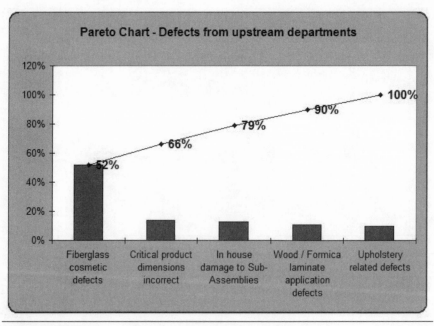

FIGURE 15-11.

You: Quite a bit of information? Quite a bit, but very interesting and telling. Let's get to analyzing throughput. Things should get interesting now.

Analyze: Throughput

You: Let's begin to take a look at the data, determine what they mean, and begin to develop action plans for the Improvement stage. We are going to identify the root causes of the issues on the line and confirm them with data. The outputs of our analysis will form the basis for solutions we will implement in the Improve stage. Let's review.

Here are some of the data, information, and charts we have obtained along with some further tasks of analysis.

- Sales has orders to support six units per month; the plant is struggling to produce one unit per month.
- There are a lot of change orders to product in process because of order cancellations and missed deliveries.
- Workers are having to be sent out to the field to rework defective product, which puts production even farther behind, drives variances higher, and slows throughput.
- There appears to be a lot of work being accomplished in Final Assembly that could be done in offline departments.
- Benchmark visits show significantly higher levels of work in process (WIP) relative to other similar operations.
- WIP turns are very low.

Further Tasks of Analysis

- Identify and list all preparation work into a database or spreadsheet. Evaluate how much can be moved into offline departments.
- Identify and list any assembly work being done on the RV that can be moved to another department.
- Identify any open areas during assembly that have no one working on product.
- Identify and list all *dependent* tasks that cannot be performed until a preceding task is accomplished.

Analyze: Labor Variance

- It is obvious that crowded work environments inside of the RVs during assembly are slowing operators down, driving labor inefficiency, and driving high levels of damage (Figs. 15-12 to 15-14).

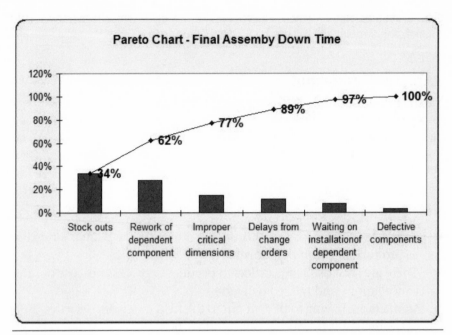

FIGURE 15-12.

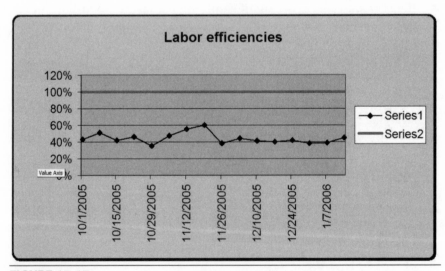

FIGURE 15-13.

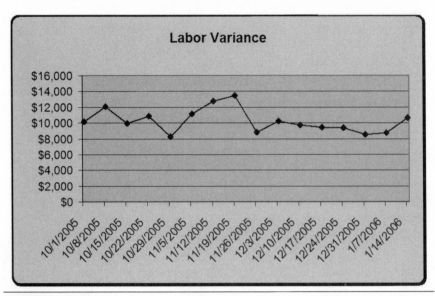

FIGURE 15-14.

- High levels of damage and scrap rates are driving stock-outs of key items and causing further delays and inefficiencies. Many components cannot be installed until after another adjoining component is installed.
- Improper critical structural dimensions are significantly lengthening installation times or delaying installation until they are corrected. Cabinetry and sub-assemblies do not line up, and additional hand-fitting is required to address misalignments, and so forth.
- Quality defects from other departments are slowing production because operators must wait on needed repairs before moving on to install components or sub-assemblies.
- Delays while waiting for definition of change orders, and instances where some components must be uninstalled altogether and replaced with a different option.
- Hours of rework are driving inefficiencies.
- Operators are spending hours assembling components inside of RVs before installation.
- The plant is dirty and unorganized. Operators often spend a great deal of time looking for parts that are stored from location to location.

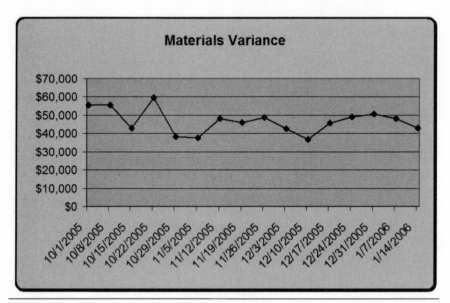

FIGURE 15-15.

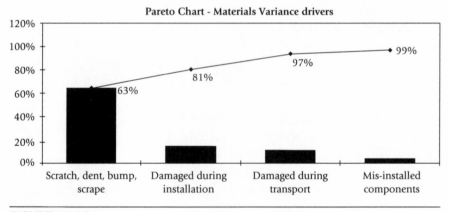

FIGURE 15-16.

Analyze: Materials Variance (Figs. 15-15 and 15-16)

- Crowded work environments inside of the RVs during assembly are driving high levels of damage. Operators are bumping into items easily susceptible to damage. Tools, components, airlines, power cords, stools, and so forth, are coming in contact with items and causing damage.
- Transporting numerous items into RVs for installation is causing damage.

- There are high levels of WIP because of a lack of schedule attainment. Materials are delivered in quantities that match the scheduled rate of production. When the schedule is not achieved it piles up and often gets damaged.

IMPROVE PHASE

You: The next phase is the Improve phase of the DMAIC process. Our goal is to try out and implement solutions that address root causes. Tested actions should eliminate or reduce the impact of identified root causes. The objective is to demonstrate with data that your solutions resolve the issues and improve performance. This phase can be very rewarding and enjoyable as everyone works together to apply their creativity to developing solutions.

Here are the initial improvements that the team determined for the key problems identified in the Project Charter:

Improve: Quality

- Set up a Quality improvement team to accomplish the following:
    - Develop a list of Critical to Quality checks derived from product specifications, process standards, product standards, warranty claims, and customer feedback. Develop sublists for each phase or gate of the process. Instruct the Quality Auditors to eliminate the freestyle-type audit and audit the product according to the Critical to Quality checklists.
    - Implement a formal quality system based on adhering to consistent product and process standards, reducing and eliminating variability in all processes, and continuous improvement.
    - Formally train and certify operators in the proper application of sealant and adhesive.
    - Formally train and certify operators in the proper assembly or installation of plumbing and hose components.
- Set up a Lamination Quality improvement team to accomplish the following:
    - Determine critical structural dimensions for hulls and decks.
    - Develop fixtures to fail-safe and ensure compliance.
    - Require Quality Auditors and Supervisors to audit and verify actual and proper use of fixtures.
    - Review top cosmetic defects to determine process improvements to significantly reduce or eliminate (Figs. 15-17 and 15-18).

Final Assembly Critical to Quality First Time Yield

	Critical to Quality Check	Standard	Operator	Supervisor	Quality	Y/N
1	Frame tab installation	Per specifications. Straight, symetrical from side to side. All connections properly executed.				Y N
2	Exterior hardware installation	Per specifications. Proper thread reveal. Proper sealant. Proper torque.				Y N
3	Chasis installation					Y N
4	Plumbing					Y N
5	Windshield seal					Y N
6	Fuel fill hose hook up					Y N
7	Fuel vent hose hook up					Y N
8	Fuel tank pressure test					Y N
9	Electrical connections					Y N
10	Water tank pressure test					Y N
11	Engine alignment					Y N
12	Water purifier installation	Water flow in alignment with arrows on strainer.				Y N
13	Sound foam installation					Y N
14	Cables installation					Y N

FIGURE 15-17.

Laminated component Critical to Quality First Time Yield

	Critical to Quality Check	Standard	Operator	Supervisor	Quality	Y/N
1	Mold preparation	Molds are clean of debris, waxed, and taped.				Y N
2	Beam location	All reinforcement beams are in place per documentation				Y N
3	Beam heights	Per documentation				Y N
4	Panel structure location	Per documentation				Y N
5	Plumbing openings	All plumbing portals in place and unobstructed				Y N
6	Cut outs	Correct diameter and location per documentation				Y N
7	Harness portals	Correct diameter and location per documentation				Y N
8	Interior fiberglass surface	Smooth and free of burrs and unsightly bumps etc.				Y N
9	Window cutouts	Correct size to documentation. Neat and clean cuts.				Y N
10	Door and entry cutouts	Correct size to documentation. Neat and clean cuts.				Y N
11	Hatch cut outs	Correct size to documentation. Neat and clean cuts.				Y N
12	Floor construction	Thickness within specified range. Average thickness variance < 1/8". Free of hollow spots.				Y N
13	Fixture application	All fixtures per documentation are in use				Y N

FIGURE 15-18.

- Set up a process improvement team to focus on driving down root causes of leaks, and implement corrective actions.
- Set up a process improvement team to focus on driving down root causes of Fit and Finish-related quality defects and implement corrective actions.
- Identify and correct all defects in each phase or station before moving up in the process.
- Aggressively cover and protect all fabricated components throughout the process.
- Begin to measure the percentage of first-time pass for all areas and RVs.
- Set up a dashboard of Key Metrics and assign a team to lead corrective action and process improvement to drive down defects.
- Post the dashboard in a key area of the plant and meet with employees daily to review improvement progress. INVOLVE employees at every opportunity to reduce defects.

Improve: Throughput

- Set up a cycle-time reduction team to accomplish the following:
  - Relocate as much work as possible out of the final assembly operation.
  - Develop sub-assemblies to the point where they are picked up, placed into RV, and quickly installed.
  - Install the bridge on the deck before putting the deck onto the hull.
  - Install the cabin ceilings, cabinetry, windows, and windshields onto the deck before installing the deck onto the hull.
  - Move all required final assembly work as far back in the assembly process as possible.
  - Reduce the schedule rate of production to two units per month, and do not increase until this capacity is demonstrated. Then, increase incrementally until the desired capacity is achieved.
  - Apply the principles of 5S and begin to maintain a clean and organized environment. Identify storage areas for parts by each station and do not deliver until current on-hand WIP is consumed.

Improve: Labor Variances

- Develop standardized task lists based on industrial engineering-type time studies.
- Reduce the amount of work stations to a minimum.
- Place a dry erase board at the end of the line, and develop a list of any and all manufacturability issues and problems that operators are encountering during Final Assembly. Assign Manufacturing Engineering

the responsibility for prioritizing and resolving these issues. Review daily with leadership and operators. Encourage all operators to write additional issues and problems on the board as they come up (Fig. 15-19).

Improve: Materials Variances

- Develop protective covers for all sensitive items to protect them during transport and after installation in Final Assembly.
- Train operators in the importance of protecting components and eliminating damage. Disallow the placement of tools and equipment on any item during the process. Tools must either be in use or in a tool box.
- Develop covers to shield components from airlines and electrical cords.

The team implemented the improvements as outlined.

CONTROL PHASE

You: Now that we have implemented and tested the improvements, we move on to the Control phase. The objective of the Control phase is to evaluate the solutions and the plan, maintain the gains by standardizing the process, and outline steps for ongoing improvements including opportunities for replication. The output of the Control phase as implemented by the team is outlined below:

Control: Quality

- Continually review the output of the formal quality system and implement corrective action when significant defects, variation, or performance issues occur.
- Develop a *Quality Dashboard* (Fig. 15-20) and track defect rates per unit, first-time pass rates for key areas of the plant, and other key metrics.
- Post continual Pareto charts of top-occurring defects, and focus improvement teams on the "biggest bars."

Control: Throughput

- Maintain and use standardized work and labor standards to continually deploy the smallest WIP footprint possible.
- Track WIP turns, continually work to improve, and take corrective action to react to slowing of turns.
- Continually scan and search for opportunities to create sub-assemblies and move work out of the Final Assembly line.
- Track and report schedule attainment percentages, and implement corrective action when attainment falls below expectations.

Open	Completed	New	Ending
147	12	6	141
141	5	2	138
138	13	8	133
133	5	4	132
132	11	6	127
127	9	2	120
120	2	3	121
121	3	0	118
118	11	7	114
114	12	8	110
110	24	9	95
95	12	8	91
91	13	6	84
84	20	8	72
72	15	4	61
61	11	8	58
58	9	4	53
53	10	6	50
50	7	2	42
42	5	3	38
38	12	0	33
33	14	7	28
28	10	8	22
22	8	9	21
21	8	8	21

	Manufacturability Issue	Assigned	Date	ETC
1	enough	RL	3-Feb	10-Feb
2	than wall it fits against	RL	2-Mar	9-Mar
3	Fittings that come in kit for head sink do not fit	JS	5-Mar	12-Mar
4	effectively hook up wiring	JS	6-Mar	13-Mar
5	than the cooler box	JS	12-Mar	19-Mar
6	shold be female plugs	BD	14-Mar	21-Mar
7	the fasteners used to install the main gauge panel on	BD	17-Mar	24-Mar
8	the installation of an additional close out panel	JS	5-Apr	12-Apr
9	makes nearly impossible to install the refrigerator	DS	8-Apr	15-Apr
10	only 1/2" thick and the weight of the ceiling requires	DS	4-Apr	11-Apr
11	impossible to install into their recesses without	DS	15-Apr	22-Apr
12	door alignment	DS	19-Apr	26-Apr
13	going over the side of chasis	JS	20-Apr	27-Apr

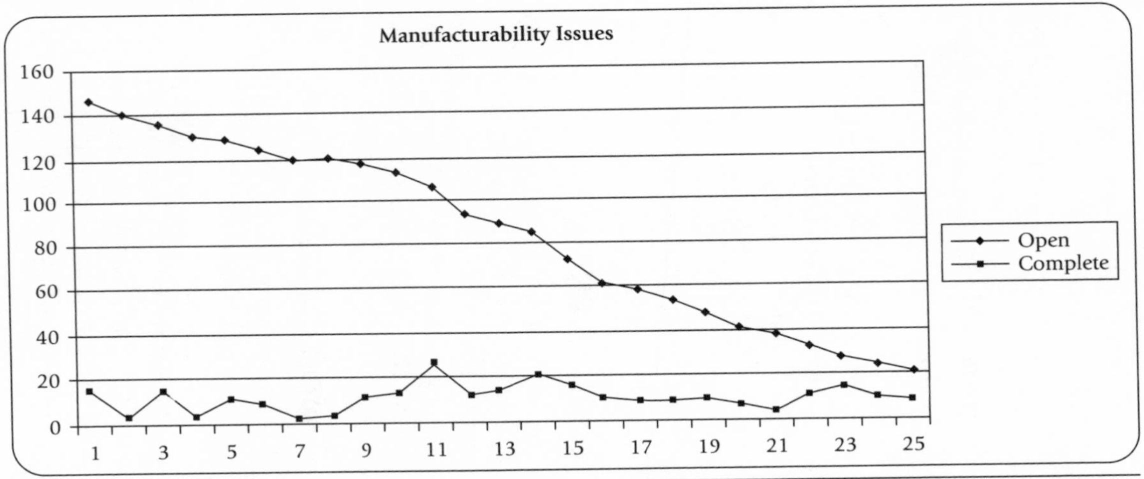

Manufacturability Issues

— Open
— Complete

FIGURE 15-19.

Dashboard - Quality - Flagship Line

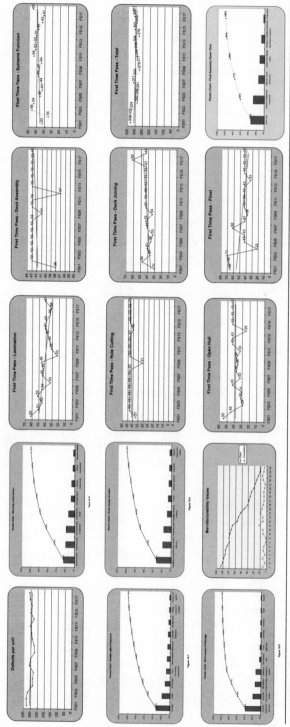

FIGURE 15-20.

Control: Labor Variance

■ Continually track labor efficiency and labor variance metrics. Set performance goals and quickly root cause and react to unfavorable trends.

■ Maintain Pareto charts and focus improvement activities on biggest drivers of variance.

■ Focus Manufacturing Engineering, employee improvement teams, and Kaizen events toward improving processes and labor content at every opportunity.

■ Continually work to eliminate any and all nonvalue-added activity.

Control: Materials Variance

■ Continually track materials variance metrics. Set performance goals, and quickly root cause and react to unfavorable trends.

■ Maintain Pareto charts and focus improvement activities on biggest drivers of variance.

■ Aggressively monitor the protection measures applied during the improve stage.

■ Maintain and enforce materials queue areas established during 5S implementation.

Okay, we've taken some real-life situations, simplified them, and embellished them to effectively demonstrate an application of applying Lean Six Sigma methodologies at a higher level. Let's assume you, as the plant manager, took all of the actions indicated in the Improve and Control stages of the DMAIC process. Most likely all of your metrics started turning in the right direction and your team began to realize successes in turning this *flagship line* around.

Is this approach the *Six Sigma* continuously talked about throughout manufacturing? Not exactly. But it is the DMAIC process, and it did help this plant improve quality, shorten cycles, and reduce costs, which are three of the primary goals of Lean. Brainstorming, affinity diagrams, process maps, SIPOC diagrams, Pareto analysis, and process improvement are effective approaches. They are all legitimate tools under the Lean Six Sigma umbrella.

The natural progression of events for this plant is to continue to focus on implementing Lean to drive waste out of its operations and then apply Six Sigma methodologies to drive variance out of the process and improve quality. As the plant grows, it will no doubt begin to apply some of the more complex analysis, tools, and methodologies contained in Lean Six Sigma. But in the beginning the more simple tools can provide exciting results.

Chapter 16

Project: Reducing Jet Ski Warranty Costs

Okay, here's the scenario. The management team of a plant that manufactures fiberglass jet skis has completed a thorough and grueling financial review. The financial review has brought to light that warranty costs for the company are way out of line with the industry average of about 1.5%. Warranty costs have continued to climb and are averaging 5.1% of annual sales of approximately $96 million. This is not good, and it is a threat to the long-term viability of the brand, not to mention the dollars it is taking away from the bottom line. This is an excellent opportunity to apply Lean Six Sigma methodologies. This is a problem that is broad-based in the company, and there is a considerable amount of data at hand.

The general manager of the company has directed a group of key staff members to participate on a Lean Six Sigma team with the goal of reducing warranty costs to a level not to exceed 1% of annual sales. This is an aggressive goal considering where the company is at today. However, it is imperative to the company's success that significant progress is made in the next 12 months. He is serious and expects results. Every dollar saved in warranty falls right to the bottom line. No ifs, ands, or buts.

THE TEAM

- Plant Manager: Matt
- Director of Quality: Tom
- Director of Sales: Dean
- Warranty Manager: Dave
- Cost Accounting Manager: Steve
- Director of Engineering: Brandon
- Director of Materials: Glen
- Anyone else needed

The good news is that Tom, the Director of Quality, has recently attended Six Sigma training and earned Green Belt status. He is a whiz with spreadsheets and charting, and has a solid background in traditional quality management skills such as statistical process control, process capability, gauge repeatability and reproducibility, control plans, etc. Tom is a student of Lean manufacturing and has experience in organizations that have implemented the principles. He is a great people person and good leader, and is honored and excited about being selected to lead this team. The other members of the team are seasoned professionals, and all have familiarity with charting, metrics, and other concepts.

Let's get started.

General Manager: Okay, good morning everyone. As we are all aware, our warranty costs are out of control. They have reached an unacceptable level that is both disappointing to our customers and dramatically affecting our bottom line. We have to resolve this most pressing issue as fast as possible. Some of you know that I have been attending the local manufacturing association for the past year. Not a monthly meeting goes by that I don't hear someone telling exciting stories of their successes with Lean Six Sigma. I mean they are flat-out excited. As you know, our sister divisions have some success applying Lean Six Sigma. I think it's time we get in the game. This stuff is real.

I have asked Tom to lead a Lean Six Sigma project team, of which you are all members, to reduce our warranty costs. As you know, he recently completed Six Sigma Green Belt training. Tom, we are counting on your leadership, and I know you can count on the full support of this team. Let us know what you need. I stand ready to support you at every opportunity.

Tom: Thanks Bob. I am excited about leading this project. It is going to be a lot of hard work. However, we have so much to gain. I know that participating on a team project of this magnitude can take a great deal of time and effort. My commitment to you is that we will meet only as necessary, follow an agenda, and move the project along as quickly and efficiently as possible. I will publish an agenda before each meeting and minutes/assignments immediately after each meeting. What I will need from you is your full support in completing your team responsibilities. Please be on time for team meetings and be prepared.

We will be following the Six Sigma DMAIC (define, measure, analyze, improve, control) process as I've outlined below.

Define: We will define the project, determine the scope and boundaries, and collect background information on the areas and processes to be improved. A clear statement of the project will be written, a basic timeline will be created, and a business case will be developed. The result will be a Project Charter.

Measure: We will determine what information and data will be required to support the project and develop a data-collection plan. Baseline data on the current state will be determined, and metrics to measure progress will be developed.

Analyze: Data will be reviewed and analyzed through different types of analysis to determine root causes of the problem or problems. The team will study the data to gain an understanding or sense of what it means. Data accuracy will be confirmed. A search for opportunities to incorporate and apply the principles of Lean—high quality, short cycles, low cost, flow, customer value—will be conducted.

Improve: The team will develop, implement, and evaluate solutions to address or eliminate the root causes determined in the Analyze phase. Effectiveness of solutions will be verified with data.

Control: The team will develop control plans to ensure that solutions developed in the Improve phase are sustained and do not fade away. Solutions will include such actions as implementing SPC, training, procedural updates, policy updates, work instruction updates, etc.

The first meeting will be next Tuesday at 1 P.M., at which we will develop the Project Charter. See you then!

DEFINE PHASE

Tom: Good afternoon. Thanks to everyone for being on time. Here is the agenda we will follow today. We will work to finish on time or early if possible (Figs. 16-1 to 16-4).

Meeting Agenda - Define
1:00 – 2:45 PM - Complete Project Charter
2:45 – 3:30 PM – Develop a SIPOC diagram
3:30 – 4:00 PM – Develop a high level process map
4:00 – 4:15 PM – Review requirements / actions in the MEASURE phase

FIGURE 16-1.

Project Charter	
Project :	* Reduce warranty costs to 1% of sales revenues.
Project Leader :	Tom Robinson
Problems to be solved :	High warranty costs, lowered CSI scores, and lost sales
Process/es impacted :	All
Team Member/s :	Matt Edwards, Tom Robinson, Dean Everett, Dave Arlington, Steve Nervos, Brandon Rust, Glen Gaston
Project goals / deliverables :	Reduce annual warranty costs to 1%
Project Start :	5-Jun
Project End :	5-Nov
Milestones :	(completed by)
Define	12-Jun
Measure	10-Jul
Analyze	7-Aug
Improve	6-Oct
Control	5-Nov

FIGURE 16-2.

SIPOC DIAGRAM				
Suppliers	Inputs	Process	Outputs	Customers
Manufacturing	Molds / Tooling	Gel Coat application	Jet Ski's	Dealers
Suppliers	Raw materials	Fiberglass lamination		Jet Skiers
Purchasing	Component materials	Sub - Assemblies		
Engineering	Labor	Upholstery		
Dealer Service		Final Assembly		
		Customer Service		

FIGURE 16-3.

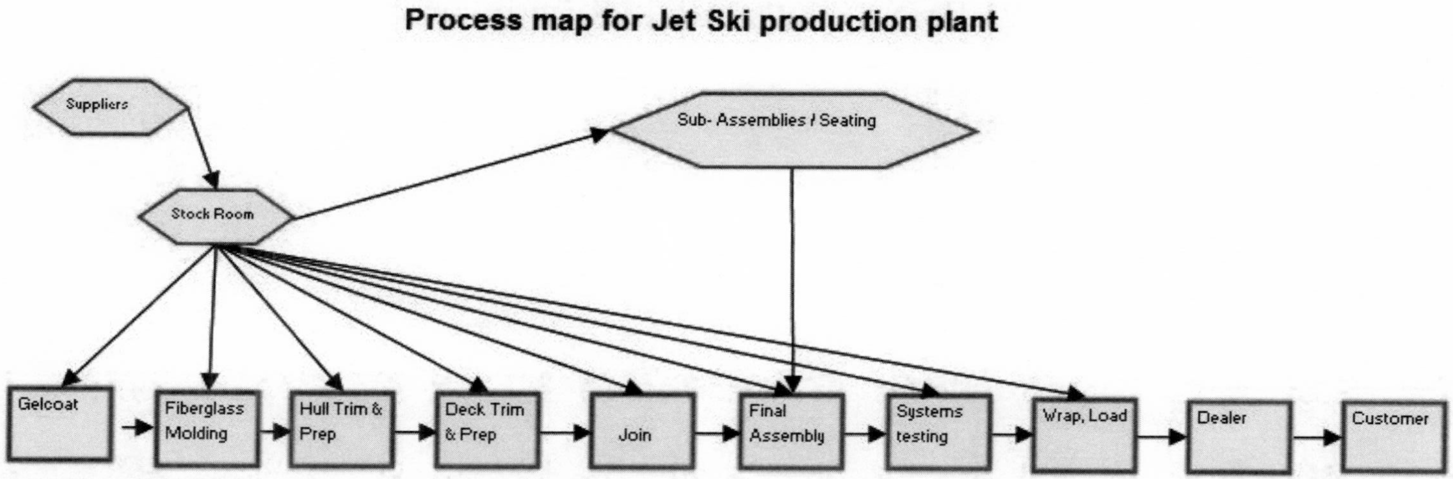
Process map for Jet Ski production plant
Suppliers
Stock Room
Sub- Assemblies / Seating
Gelcoat
Fiberglass Molding
Hull Trim & Prep
Deck Trim & Prep
Join
Final Assembly
Systems testing
Wrap, Load
Dealer
Customer

FIGURE 16-4.

Meeting Agenda - Training
8:00 - 9:00 AM - Basic charting
9:00 -10:00 AM - Pareto analysis
10:00 -11:00 AM - Flow charting

FIGURE 16-5.

Meeting Agenda - Measure
9:00 - 10:30 AM - Determine what data will be gathered in Measure phase
10:30 - 11 AM - Assign responsibilities

FIGURE 16-6.

Tom: Great job. We have a project charter, SIPOC (suppliers, inputs, process, output, and customers), and process map. I am sure they will be valuable tools as we progress through the project. Because we will be evaluating data and using charts and graphs to support analysis, I thought it would be valuable for the team to receive some training. I have arranged for a representative from our community college to provide 3 hours of on-site training next week. Please be on time and bring your laptop! Here is next week's agenda (Fig. 16-5):

MEASURE PHASE

Tom: Good morning. Thanks for the great participation in the training last week. I hoped you learned or reinforced your skills with spreadsheets and charts. As promised, we will be following the agenda I forwarded to you last week. We only have 2 hours, so let's get to it (Fig. 16-6).

Tom: You may have noticed a new team member today. Don from Information Technology has been drafted to be on the team! Because gathering and analyzing warranty data will be a big part of the team's activities, I decided to enlist his participation. Welcome Don.

Let's talk about what data we will want to gather and analyze initially. Any ideas?

Dave: I think the number warranty claims by failure type will be needed.

Tom: Excellent.

Steve: How about the frequency of claims by type?

Tom: Yes, absolutely.

Brandon: I think we need warranty claims paid by model.

Glen: How about warranty failures by part number?

Steve: How about claims by dealer by frequency and dollars paid?

Matt: I think we will need total number of warranty claims by year for the past 5 years.

Brandon: That's good. I would like to see claims by model for each of the last 5 years in frequency and dollars paid.

Tom: Don, can you please research the availability of this type of data and report back to us, say, this Friday at 1 P.M.? You can also do some research on any other existing data reports, and so forth, that might be of value.

Don: Sure.

Tom: Also, Dave, can you please look around the warranty department and see what other information or data might be available for our use?

Dave: Will do.

Tom: Okay, we will see everyone again this Friday at 1 P.M. for a 1-hour meeting to check in on the availability of data to support the project. See you then!

Tom: Good afternoon folks. Okay, as we planned, today we review the availability of data as requested by members of the team at last week's meeting. Don was tasked with researching the availability of requested data and other available data. Dave, you were tasked with checking for any other reports or data in the warranty department. Here is the agenda that everyone received (Fig. 16-7).

Tom: Okay guys. How did we do?

Don: We did great. Actually, everything you asked for is available. In fact there were reports for almost all of it already set up in the system. Also, there are some subcategories of defect categories that might be helpful. For example, on cosmetic fiberglass defects there are subcategories of air, porosity, damage, scratches, etc.

Tom: Awesome.

Dave: To be honest, I did not locate any other reports or data. Just some of what we have already discussed.

Tom: Alright. Here's what we need. Don, can you please get as much of the data into spreadsheet form as you can for the next meeting? We can then work to set up some analysis and see if we can get the data to tell us where our opportunities are. Next week's meeting is scheduled to last 4 hours, folks. Please plan accordingly.

Meeting Agenda - Measure
1:00 - 2:00 PM - Pre-liminary review of available data
Task assignments :
Don :
Warranty claims $ by failure type
Frequency of claims by failure type
Warranty claims $ by model
Frequency of claims by model
Warranty claims $ paid by part number
Frequency of claims by part number
Warranty claims $ paid by dealer
Frequency of claims paid by dealer
Frequency of Warranty claims by year for last 5 years
Warranty cost as a percent of sales for the last 5 years
Warranty claims $ paid by year for the last 5 years
Dave :
Check for availability of other reports or data on hand in Customer Service

FIGURE 16-7.

ANALYZE PHASE

Tom: Greetings folks. Today is the day we begin to analyze our data! Anyone care to guess what our number one warranty driver is? Be careful. The data know the true picture. Here's the plan. It's pretty simple (Fig. 16-8).

Tom: Well Don, how did we do?

Don: Great. I was actually able to put most of the data right into Pareto charts. Turned out the data were easily processed in plain spreadsheets. We've got some great charts to work with already. Here is what I have. I made copies for everyone (Figs 16-9 to 16-18).

Meeting Agenda - Analyze
1–5 PM - begin analysis of available data
Task assignments :
Don :
Put data into spreadsheets

FIGURE 16-8.

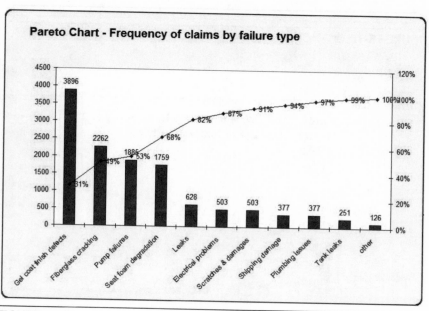

FIGURE 16-9.

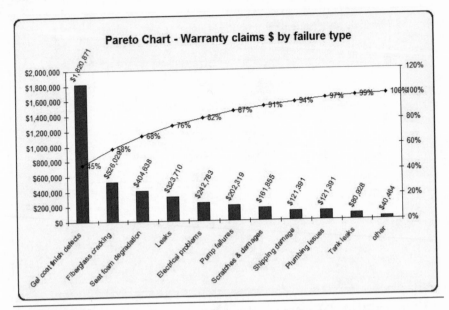

FIGURE 16-10.

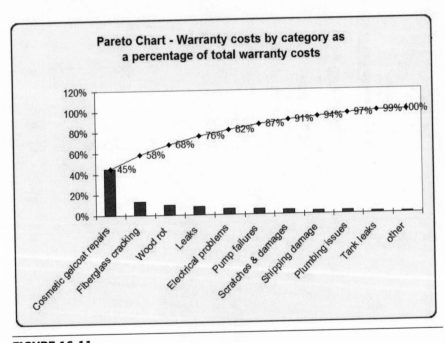

FIGURE 16-11.

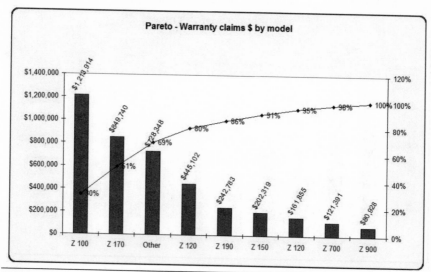

FIGURE 16-12.

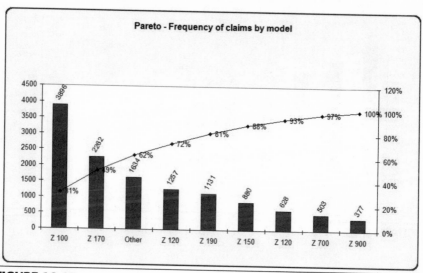

FIGURE 16-13.

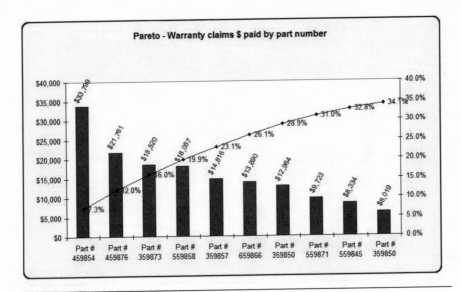

FIGURE 16-14.

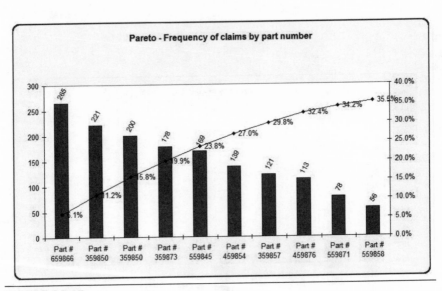

FIGURE 16-15.

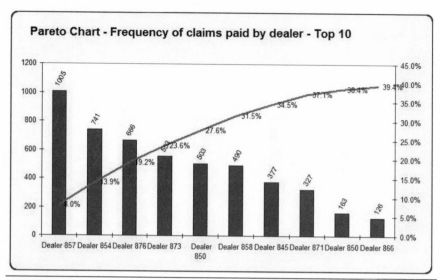

FIGURE 16-16.

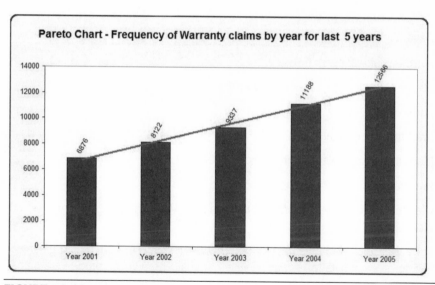

FIGURE 16-17.

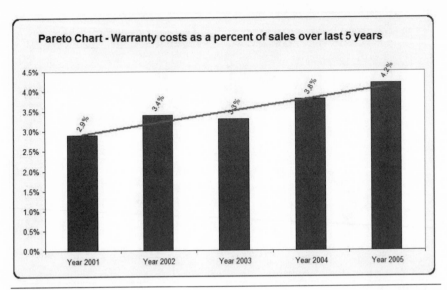

Pareto Chart - Warranty costs as a percent of sales over last 5 years

	Year 2001	Year 2002	Year 2003	Year 2004	Year 2005
	2.9%	3.4%	3.3%	3.8%	4.2%

FIGURE 16-18.

Tom: Wow, these data are awesome, Don. Thanks very much. You have saved us a lot of work! Well team, let's take a look. What are the data telling us?

Dave: Well, one thing they're telling us is that we are in big trouble with quality.

Tom: I would agree.

Steve: We better get our act together quick.

Tom: What else do we see?

Brandon: I never realized we had so many problems with fiberglass warranty claims.

Matt: It's a big problem in production too.

Brandon: Electrical problems are costing a lot of money too.

Glen: Did you see the warranty we paid on the Z100? I'll bet we've never made the first dollar of profit on that jet ski.

Tom: Well folks, we better get to work. The good news is that we have a great team and some great data to help us achieve our goal. The purpose of the Pareto analysis is to show on a relative basis what our biggest drivers of cost or defects are. The strategy is to apply your improvement efforts toward your biggest opportunities. This will give you the highest payoff for your effort. Alright, let's study the data together and work to develop an action plan of, let's say, three to five focus areas.

Steve: I think it's pretty obvious that we need to work on fiberglass gel-coat quality and cracking. Those two categories represented 58% of our warranty payout last year. Fixing that would definitely make a dent in it. A $2 million dent.

Action items - Focus Areas
Cosmetic gelcoat repairs
Seat foam degradation
Fiberglass cracking
Leaks
Electrical problems
Researsh pump suppliers to find more reliable pumps
Develop protection for products during the process

FIGURE 16-19.

Meeting Agenda - Analyze continued
1:00 – 3:30 PM - Continue to analyze and discuss warranty data

Figure 20

FIGURE 16-20.

Matt: Easier said than done, but you're right.

Tom: Okay, what else are we looking at?

Matt: Let's just take the top five items as focus areas. Maybe we could set up some Lean Six Sigma teams to improve in those areas.

Brandon: I'd like to suggest that we research pump suppliers and get some more reliable pumps. Obviously, the ones we are using are failing at a high rate. If we find suitable replacements, we could get them into production fairly quickly.

Tom: I think that's an excellent idea. It's on the list.

Tom: Gentlemen, we have to address the electrical issues. That situation worries me from a safety perspective. I mean we haven't had a serious situation, but with all those claims it's just a matter of time. We need to dial in on that.

Tom: Okay folks, there is our initial priority list. I think it's a good start (Fig. 16-19).

Tom: Here is what I am going to ask the team to do. Between now and next week's meeting, I would like you to spend some time reviewing warranty claim records, photos, and details. We need to really understand this information. Then be thinking of what approaches we should take in addressing our warranty costs. See you next week (Fig. 16-20).

Tom: Okay guys, nice to have everyone. By the way, thanks for your hard work and support on the project so far. You all have a copy of our agenda for today, which is rather simple. I trust everyone had a chance to review the warranty data in more detail. Any comments?

Dave: Well, Brandon and I spent an afternoon reviewing claim data, pictures, and information. It was quite revealing. We are amazed at the amount and severity of cosmetic gel-coat defects that surface at the dealership and after customers buy jet skis. It is obvious that jet skis are leaving with some defects, but a lot of defects are appearing later in the product cycle. We have a problem. It is real. We also took a look at current production. We are spending a great deal of money on internal rework. We're doing too much, and very often the defects we are seeing in the field are places where we reworked them in-house, and the repair has resurfaced or become visible.

Matt: Steve and I actually called some dealers and customers regarding the electrical problems. They were very appreciative that we called, but expressed aggravation at the problems they had. They buy their jet skis for fun and expect things to work. There are a lot of instances where components stop working, or actually get fried from shorts and improper wiring, but mainly components that did not work properly or failed. We have some ideas.

Brandon: I looked at the seat foam degradation. Some of our competitors have replaced sewn seat covers with welding applications and higher quality vinyl. This is a big deal. We need to fix it.

Tom: Great job, folks. That is exactly the level of detail we need to get into. Let's develop an action plan. Give me your thoughts.

Dave: We absolutely have to set up a fiberglass rework and warranty reduction team. This represents $1.8 million in warranty costs, which would be a sizeable cost reduction in the plant.

Tom: Okay, action item one is to set up a fiberglass rework and warranty reduction team.

Dave: Let's set up a separate team for root causing and eliminating cracking.

Tom: Got it.

Brandon: I would be happy to lead a "fiberglass cracking elimination team."

Glen: I can lead a damage elimination team.

Dave: We need to have a leak team and an electrical team.

Glen: Materials will source some more reliable pumps.

Tom: Alright team, here is a list of the project teams we will be leading. As you will note, I am going to lead the electrical team (Fig. 16-21).

Lean Six Sigma Warranty Reduction Project - Sub-Teams	
Team	Leader
Fiberglass rework and warranty reduction team	Matt
Fiberglass cracking / structural improvement team	Brandon
Seat foam degradation team	Brandon
Electrical warranty elimination team	Tom
Damage elimination team	Glen
Supplier warranty elimination team - pumps	Dave

Figure 21

FIGURE 16-21.

Meeting Agenda - Analyze continued
1:00 – 4:00 PM - Continue to analyze and discuss warranty data

Figure 22

FIGURE 16-22.

Tom: The plan is that we will each lead a team. I will assist you with your team's strategy, and Don will assist with any Information Technology requirements you may have. We will meet each Thursday afternoon for 3 hours during which we will each provide updates of your team's progress and receive suggestions and critique from your teammates. Feel free to bring in your team to participate in the review. Just let us know ahead of time.

See you next Thursday!

Tom: Okay, you have the agenda. First up is the fiberglass cracking and structural improvement team (Fig. 16-22).

Brandon: Well, we looked at all of the data and found the following (Fig. 16-23):

Brandon: The greatest amount of claims are on transoms where the nozzles bolt on, followed by seat frames rusting. There is a great deal of cracking everywhere we attach hinges, and access plates are cracking on their edges on nearly every model.

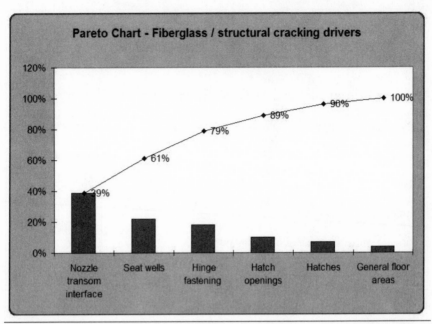

FIGURE 16-23.

The defects tend to be equally occurring across all models. Here is a summation of other data we gathered:

■ The transoms are laminated with bulk laminates (normal-thickness applications as called for in materials specification and application formulas used by engineering).

■ There are some tight corners that may impede proper application of fiberglass and yield weak areas.

■ There are questions about the effectiveness of the clamping mechanisms used in constructing the transom coring. There may be uneven pressures causing weak spots or voids.

■ The transom coring thickness is at the low end of the thickness ranges from engineering calculations.

■ There are instances of adhesive cracking from improper activation. Operators mix the activator into the adhesive by hand, which could lead to uneven or improper activator blends.

Brandon: Next week we will present our intended improvements.

Tom: Great job! Let's move on to the seating foam degradation team. Now that's quite a name! We need T-shirts! Brandon, you're up again.

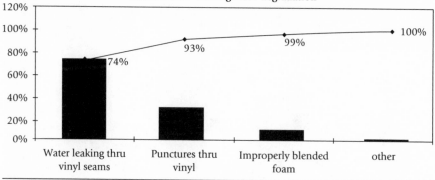

FIGURE 16-24.

Brandon: Well, we're together once again. We did a Pareto analysis, and this is what we got (Fig. 16-24):

Brandon: As you can see, the Pareto analysis showed us that weak vinyl seams are a big problem. Seats are being easily punctured in the field.

Brandon: Our other research and information provided the following: A particular area of concern is where thru-hulls are installed. If they're not sealed, they leak a very high percentage of the time. We did learn that there were very few failures when sealant was injected into holes before installing a screw or fastener.

Brandon: We will develop a list of improvements this week and review them next week with the group.

Tom: Another great job. Thanks for the effort. Let's move on to the electrical warranty elimination team. That's me! Well, we followed the same path as Brandon and his teams. Here is our Pareto (Fig. 16-25):

Tom: The Pareto indicated improper installation, corroded connections, defective components, and moisture-related shorting as the top drivers.

Other Data and Information Obtained

- Schematics for electrical installations were weak, and there is not a solid process in place to manage changes to specifications and ensure suppliers and installers are up to date.
- Connections covered with heat-shrink are corroding less and not experiencing moisture-related failures.
- Use of improper crimpers is a problem, and improper crimping when the correct crimper is used.
- There are often mismatches between harness wiring and component wiring driving confusion.

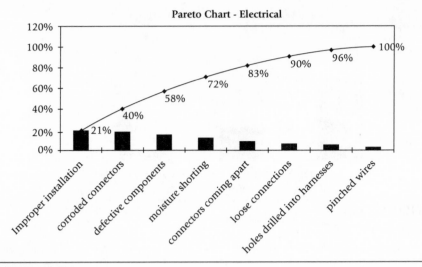

FIGURE 16-25.

Tom: We already have quite a few ideas and are excited about developing our improvement strategy. See you next week.

Tom: Okay, now for the damage elimination team. Glen, are you guys ready?

Glen: Are we ready to do some damage? We have been working hard. Our data yielded the following Pareto (Fig. 16-26): Our Pareto showed in-process movement, damaged during shipment, tool contact during production, and loose gear moving around during shipment as the key drivers.

Other Information Obtained

- Shrink-wrap improperly affixed can move around and scratch as it vibrates during shipment.
- When shrink-wrap comes loose, dirt and debris get underneath and the wind action causes abrasion between the wrap and the jet ski.
- Observations in production included operators laying screw guns, drills, knives, saws, and many other tools onto jet ski surfaces.
- Jet skis often came in contact with ladders and fixtures on the line during movement.
- Operators sometime bump components into other parts of the jet skis when bringing them near the assembly line.

Glen: We'll be ready to recommend improvements next week.

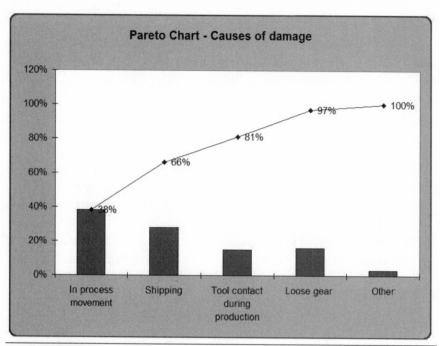

FIGURE 16-26.

Tom: Last but not least. Dave are you ready to talk to us about supplier warranty elimination team's efforts on eliminating pump warranty?

Dave: We are. Actually, it was quite a revelation that one category of components was driving 5% of our total warranty costs. This is a great opportunity. Here is what we found:

- Most pump failures are simply pumps failing from reliability issues.
- We tend to specify pumps at the lower end of the capacity spectrum.
- Most of the pumps we use tend to cycle longer.
- Our supplier recommends that we specify larger pumps.
- Our supplier could not provide any reliability testing data.
- We have other suppliers that have provided reliability testing data indicating higher levels than we are experiencing.

Dave: We will continue to analyze and present our recommendation next week.

Tom: I cannot thank everyone enough for the effort. We look forward to starting the Improve stage next week.

IMPROVE PHASE (FIG. 16-27)

Tom: Okay folks, we have a lot to do. Let's get started. Today, we are looking forward to hearing recommendations for the improve stage. Brandon, you are first. Let's hear from the fiberglass cracking team.

Brandon: Okay, our team worked hard this past week, and here is our improvement plan. We plan to take the following actions:

1. We reviewed the transom laminate schedule with engineering, and they initiated a design change to replace the current general application adhesive used in the structure with a high-strength blended adhesive.
2. Engineering has initiated a design change to add additional layers of fiberglass knit to the lamination schedule on all transoms. They also increased the coring material thickness by approximately 25%.
3. We engaged manufacturing engineering to improve the clamping process. In response, they designed an air cylinder-clamping mechanism that provides increased clamping pressure over several points, providing a much more even and effective clamp. This should eliminate voids and weak spots caused by uneven clamp pressure from the previous clamp.
4. We obtained an adhesive gun mechanism to use in place of hand mixing adhesive. The gun has a high reliability, and given it is maintained and routinely calibrated it will yield adhesive with an even catalyst dispersion.
5. Engineering has agreed to add a high-strength fiberglass knit to all hatch-opening corners.

Meeting Agenda - Improve
1:00 - 1:30 Fiberglass cracking / structural improvement team
2:00 - 2:30 Seat Foam degradation team
2:30 - 3:00 Electrical warranty elimination team
3:00 - 3:30 Damage elimination team
3:30- 4:00 Supplier warranty elimination team - pumps

FIGURE 16-27.

6. Engineering has added solid coring material behind all hinge locations. Models with this design have yielded very few hinge pull failures in the past.

Tom: Awesome job folks. Great job! I am excited about the results we know you will get. Okay, let's hear from the seat foam degradation team.

Brandon: The seat foam degradation team has met three times in the past week. It was a challenge, but our team will implement the following improvements to address seat foam degradation:

1. In the short term we have updated internal product specifications with detailed instructions on the requirement to apply sealant on all seams. We have begun to coordinate the introduction dielectric welding as replacement for sewing. If done every time, it should be highly effective.
2. We have worked with purchasing and engineering to specify a new seat covering material with a strong backing material that will nearly eliminate punctures. Testing is currently under way.
3. Our supplier quality leader has worked with our foam supplier's quality team, and jointly they developed a control plan to eliminate improper blending of foam.

Tom: Wow, another awesome job guys. Thanks for the effort. Well, I guess I should introduce myself and the electrical warranty team. We too, have had a busy week. Busy, but rewarding. Here is our improvement plan:

1. We contacted engineering and arranged to begin to review all electrical documentation for accuracy. They suggested and agreed to inserting comments to clarify most connections and doubled the size of digital reference pictures and diagrams in all specifications. This review is about 25% complete, and we anticipate having all documentation reviewed and updated in 4 weeks.
2. Suppliers will also receive a copy of updated documentation for components that they supply.
3. We have set up a meeting with our ISO coordinator to review our document control process. Any improvements to the control process will be implemented immediately and will be included as a focus item in all future quality audits.
4. We have submitted an Engineering Change Request to mandate that all connections be covered with heat-shrink.

5. All operators will be instructed to notify a Quality Auditor any time they identify any mismatch in wire coloring or other similar problems. The auditor will research and engage engineering or the supplier as required to address the issue.

6. A preliminary review of jet skis indicates the potential to relocate many harnesses by 2 to 3 inches lower, which will move them out of the reach of most fasteners and we have replaced the screw-type fasteners with rivets.

Glen: Great job, Tom. You know, it is amazing that most of our proposed solutions require little if any technology or new equipment.

Tom: You're welcome, Glen. It's true, so many of the solutions are relatively simple. Well Glen, is the damage team ready?

Glen: We are. We are happy to report that our brainstorming, teamwork, and collaboration have yielded some important improvements that we are very optimistic will help get us results. Here are our intended improvements:

1. We will work with the shipping department and our shrink-wrap supplier to improve our shrink-wrap application process. We will then train the operators in the improved process. They are scheduled to meet with us next Tuesday.

2. We are going to engage the plant leadership group to mandate that no one place any tools or items on product during production. We will require that tools either be in tool boxes, in use, or sitting on an approved platform.

3. We have set up a team to apply foam and padding to all surfaces on assembly lines that can come into contact with the product.

4. We are setting up a team to develop padding and protection in areas that are susceptible to damage or abrasion when bringing components into the assembly area for installation.

5. We will review loose gear stowage and develop controls to stop shifting during transport. If necessary, we will design shipment crates.

Tom: Thanks Glen. Another nice job. Dave are you ready?

Dave: We are.

1. We have engaged engineering regarding pump capacity. They have preliminarily agreed to consider increasing pump-capacity specifications to higher outputs, which should mean they will run for shorter lengths of time.

2. Engineering will participate in discussions with three different suppliers next week and review each supplier's pump offerings. Each supplier conducts its own internal reliability testing and will provide the results and pertinent data. Two of the three suppliers will unconditionally warranty their pumps for 10 years. The objectives are to resource and re-specify pumps to all models.

CONTROL PHASE

Brandon (Fiberglass Cracking/Structural Improvement Team): Here is an overview of our Control plan.

- Use of the transom clamp fixture will be included in the quality process audit.
- Add the adhesive gun to the equipment calibration schedule portion of the quality process.
- All specifications and work instructions will be updated to reflect process and product modifications.

Brandon (Seat Foam Degradation Elimination Team):

- Add a critical product quality audit to verify the presence of sealant in all screw holes, and set up a training certification for all operators drilling holes into structure.
- Add a critical product quality audit to verify the presence of gel coat in all thru-hull holes, and set up a training certification for all operators installing thru-hulls.

Tom (Electrical Warranty Elimination Team):

- Add a Critical to Quality product audit to verify the presence of heat-shrink on all connections.
- Set up periodic training for operators installing electrical components.

Glen (Damage Elimination Team):

- Set up periodic training to cover importance of protecting product during process with specified protective measures.

Dave (Supplier Warranty Elimination Team: Pumps):

- On a yearly basis, the pump supplier will provide copies of durability testing on all pumps to confirm a minimum of a 5-year reliability window.

The team here has applied an array of tools from the Lean Six Sigma tool box. It is important to note that the Lean Six Sigma methodology is not a complex process. It is a process consisting of tools ranging from relatively simple to complex. This team was relatively inexperienced at Lean Six Sigma. If they continue to apply the tools, over time they will become more and more skilled. At the same time they will be building them into their culture. After a time, they may choose to hire or train a Six Sigma Black Belt to provide leadership and training in applying more complex Six Sigma tools.

Chapter 17

Project: Eliminate Rework–
Fiberglass Bath Tubs and Showers

This chapter will take you through a focused effort to eliminate rework in a fiberglass bath tub and shower stall manufacturing plant. Most every manufacturing plant has to deal with reducing and eliminating rework. This factory is no different. Let's join the team.

You: Good morning. The purpose of this meeting is to generate a discussion and strategy to eliminate the high levels of cosmetic fiberglass rework we are dealing with. We all know the cost of this rework is hitting our bottom line hard. In addition, this rework is hitting us twice in the form of warranty. Many of the warranty claims are for labor to rework our rework! Last year more than half of total warranty costs were from claims related to fiberglass rework. The repair areas are resurfacing dull spots, cracking, fading, and deterioration. This is a significant issue. Our average weekly payroll for tooling maintenance and fiberglass repair is more than $50,000 per week.

Eighteen months ago we purchased and set up two robotic gel-coat cells. Although we saw improvement immediately after installation, the defect rate is climbing, and we are nowhere near the rate we should be experiencing. Our gel-coat application and fiberglass lamination processes are obviously out of control. As Director of Quality,

I have been asked to lead a Lean Six Sigma project to bring these processes into control and drastically reduce the costs associated with this situation. You guys know the routine. We'll meet this coming Tuesday and define the project with a Project Charter. I'll see you next week.

THE TEAM

- Director of Quality: Bill
- Fiberglass Manager: Joe
- Finish Supervisor: Ken
- Manufacturing Engineering Manager: Julio
- Finance Manager: Frank

Define Phase

You: Good afternoon. We are here today to develop a Project Charter for the fiberglass rework project. Here is the agenda we will follow (Figs. 17-1 to 17-3):

You: Okay, nice job. I think we're getting this DMAIC (define, measure, analyze, improve, control) thing down. We have a charter, SIPOC (suppliers, inputs, process, output, and customers) diagram, and a high-level process map. See you next week when we will begin the measure phase.

Measure Phase

You: Okay guys, today we start the measure phase (Fig. 17-4). To begin, we need to determine what data we need, and what we are going to measure.

Joe (Fiberglass Manager): This is unbelievable. I thought that these gel-coat robots were supposed to produce near-perfect application thicknesses. Heck, we had better luck with operators spraying it by hand. I would like to know just what the actual rework level is. Are we getting worse?

Frank (Finance): We are. Our gel-coat Finish department payroll is over budget, and it's not improving. I will get the payroll dollars associated with the rework department.

You: We will need the number of tubs and shower stalls per week, etc. Also, can you pull the warranty data on gel-coat claims? I have the number of gel-coat defects per tub and shower stall. We have been measuring that for some time.

Let's get a list started:

- Payroll dollars for gel-coat rework
- Number of gel-coat defects per tub
- Gel-coat–related warranty data

Meeting Agenda - Define
1:00 – 2:45 PM - Complete Project Charter
2:45 – 3:30 PM – Develop a SIPOC diagram
3:30 – 4:00 PM – Develop a high level process map
4:00 – 4:15 PM – Review requirements / actions in the MEASURE phase

FIGURE 17-1.

Project Charter	
Project :	Fiberglass Rework & Warranty Cost Reduction Project
Project Leader :	Bill Trudell
Problems to be solved :	Hi levels of fiberglass rework/costs during the manufacturing process, and high warranty costs associated with cosmetic fiberglass issues
Process/es impacted :	Final Assembly, Fabrication
Team Member/s :	Bill, Joe, Ken, Julio, Frank
Project goals / deliverables :	Achieve a significant reduction in fiberglass rework , repair, and warranty related costs.
Project Start :	1-Jan
Project End :	31-Mar
Milestones :	(completed by)
Define	8-Jan
Measure	5-Feb
Analyze	5-Mar
Improve	28-Feb
Control	31-Mar

Figure 2

FIGURE 17-2.

Process map for Gel coat & Fiberglass Lamination

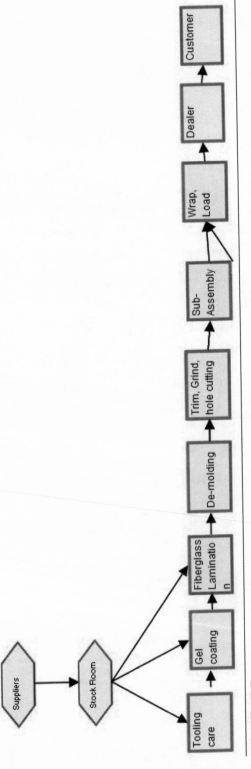

FIGURE 17-3.

Meeting Agenda - Measure

9:00 - 10:30 AM - Determine what data will be gathered in Measure phase

10:30 - 11 AM - Assign responsibilities

FIGURE 17-4.

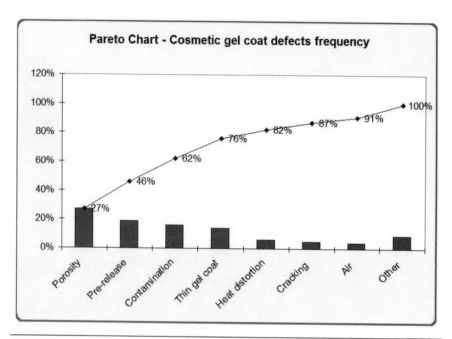

Pareto Chart - Cosmetic gel coat defects frequency

FIGURE 17-5.

You: Okay, let's get started. Let's see what we have. We pulled together some data from our Quality Assurance process and created Pareto charts.

Here is what the initial Pareto analysis indicates:

- Top 5 gel-coat defects by frequency of occurrence are
  - porosity, pre-release, thin gel coat, heat distortion, cracking
- Top 5 generators of fiberglass rework are
  - cracking, thin gel coat, heat distortion, porosity, contamination
- Top 5 generators of fiberglass-related warranty costs are
  - cracking, thin gel, air, halos, scratches
- The fiberglass rework payroll is self explanatory. We are way over budget and spending excessively on rework (Figs. 17-5 to 17-8).

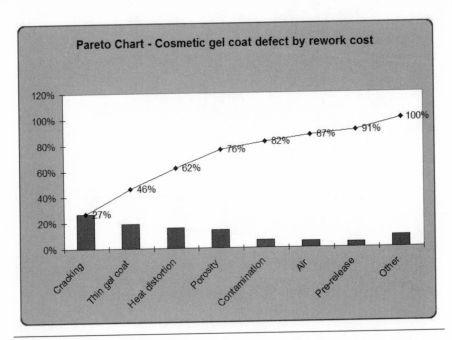

FIGURE 17-6.

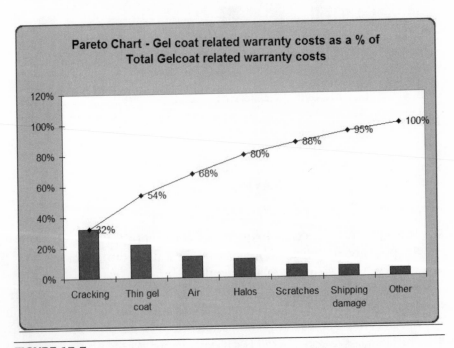

FIGURE 17-7.

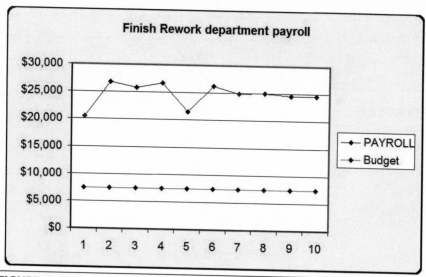

FIGURE 17-8.

Ken (Finish Supervisor): Bill, don't take this the wrong way, but those charts you have don't seem to relate to what is going on out there on the floor.

You: What do you mean?

Ken: Well for one thing, your chart says that our biggest problems are porosity and pre-release. To be honest, we spend more time working on cracking and thin gel coat. Something isn't adding up. We spend hours and hours on these two defects alone. It just doesn't make sense. I think you're looking at how many times we are working on defects, as opposed to how long we are working on them.

You: Ken, you are making some good points. I think we better step back and take a look at our measurement system. You are correct. Our product auditors are recording how many instances we have of porosity, pre-release, etc. Let's try this. Julio, can you give us the surface area of all of the parts we produce?

Julio (Manufacturing Engineering Manager): Sure. It's in our CAD files. I'll have it next week.

You: Meanwhile, let me meet with the Quality team and put some thought into improving our measurement system. Frank, let's keep tracking the payroll data. I have some ideas.

Frank: No problem.

You: Gentleman, this concludes our meeting. We will meet again next week, and I will present our recommendation on our measurement system (Fig. 17-9).

Meeting Agenda - Measure
1:00 – 2:45 PM - Review measurement system
2:45 – 4:00 PM – Develop action plan to implement

FIGURE 17-9.

Model	Surface area Sq inches	SA SQ FT
TUB GRP 1	6048	42
TUB GRP 2	6336	44
TUB GRP 3	7632	53
STALL GRP 1	6480	45
STALL GRP 2	6768	47
STALL GRP 3	7056	49

FIGURE 17-10.

You: Good afternoon. Well, I'm kind of excited today. I met with our Quality team last week, and I think we have come up with a pretty solid strategy. I have an overview of our recommended approach to measuring our process and associated rework. First, thank you Julio, for obtaining the surface areas for all models. Here it is in table form (Fig. 17-10):

Frank: I put together a chart of our weekly payroll for Finish rework. As you can see, we are way over budget and have seen no improvement (Fig 17-11).

You: Guys, this is excellent information. Here is what we'll do. We will begin to track the payroll dollars per square foot of fiberglass surface area produced. This will be a relative measurement that will be relative to production rates and tub size.

The bottom line is that we will either be paying more or less over time to produce a square foot of fiberglass. I think this will be very meaningful.

Alright, let's review our proposed gel-coat finish measurement system. Here it is.

Measurement System Overview (Figs. 17-12 to 17-14)

You: Okay, I will present to the Quality team, and we will begin immediately measuring with this system. Let's meet in 2 weeks to review the results.

Frank: I will have our Finish payroll dollars to SF of fiberglass-produced metrics then.

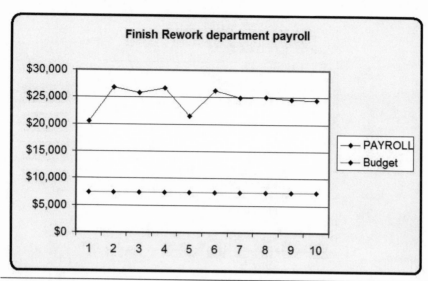

FIGURE 17-11.

Gel coat Finish Measurement system overview
* Determine the surface area for all fiberglass parts that will be produced and set up a database or spreadsheet
* Each square inch of fiberglass surface area is an opportunity for a defect
* Any square inch of fiberglass that has any type of defect is considered 1 defect
* All defects will be measured in square inches
* If a crack is 9" in length, it represents 9 defects
Auditor will indicate on data collection form the defect identification # X Sq Inches
Product Auditors will complete a datat collection form and reference the defect ID# and location on a product map. They will record the square inches of each defect in the corresponding block.

FIGURE 17-12.

There are 11 types of defects

ID	DEFECT TYPES
1	Air
2	Contamination
3	Cracks
4	Damage
5	Heat distortion
6	Mold marks
7	Overspraty
8	Porosity
9	Pre-release
10	Thin gel coat
11	Other

FIGURE 17-13.

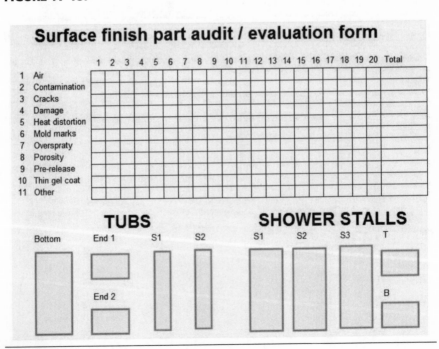

FIGURE 17-14.

Meeting Agenda - Analyze
1:00 – 2:45 PM - Review measurement data
2:45 – 4:00 PM – Begin action plan for IMPROVE stage

FIGURE 17-15.

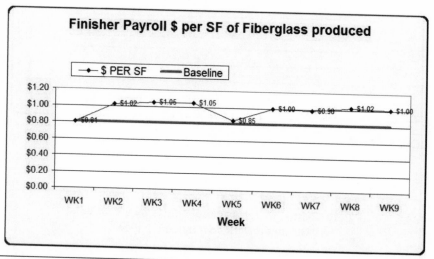

FIGURE 17-16.

Analyze Phase (Fig. 17-15)

You: Greetings. Let's get right to business. We have some data to analyze. Here is what we have so far:

Frank: As you can see we are spending about $0.55 per square foot in rework (Figs. 17-16 and 17-17).

You: We have also provided the first-time pass data for the process. Here are some Pareto charts for the process (Fig. 17-18).

You: There are some differences between frequency and amount of rework for each type of defect. Looking at the rework as a percentage of total Pareto, we need to focus on thin gel coat, cracking, porosity, contamination, and heat distortion. This is a good time to welcome Ray to the team. Ray, because you lead the equipment maintenance team your knowledge of the robots and other equipment will be very valuable and helpful.

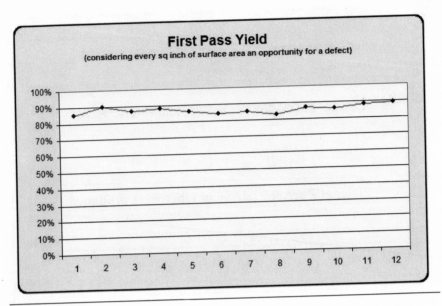

FIGURE 17-17.

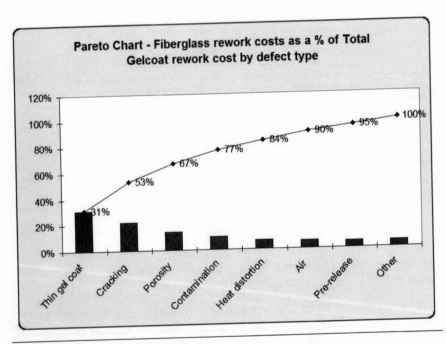

FIGURE 17-18.

Meeting Agenda - Analyze
1:00 – 2:45 PM - Review measurement data
2:45 – 4:00 PM – Begin action plan for IMPROVE stage

FIGURE 17-19.

Ray: Great to be here. I am looking forward to working with you guys. I don't know much about this Lean Six Sigma thing, but I am willing to learn if you can put up with me.

You: We're all in it together Ray. We're a team. According to the Paretos, I am going to ask the quality assurance team to start measuring and tracking gel-coat thickness, heat temperatures during lamination, and resin content, because we all know that resin-rich parts generate excessive heat. Ray, I would like to ask that you participate in some brainstorming sessions with Julio, Joe, and the robot operators to help root cause the thin gel, cracks, porosity, contamination, and heat. See you all next week (Fig. 17-19).

You: Greetings, let's get right to reviewing our data. We have a lot to do. Here are the additional data we have (Figs. 17-20 to 17-27).

You: Well, I think we can draw several conclusions from our data at this point:

- Our process is yielding a significant variance in gel-coat thickness. It is yielding both thin and thick relative to our design specifications.
- Our process is continuously yielding fiberglass parts that have more than the upper limit of 65% resin. This is one causal factor in heat distortion.
- Our parts are exceeding our upper limit on peak exotherm or temperature during our fiberglass lamination process. This is one effect of exceeding the resin content specification.

You: Here is our agenda for the next meeting at which we will begin the Improve phase. Your homework assignment is to develop a list of any and all ideas you have to eliminate each of these defect situations. The more you prepare, the more successful we will be. See you then.

Improve Phase (Fig. 17-28)

You: Welcome. Today we begin the Improve phase of the DMAIC process. This is going to be a busy afternoon. Our objective is to develop an improvement plan for each of the defects we are focusing on.

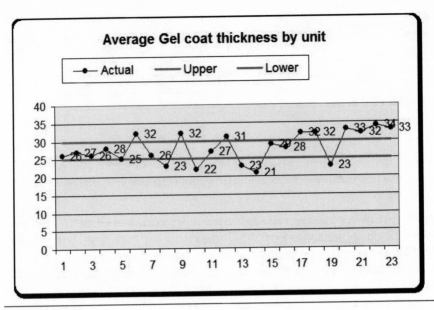

FIGURE 17-20.

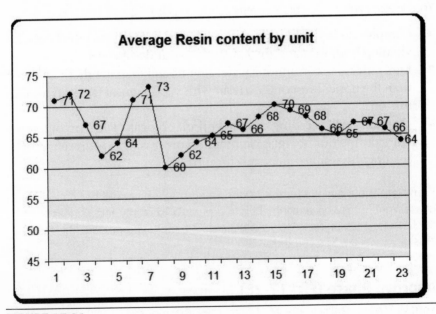

FIGURE 17-21.

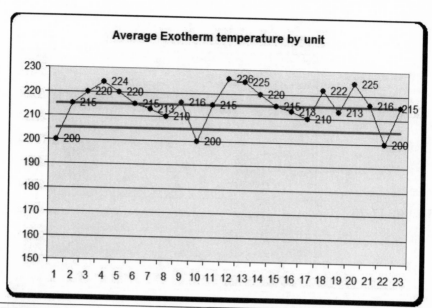

FIGURE 17-22.

Cause & Effect Diagram			
Thin Gel Coat			
Man	**Machine**	**Methods**	**Materials**
Incorrect pump pressures	failed pump seals		gel coat viscosity too low
Incorrect tip size	misapplication		
mold not in correct position in spray chamber	Excessive air movement in spray chamber		
	Fluid line expansion		
	Robot malfunction		

FIGURE 17-23.

Cause & Effect Diagram			
Gel coat cracking			
Man	**Machine**	**Methods**	**Materials**
Incorrect settings on equipment drive excessive thickness		Rough handling of parts	Out of date gel coat
Incorrect pump pressures generate excessive materials thickness	Inaccurate machine code drives misapplication generating excessive materials thickness		
Incorrect tip size generate excessive materials thickness		Tension during pulling	Materials out of specification
mold not in correct position in spray chamber cause materials pile up	Robot malfunction	Tension while turning parts	
Incorrect catalyst ratio			

FIGURE 17-24.

Cause & Effect Diagram			
Porosity			
Man	Machine	Methods	Materials
Exsessive pump pressures generate excessive materials thickness	Insufficient gas off time between machine passes		Out of date catalyst
Incorrect tip size generate excessive materials thickness	inaccurate machine code drives excessive materials thickness		Catalyzt out of specification
	Inaccurate machine code applies past point of diffusion		Incorrect catalyst
Mold not in correct position in spray chamber cause materials pile up	Inadequate or improper spray fan during dispersion of gel coat		

FIGURE 17-25.

Cause & Effect Diagram			
Contamination			
Man	Machine	Methods	Materials
Containers left open gathering debris	Moisture in air lines	Debris in air during spraying	Supplier provides contaminated materials
Debris left on surface of tooling prior to application	Oil or lubricants from air compressors in air lines		
Tooling cleaned with contaminated rags			

FIGURE 17-26.

Cause & Effect Diagram			
Heat distortion			
Man	Machine	Methods	Materials
Insufficient roll out of resin during lamination	Bad pump seal yielding excessive catalyst	Applying additional layers of glass before reaching peak exotherm of previous layer	Incorrect catalyst
Application of excessive amounts of resin	Equipment out of calibration	Failure to use a nap roller	Resin out of specification
Improper / excessive catalyst settings		Failure to use a squeegee	
Improperly agitated materials		Excesive shop temperature	
Resin allowed to pool during application		untrained operators	

FIGURE 17-27.

Meeting Agenda - Improve	
1:00 - 1:30 Thin Gelcoat	
2:00 - 2:30 Gel Coat cracking	
2:30 - 3:00 Porosity	
3:00 - 3:30 Contamination	
3:30- 4:00 Heat distortion	

FIGURE 17-28.

The team developed and immediately implemented the following improvement plans:

Improvement Plan: Thin Gel Coat

- Review correct pump pressures with robot setup team.
- Install warning system to alert to low or high pressures.
- Review proper tip-size application with robot setup team.
- Verify serviceability of seals. Review maintenance schedule on seals.
- Install warning buzzer to signal an open door on chamber when robots initiate spraying.
- Inspect all fluid lines, and verify their review is in the maintenance plan.
- Increase and verify gel-coat sampling for viscosity testing.
- Develop fixture clamp to lock down tooling in place during spray process.
- Add reviews and actions to standardized work and process checklists of operators.

Improvement Plan: Gel-Coat Cracking

- Review correct equipment settings with robot setup team.
- Install warning system to alert to low or high pressures.
- Review proper tip-size application with robot setup team.
- Develop fixture clamp to lock down tooling in place during spray process.
- Request Engineering to review/update all code on a monthly basis.
- Retrain parts pullers in proper pulling procedures to eliminate cracking.
- Review location of pull tabs on parts to specified locations.
- Review materials' shelf-life date location with operators.

Improvement Plan: Porosity

- Review correct equipment settings with robot setup team.
- Install warning system to alert to low or high pressures.

- Review proper tip-size application with robot setup team.
- Develop fixture clamp to lock down tooling in place during spray process.
- Review machine code and audit time lapse between robot spray passes to ensure that it is within the 3- to 5-minute specification.
- Implement signal and pause requiring operator to verify proper spray fan of gel coat during application.
- Implement signal to verify gel coat is contacting tooling at point of dispersion.
- Review materials' shelf-life for catalyst date location with operators.
- Review specified catalysts with operators and post visual chart in spray chamber.
- Add reviews and actions to standardized work, and process checklists of operators.

Improvement Plan: Contamination

- Emphasize to operators to keep containers covered and closed at all times.
- Retrain operators and emphasize verification of tooling being properly prepped and clean before spray process.
- Require use of fresh rags on all tooling. Rag must go from box to tooling.
- Install additional dryers on air compressors.
- Install moisture alarms on air lines.
- Changeover to compressor lubricant approved by gel-coat manufacturer.
- Install alarm to ensure door to chamber is closed during spray process.
- Require supplier to add final analysis/check to ensure no contamination.

Improvement Plan: Heat Distortion

- Retrain operators on proper resin rollout.
- Install electronic resin monitors that digitally display resin content during application.
- Retrain crew leaders to ensure no resin pooling exists, and use nap rollers.
- Install alarm to signal improper catalyst level.
- Add material agitation check to daily process audit.
- Reinforce daily equipment calibration.
- Have process auditors signal when peak exotherm has been reached to signal operators' approval to apply next layer.
- Ensure plant air make-up system is running at all times and doors are closed to ensure proper function to control temperatures in plan.
- Add secondary materials testing on a daily basis in addition to incoming testing.

You: Welcome. Well, let's see how we're doing (Figs. 17-29 to 17-32).

You: Guys, these are awesome results! We are making great progress. Our process is coming under much better control. However, we are still varying on gel-coat thickness, even after taking all of the actions in our improvement plan. Ray, I am going to ask that we do another brainstorming session with our maintenance and setup crew. We need to study the whole gel-coating process carefully. Julio, please join them again.

Julio: I will. Glad to help.

You: See you guys next week.

You: Greetings folks. Okay, how did we do ?

Julio: We found some interesting results. We also called some of the other plants and our robot manufacturer. We found some new causes (Fig. 17-33).

Ray: We now have another improvement plan.

Improvement Plan: Gel-Coat Thickness Variation

- Implement daily laboratory inspection of all tips to check for wear and damage.
- Replace robotic arm bushings immediately, and increase maintenance inspection to once every 40 hours.

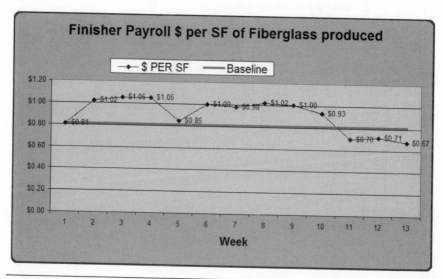

FIGURE 17-29.

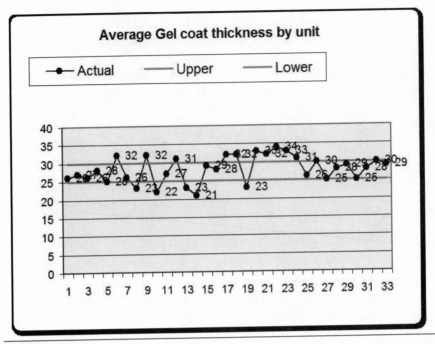

FIGURE 17-30.

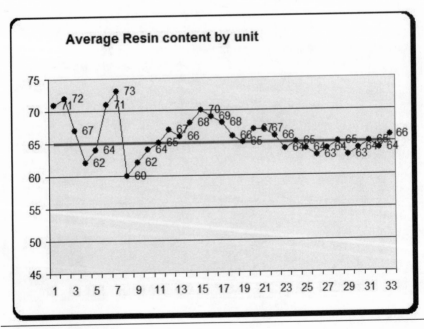

FIGURE 17-31.

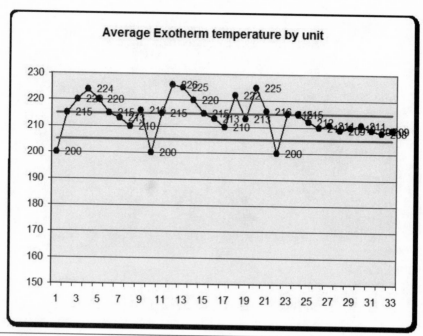

FIGURE 17-32.

Cause & Effect Diagram			
Thin / Thick Gelcoat - Second pass			
Man	Machine	Methods	Materials
	Spray tip wear		
	Damaged spray tips		
	Robotic arm bushings worn		
	Fixture locators bent / damaged		
	Improper spray angle		

FIGURE 17-33.

- Inspect fixture locators for damage daily and replace or repair immediately if required.
- Add verification of proper spray angle to daily equipment setup.

Once again the team implemented the plan. Here are the final results (Figs. 17-34 to Fig. 17-36). What a great effort by this team! This team took the basic tools of Lean Six Sigma and applied them toward reducing an area of rework, and they got results. No doubt they will continue to build on their successes and achieve even higher levels of improvement.

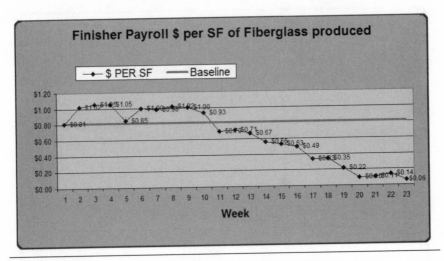

FIGURE 17-34.

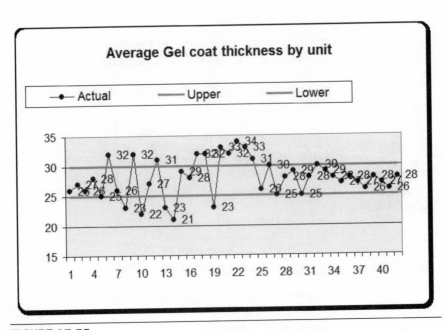

FIGURE 17-35.

DASHBOARD - Gelcoat Process

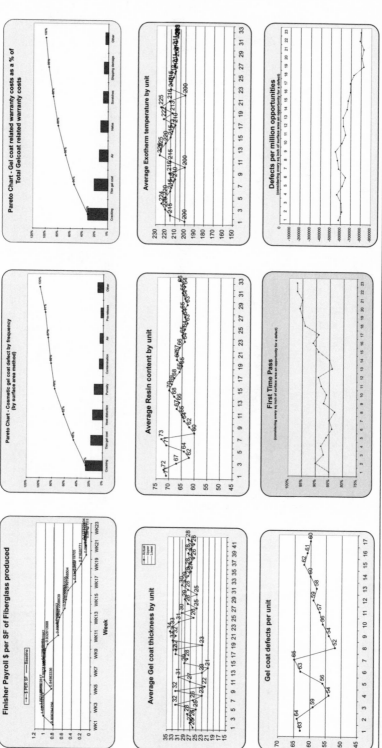

Chapter 18

The Psychology of Lean Six Sigma

With all of the discussion about current state, value stream maps, Kaizen, DMAIC, Pareto, metrics, and the other tools, it is important to remember that it is the mindset or psychology that brings it all together.

The psychology of Lean Six Sigma is not just about improvement. It's not even about continuous improvement. It is about *relentless* improvement. To truly be successful in applying or implementing Lean Six Sigma, you and your organization have to have the mindset of relentless improvement. This means a never-ending stream of efforts to drive improvement into your organization, product or service quality, and profitability.

Relentless improvement, yes relentless improvement. What could be better than relentlessly focusing your company on pleasing customers and giving them products that perfectly match their expectations at the lowest possible costs without having to wait for them for a long period of time? This is a tall order, but the tools and methodologies of Lean Six Sigma will help you fill it. Lean Six Sigma will give you practical tools to make it a reality.

The psychology of Lean Six Sigma is about focus, a clear focus for your team. It provides a set of principles to ground the organization's efforts.

Lean Six Sigma clears up the fog of the daily battlefield of manufacturing or business. It does so by providing principles to live by:

- High quality
- Low cost
- Short cycle times
- Flexibility
- Customer-defined value
- A never-ending stream of efforts to eliminate waste and nonvalue-added activities
- Relentless improvement

Lean Six Sigma is the toolbox that you use to realize your gains. As the president, general manager, or manager, it will start with you. Your organization's success will be directly tied to your personal commitment. It has to be a religious-type conversion that results in a personal commitment to a new way of thinking and running your business.

What does this commitment mean? It means that you will become a scholar of Lean Six Sigma. You will read all you can and attend training. You will provide the resources and time to train everyone in the organization in Lean Six Sigma as required. This is one of those "the speed of the team is the speed of the boss" scenarios. There will be many in your organization who will immediately embrace this new philosophy, probably the 20% who always support change. The remaining 80% will key off of you and the other leaders. Their commitment will be greatly influenced by your passion about it. As the leader, all eyes will be on you. Take every opportunity to get out on the floor to sell and explain the philosophy. Bring it up in meetings, and stop in people's offices and workstations to talk about it for a few minutes. Show your excitement.

The commitment to training is a critical success factor. This means that time and resources will be expended. You will have to not only allow but also encourage employees to attend training to learn brainstorming, how to conduct a Kaizen event, or how to understand the information on a dashboard. Your commitment will be rewarded. I assure you that as a leader you will be rewarded sooner or later when you happen to go by a room and see a group of employees in a brainstorming session or reviewing a Pareto analysis to determine where to focus their improvement efforts. You will be rewarded when you begin to receive letters from customers telling you how much they enjoy your product. You will be rewarded with increased profitability.

The final ingredient in the psychology of Lean Six Sigma is passion. Applying Lean Six Sigma is like learning to play the violin. It is hard, very hard. But if you are determined and passionate about learning, you will be rewarded with beautiful music. As a leader, you must display passion and excitement. It will rub off on your team. After all, if exciting your customers with unbelievable quality and watching your employees and your organization reach their full potential, all while making great profits, don't get you excited, why are you there?

INDEX

Page numbers followed by *f* indicate a figure

ABOUT THE AUTHOR

Bill Carreira is president of Carreira Consulting, working with clients as an educator, mentor, and facilitator of lean manufacturing methodologies. With over 30 years of experience in manufacturing, engineering, and P&L management, Bill has worked with both fortune 500's and small, closely held firms across a broad range of industries. Bill's first book "**Lean Manufacturing That Works,**" published by AMACOM Publishing House, November 2004, enjoys best seller status as well as numerous positive accolades, such as "**One of the best business books of 2004; CEO Magazine.**" He lives in Sarasota, Florida and can be reached at **carreiraconsulting.com.**"

Bill Trudell has 20 plus years of experience in a variety of manufacturing and service roles in Fortune 500 companies ranging from Assembly line worker, Division Materials Manager, Plant Manager, Vice President of Quality, and Vice President of Operations. Throughout his career he has focused on continuous improvement and learning. Early on he became a student of Just in Time and Lean, and later Six Sigma. He has earned a Lean 101 certificate, is an ASQ certified Six Sigma Black Belt, and has earned APICS CPIM, ISM C.P.M., and ASQ CQA certifications. He is currently an executive with a manufacturing company in Sarasota, Florida, and manages Val-stream Improvement (www.val-streamimprovement.com)—a private consulting practice.